MINERALS
of New York State

David E. Jensen

WARD
PRESS

Ward's Natural Science Establishment, Inc.
Rochester, New York • Monterey, California

Library of Congress Catalog Card Number: 78-66426

ISBN: 0-932142-00-1

PRINTED IN THE UNITED STATES OF AMERICA
BY W. F. HUMPHREY PRESS, INC., GENEVA, NY

Quartz, "Herkimer diamonds"   Herkimer Co.

Dedicated to my wife Kay

Preface

This report on the Minerals of New York State is partially a summary of published knowledge. Credit is due the hundreds of authors whose work since the late 18th century has made this report possible. Personal observations in the field have been supplemented by viewing numerous museum and private mineral collections in this country and Europe since 1930.

Local Indians were the first to utilize minerals as tools, weapons and ornamentation long before white settlers set foot in the area. It is reported that in the mid 1600's missionaries from Canadian settlements visited the vicinity of Onondaga Lake where there were salt marshes. However, the occurrence of salt as an economic mineral of the state was not established until 1863.

Iron ore was reported in the Highlands of southeastern New York in 1740. Deposits of magnetite ore in the Adirondacks were worked before 1800. Prospectors searching for silver near Lake Sanford in Essex County discovered magnetite in 1826, but an excess of ilmenite delayed economic use of the ore in making iron. The development of the many iron mines as well as other mines and quarries in the state spurred further survey work. Investigations in the field and in laboratories were followed by scientific reports on the geology and the minerals of different areas.

Attention was given to the mineralogy of the state as early as 1790 when Dr. Samuel Latham Mitchill of New York wrote A Sketch of the Mineralogical History of the State of New York. Mineralogy of New York by Dr. Lewis Caleb Beck was published in 1842. This was the first state topographical mineralogy. Another milepost in the mineralogy of the state was reached in 1903 when the New York State Museum published a List of New York Mineral Localities by Herbert P. Whitlock.

Many early studies of minerals were made long before the advent of sophisticated equipment such as the X-ray and the electron microprobe. Mineral identifications were once made chiefly by sight with the aid of a hand lens. External crystal forms and common physical properties were the basic features to be observed. Optical identification methods and simple chemical analyses gradually became aids to the identification of minerals. Many minerals that were reported in early literature could merit reexamination using modern analytical methods.

1

Some mineral names that appeared in early reports of mineral occurrences in the state are now obsolete and are seldom used as more accurate identifications have been made. Detailed chemical studies of the members of the tourmaline group have expanded the occurrences of uvite, a little known member of the group to the brown tourmalines of St. Lawrence and Warren counties as well as most of the black tourmalines of Pierrepont. All had previously been identified as other members of the tourmaline group (Dunn et al.–1977).

A century and a half ago there were very few mineral collectors in New York state. Today there are thousands, most of whom are hobbyists. As classic mineral localities become exhausted, the interest in specimens that were collected years ago may increase. Additional study may reveal additional interesting facts that had not been noticed previously. A good reference library is a most useful asset for the amateur as well as the advanced collector. The following books are suggested for general reference use in connection with this book. Many others are listed in the bibliography p. 180.

Encyclopedia of Minerals by Roberts, Rapp, Weber 1974, 848 p.

Dana's Textbook of Mineralogy, 4th ed. Dana-Ford 1932, 851 p.

Dana's Manual of Mineralogy, 19th ed. Hurlbut and Klein 1977, 352 p.

Mineralogy, Kostov 1968, 587 p.

Glossary of Mineral Species, Fleischer 1971, 1975.

Chemical Index of Minerals, Hey 1955:

Appendix 1963; second appendix 1974.

Elements of Mineralogy, Mason and Berry 1967, 550 p.

Mineralogy, A First Course. Sinkankas, 1966, 587 p.

Acknowledgements

I am deeply indebted to Clifford Frondel, who critically read my manuscript and offered numerous suggestions which have been incorporated into the text. Brian Mason read the section on meteorites. Pete J. Dunn read the section on tourmaline, and Donald D. Hogarth read the sections on haüynite and lapis lazuli.

Assistance is also gratefully expressed to Fred C. Amos, Clifford J. Awald, Steven Bryson, David B. Dill, Jr., Robert M. Eaton, Donald W. Fisher, William C. Gamble, E. Wm. Heinrich, Richard S. Laub, Nina Lockwood, J. C. H. Martens, Bea Redfield, George Robinson, Elmer B. Rowley, John Sinkankas, Bertis J. VanderSchaaf III, Timothy J. Westbrook, Charles F. Wray, Neal Yedlin and John M. Youngpeter.

All photographs were made by Katherine H. Jensen, except where otherwise credited.

Violet Morgan, Dawn Brunke and Katherine H. Jensen shared the typing task.

Good reference libraries are essential in the search for knowledge. The following have been especially helpful in obtaining information about the minerals of the state: the Reference Library of the Buffalo Society of Natural Sciences; the Geological Libraries at Columbia University, Harvard University, and the Smithsonian Institution; both Rush Rhees Library and the Geological Library at the University of Rochester; the main Public Library of Buffalo and Erie County; and the Crandall Public Library (Holden Research Room) at Glens Falls.

Table of Contents

BLACK and WHITE ILLUSTRATIONS

Magnetite, octahedral crystal
Mineville, Essex Co.
Magnetite
Monroe, Orange Co.
Magnetite, dodecahedral crystals
Tilly Foster Mine, Putnam Co.
Microcline
Bedford, Westchester Co.
Millerite
Antwerp, St. Lawrence Co.
Muscovite enclosing iron oxides
Batchellerville, Saratoga Co.

Phlogopite, crystal plate
Oxbow, Jefferson Co.
Phlogopite, cleavage of a multiple
crystal
Pierrepont, St. Lawrence Co.
Phlogopite crystal in dolomite
Pierrepont, St. Lawrence Co.
Polycrase
Overlook, Saratoga Co.
Pyrite
Schoharie Creek, Schoharie Co.
Pyrolusite in Talc
near Fowler, St. Lawrence Co.
Pyroxene—Augite
Russell, St. Lawrence Co.
Pyroxene—Diopside (Malacolite)
Sing Sing, Westchester Co.

Quartz enclosing air bubble
Herkimer Co.
Quartz—Flint in various stages of be-
ing made into arrowheads
Coxsackie, Greene Co.
Quartz, Herkimer "diamonds"
Herkimer Co.
Quartz, Herkimer "diamonds"
Herkimer Co.
Quartz crystals
Saratoga Co.
Quartz—crystallized
Ellenville, Ulster Co.
Quartz—crystals
Antwerp, St. Lawrence Co.
Quartz, drusy on calcite
Anthony's Nose, Westchester Co.
Quartz—Chalcedony
Rochester, Monroe Co.

Quartz conglomerate
Olean, Cattaraugus Co.
Quartz, Banded Jasper and Pyrite
Lewis Co.

Scapolite
Newcomb, Essex Co.
Scapolite
near Pyrites, St. Lawrence Co.
Serpentine, with Chrysotile veins
Thurman, Warren Co.
Serpentine pseudomorph after
Chondrodite
Tilly Foster Mine, Putnam Co.
Sillimanite with Magnetite in Gneiss
Benson Mines, St. Lawrence Co.
Snow crystals
(Photo by Dr. Lothar Engelmann)
Sphalerite veins in Marble
Balmat, St. Lawrence Co.
Spinel crystal
Amity, Orange Co.

Titanite (Sphene)
Putnam Co.
Titanite (Sphene)
Tilly Foster Mine, Putnam Co.
Tourmaline, Schorl
Bedford, Westchester Co.
Tourmaline, Uvite
Pierrepont, St. Lawrence Co.
Tourmaline, Uvite
Richville, St. Lawrence Co.

Uraninite and Thucholite in Quartz
DeKalb, St. Lawrence Co.

Vesuvianite
Olmsteadville, Essex Co.

Wollastonite and Andradite Garnet
Willsboro, Essex Co.

Crystal drawings of calcite by
Dr. H. P. Whitlock
from N.Y. State Museum Memoir
13, 1910
Calcite, Rossie, St. Lawrence Co.
Calcite, Rondout, Ulster Co.

Fresh water pearls
Gorham, Yates Co.

FULL COLOR ILLUSTRATIONS
Following Page 92

Amphibole, var. Tremolite (hexagonite)
  Fowler, N.Y.
Ankerite with quartz on hematite
  Antwerp, N.Y.
Ankerite with quartz and hematite
  Antwerp, N.Y.
Apatite crystals
  Pyrites, N.Y.
Apatite in calcite
  Rossie, N.Y.
Artinite
  Staten Island, N.Y.
Calcite crystal on dolomite crystals
  Penfield, N.Y.
Celestite
  Chittenango Falls, N.Y.
Chondrodite
  Tilly Foster Mine, Brewster, N.Y.
Chrysoberyl-twin crystal
  Saratoga County, N.Y.
Danburite crystal group
  Russell, N.Y.
Dolomite crystal group
  Penfield, N.Y.
Fluorite with dolomite crystals
  Penfield, N.Y.
Garnet with hornblende
  Gore Mt., N.Y.
Gieseckite after nepheline
  Natural Bridge, N.Y.
Hematite-botryoidal
  Antwerp, N.Y.

Hematite-oolitic
  Clinton, N.Y.
Labradorite
  Saranac Lake, N.Y.
Labradorite-closeup
  Saranac Lake, N.Y.
Lapis lazuli
  Edwards, N.Y.
Microcline-Amazonite
  Valhalla, N.Y.
Millerite
  Antwerp, N.Y.
Pyroxene-augite
  Star Lake, N.Y.
Pyroxene-augite
  Fine, N.Y.
Pyroxene-augite
  Pyrites, N.Y.
Pyroxene-diopside
  De Kalb, N.Y.
Pyroxene-diopside (coccolite)
  Cascadeville, N.Y.
Scapolite (wernerite)
  Olmstedville, N.Y.
Spinel and chondrodite
  Amity, N.Y.
Sulfur on dolomite
  Monroe Co., N.Y.
Zircon
  Rossie, N.Y.
Pyritized Nautiloid, Tornoceras sp.
  Alden, N.Y.

History of
New York State
Mineralogy

PALEO-INDIANS

The first people to collect and use minerals in the State were probably Paleo-Indians who discovered that flint, suitable for making sharp implements, was abundant in the hillsides along the Hudson River near Coxsackie. Parker (1924) reports on the great Algonkian flint mines at Coxsackie where a great abundance of worked flint and waste material was literally a "mountain of arrowheads". It was estimated that activity began at the flint mines at least 5,000 years ago and probably 50 to 100 people worked intermittently on the hill during busy seasons when such work was possible and necessary. "Flint Mine Hill" is principally composed of Normanskill shale which consists of chert (flint) and shale. The chert is varicolored from black and green to gray. The hammerstones used to chip the flint were cobbles of convenient size.

Flint is a name widely used by archeologists for material used for siliceous artifacts. It is a synonym of chert, a dense dark gray, black or colored chalcedony.

STATE GEOLOGICAL SURVEY

(Merrill-1906; Kaplan-1965; Fisher-1976, 1977)

On April 15, 1836, The New York State Assembly authorized a Geological and Mineralogical Survey at the suggestion of Amos Eaton and Edward Hitchcock. This was promoted by John Dix, the Secretary of State and by Governor Marcy. The State was divided into four districts: W. W. Mather was placed in charge of the first (Eastern); Ebenezer Emmons, the second (Northern); Timothy A. Conrad, the third (Central); and Lardner Vanuxem, the fourth (Western). The mineralogical and chemical work of the survey was put in charge of Dr. Lewis Caleb Beck. Dr. John Torrey became the botanist while Dr. James E. DeKay accepted charge of the Zoological Department. At the end of the first season, Conrad resigned to become paleontologist of the survey. James Hall, who had been Emmon's assistant, was put in charge of the Fourth district and Vanuxem was transferred to the third. Hall also soon became State Paleontologist.

Annual reports were made with the final reports issued in 1842–1843. In the Paleontology of New York (1846–1894), Hall produced

11

15 quarto volumes comprising 4,320 pages and 980 lithograph plates of fossils. This was a superb accomplishment in the annals of American geology. In 1842, Beck's Mineralogy of New York was published. This 536 page quarto volume was illustrated with 533 crystal drawings and 7 plates.

Since 1888, many Bulletins and other publications of the New York State Museum have contained excellent scientific reports on the mineralogy, geology and paleontology of many parts of the state. Authors include H. L. Alling, A. F. Buddington, J. M. Clarke, H. P. Cushing, D. W. Fisher, W. Goldring, J. F. Kemp, W. J. Miller, D. H. Newland, R. Ruedemann, C. H. Smyth, Jr., and H. P. Whitlock.

The State Science Survey is currently comprised of three units: (1) The Anthropological Survey; (2) The Biological Survey; and (3) The Geological Survey. The New York State Museum and Science Service has issued the following publications on Geology and Paleontology; (a) Museum Bulletins; (b) Special Publications; (c) Map and Chart Series; (d) Museum Circulars; (e) Museum Handbooks; (f) Museum Memoirs; (g) Annual Report of the New York State Museum and Science Service. Many are out of print; (e) was discontinued with #19, 1942; (g) is not published continuously.

Recent active research investigations pursued by the staff of the Geological Survey include the study of subsurface strata, environmental, geology, earthquake and seismic studies and geochemical investigations as related to stream pollution and genetic rock studies.

At the present time, there are no mineral or fossil exhibits available (per se) to the public for viewing. Researchers may study portions of the collections that interest them.

MAJOR CONTRIBUTORS TO NEW YORK STATE MINERALOGY AND GEOLOGY

Harold Lattimore Alling (Jensen-1961)

Harold Lattimore Alling was born February 7, 1888 in Rochester, New York. He graduated from the University of Rochester in 1915 with honors in Geology.

The Alling family had a summer camp near Keene Valley in the Adirondack Mountains. One summer he learned that Professor James Kemp of Columbia University was doing field work near Keene so he volunteered his services as Professor Kemp's field assistant. This association established a lively and lasting interest in the geology of the Adirondack region. He entered Columbia University obtaining his A.M. degree in 1917 and his Ph.D. in 1920.

From 1917 to 1920, Harold Alling served as geologist for the New York State Museum. In 1917, he made a thorough survey of the Adirondack graphite deposits. Returning to the University of Rochester in 1920, he became chairman of the Geology Department from 1924 to 1953.

Continuous research on feldspars and summer field work in the Adirondacks led to the publication of dozens of mineralogical and geological reports. He retired in 1953 and died July 27, 1960.

Lewis Caleb Beck (Merrill-1906)

Lewis Caleb Beck, M.D. was born in Schenectady, New York October 4, 1798. He graduated from Union College in 1817 and from 1830 to 1853 he was Professor of Chemistry and Natural History at Rutgers University. He was also Professor of Chemistry at Albany (NY) Medical College from 1840 to 1853. Beck became Mineralogist of the New York State Geological Survey in 1836. In January 1840, he submitted a report to the Assembly of the State of New York on the Mineralogical and Chemical Department of the Geological Survey. He included a report of the mineralogy of each county in the state. Mineralogy of New York, published in 1842, was the first state topographical mineralogy. Beck died April 20, 1853.

John Stafford Brown

John Stafford Brown was born September 26, 1894 in Thomas County, Kansas. The Missouri School of Mines awarded him a B.S. in 1917 and later in 1935 an E.M. degree. He obtained his M.S. from George Washington University in 1922 and his Ph.D. from Columbia University in 1925. He was geologist on the Missouri Geological Survey 1917–1919 and joined St. Joe Lead Company (now St. Joe Minerals Corporation) at Edwards, New York in 1928, becoming Chief Geologist of the company in 1947. He held this position until retirement in 1959. While at Edwards, he made many major contributions to the mineralogy and geology of the Edwards-Balmat zinc district of St. Lawrence County. (See bibliography, p. 180.)

Arthur Francis Buddington (Hess-1962; Byrne-1975; American Men of Science)

In the present century, Dr. Arthur Francis Buddington made many very significant contributions to the mineralogy and geology of the northern part of the state. Born in 1890, he was Professor of Geology at Princeton University from 1920 to 1959. He spent 24 summers with the U.S. Geological Survey and 16 summers as Geologist for the New York State Museum. He was an exceptional field geologist and it is reported that he studied many thousands of rock outcrops and walked thousands of miles, chiefly in the Adirondacks. After a summer's field

Dr. Lewis Caleb Beck
Photograph of a painting at Rutgers University, New Brunswick, N.J.
(Taken by Essex Blue Printing Co.)

work he would return to Princeton where he would continue detailed chemical and petrographic studies of the samples he had collected. He was a prolific writer and a selection of his publications is listed in the bibliography on p. 180. An ammonium feldspar was named buddingtonite in 1946.

Parker Cleaveland (Merrill–1906)

Parker Cleaveland was born January 15, 1780 and died October 16, 1858.

Six years after graduating from Harvard College in 1799, Parker Cleaveland became Professor of mathematics, natural philosophy, and mineralogy at Bowdoin College, Brunswick, Maine. The first edition of his Treatise on Mineralogy and Geology appeared in 1816. The second edition was published in two volumes in 1822. This was the first attempt by an American at a systematic treatise on mineraology. He corresponded with other American mineralogists of his time exchanging specimens and getting locality information. His collection is still preserved at Bowdoin College, Brunswick, Maine. Cleavelandite, a platy albite was named after him in 1823.

The Danas and Dana's System of Mineralogy (Gilman–1899)

Mineralogists the world over have associated the name Dana with comprehensive and standard texts of mineralogy. Born on February 12, 1813 in Utica, New York; James Dwight Dana graduated from Yale College in 1833. In 1836, Dana became assistant to Professor Benjamin Silliman in chemistry. Ten years later he became an Editor of the American Journal of Science and in 1850 he was appointed Professor of Natural History at Yale College.

Dana was a prolific writer of scientific publications. The first edition of his *System of Mineralogy* was published in 1837 when he was but 24 years old. The second edition appeared in 1844, the third edition in 1850, the fourth edition in 1854, and the fifth edition in 1868. The sixth edition published in 1892 was largely due to the able assistance of his son, Edward Salisbury Dana, who later wrote Dana's *Textbook of Mineralogy*. The fourth edition of the latter, revised and edited by Professor William E. Ford, was published in 1932. A fifth edition by Gaines, Winchell and Skinner was published in 1978. The calcium borosilicate, danalite was named after J. D. Dana in 1866. J. D. Dana died April 14, 1895.

The six editions of Dana's *System of Mineralogy* represent a monumental series of treatises on mineralogy by an American author. The 6th edition is still considered a mineral collector's "bible" as it contains a great wealth of information about minerals. Important world localities were given. Several pages were devoted to mineral localities in New York State.

1944 saw the publication of Volume I of the seventh edition of Dana's *System of Mineralogy* on Elements, Sulfides, Sulfosalts, Oxides, by Charles Palache, Harry Berman and Clifford Frondel—all of Harvard University.

In 1951, Volume II of the seventh edition by the same three authors on Halides, Nitrates, Borates, Carbonates, Sulfates, Phosphates, Arsenates, Molybdates, etc. was published.

In 1962, Volume III of the seventh edition on the Silica Minerals was published by Clifford Frondel.

Amos Eaton (Merrill-1906; Fenton and Fenton-1953; Fisher-1978)

Amos Eaton was born two centuries ago, May 17, 1776. He graduated from Williams College in 1799, then practiced law for several years, before studying Natural History at Yale University. He was a popular speaker and in 1817 was invited to introduce courses in Natural History at Williams College. A year later he was invited by De Witt Clinton, Governor of the State of New York, to give a series of lectures on Natural History before the State Legislature. He became official lecturer at the Troy Lyceum of Natural History which was later to become Rensselaer Polytechnic Institute. Eaton's "Index to the Geology of the Northern States" (1818) was followed by "A Geological and Agricultural Survey of the District Adjoining the Erie Canal" (1824). Both were milestones in the geological history of this country.

Clifford Frondel

Clifford Frondel was born in New York City, January 8, 1907. After studying at the Colorado School of Mines and Columbia University, obtained a Ph.D. in crystallography at the Massachusetts Institute of Technology in 1939. Joining the Mineralogical faculty at Harvard University that same year, he became Professor of Mineralogy in 1954. He was also Curator of the Harvard Mineralogical Museum. Dr. Frondel has authored or co-authored over 100 scientific books and papers. Several of these are landmarks in mineralogic literature. His interest in the minerals of the state developed when he was living in New York City and had an opportunity to study the collections at the American Museum of Natural History. He is widely known as co-author of Volumes I and II of the seventh edition of Dana's System of Mineralogy and author of Volume III, Silica Minerals. An iron manganese phosphate hydroxide was named frondelite in 1949.

James Hall (Fisher-1976)

James Hall was born in Hingham, Massachusetts on September 12, 1811. His early interest in natural history was aroused when, as a youth, he assisted the organizers of the Boston Society of Natural History. In 1830, Hall enrolled in the Rensselaer School (which later became the Rensselaer Polytechnic Institute). There, he studied Geology and Natural History under Amos Eaton. After graduating from the Rensselaer School in 1833 with an M.A., he taught chemistry there until 1836. The New York State Geological and Mineralogical Survey was established in that year and Hall received an appointment as a junior member of the newly formed survey. Endowed with prodigious energy, a great devotion to science and exceptional competence, Hall was able to produce an extensive series of reports on the geology and paleontology of the state. From 1846 to 1894, Hall produced 15 quarto volumes comprising 4,320 pages and 980 lithograph plates of fossils. These great volumes remain an enduring monument to his achievements. Hall died on August 7, 1896.

James Furman Kemp

James Furman Kemp was born August 14, 1859 and died November 17, 1926. For 35 years he was Head of the Geology Department at Columbia University carrying out field studies in the eastern Adirondacks. Many of his students at Columbia and his assistants in the field later became noted geologists. In 1924, a manganese oxychloride was named kempite.

James G. Manchester (Hawkins-1948)

Individuals who develop an interest in minerals as an avocation often make significant contributions to their adopted scientific hobby field. James G. Manchester was born in Fall River, Massachusetts on September 20, 1871. An excellent typist and stenographer, he received the highest award in these skills at the Columbian Exposition in 1893. He was appointed Assistant Treasurer of the New York Mutual Life Insurance Company and later became the Assistant Director of its Real Estate Division.

Adopting mineralogy as a hobby, he soon acquired a fine collection and donated many minerals to museums. He became active in the New York Mineralogical Club and served as its president. Two of his books, Minerals of Broadway in 1914, and The Minerals of New York City and its Environs in 1931, were published by the New York Mineralogical Club. Manchester died June 28, 1948. His collection is still preserved in the public library of Fall River, Massachusetts.

Samuel Latham Mitchill (Merrill-1906)

Documentation of the mineralogy of the state of New York began as early as 1797 when "A Sketch of the Mineralogical History of New York" by Dr. Samuel Latham Mitchill was published in the *Medical Repository*. Dr. Samuel Latham Mitchill became Professor of Chemistry and Natural History at Columbia College in 1792. Later he was Professor of Natural History and Botany at the University of the State of New York. Dr. Mitchill was a founder and the first president of the Lyceum of Natural History in the City of New York. Samuel Latham Mitchell was born August 20, 1764 and died September 7, 1831.

David Hale Newland (Ruedemann & Goldring-1944)

David Hale Newland was born April 7, 1872 and died October 18, 1943. He graduated in 1894 from Hamilton College where he had studied geology under C. H. Smyth, Jr. Graduate studies in geology were continued at German universities in Munich and Heidelberg. Newland was a member of the New York State Geological Survey from December 1, 1904 until June 30, 1920 when he resigned to do consulting work. He rejoined the Geological Survey of the state as State Geologist continuing in this position until his retirement June 30, 1940. Newland began field work in the Adirondacks in 1898. He was primarily an economic geologist. His numerous reports on the economic minerals and rocks of the state were milestones in this field of information.

Heinrich Ries (Moore-1952)

Heinrich Ries was born in Brooklyn, New York April 30, 1871. After studies in city schools, in Germany and at the Columbia School of Mines, he received his doctorate from Columbia University in 1896. His career in teaching began at Columbia where he held an Assistantship in Mineralogy. He went to Cornell University as Instructor in Economic Geology in 1898 and eight years later became Professor of Economic Geology. In 1914, he was made Head of the Department of Geology, a position he held until his retirement in 1939. His early publications included a report on the monoclinic pyroxenes of the state. Several editions of his Economic Geology that were published covered descriptions of several mines and quarries in the state. He died April 11, 1951.

Elmer B. Rowley

Elmer Rowley was born April 17, 1909 in North Westminster, Vermont. After graduation he was associated with the Glens Falls Insurance Company until retirement in 1970. In 1972, Mr. Rowley became Curator of the Mineral Collections at Union College in Schenectady. Acquiring an interest in mineralogy in the mid-1930's, he attended lectures at Harvard University and studied its research mineral collection whenever possible. From 1948, Elmer Rowley taught adult education classes in mineralogy and geology at Glens Falls High School. He became a charter member and co-sponsor of the Capital District Mineral Club of Albany, New York. His continual interest in the mineral occurrences of the Adirondack Mountain region led to the discovery of several species that had not previously been reported in the state. His enthusiasm for teaching mineralogy to amateurs and his appreciation of fine mineral specimens has been an inspiration to many.

Benjmain Martin Shaub (American Men of Science)

Benjamin Martin Shaub was born in New Freedom, Pennsylvania, January 12, 1892. At Cornell University, he received his M.E. in 1925 and Ph.D. in 1929. He was Assistant Professor of Mineralogy, Petrography and Petrology at Smith College from 1931 to 1941. From 1941 to 1946 he was a Colonel with the U.S. Army Ordnance Department. In 1946, he returned to Smith College as Associate Professor until his retirement in 1958. His photographic and drafting talents ever enhanced his published contributions in mineralogy which included many reports on mineral occurrences in New York State.

Charles Upham Shepard (Merrill–1909; Lange–1975)

Professor Shepard was born June 29, 1804 at Little Compton, Rhode Island. He attended Brown University for two years then transferred to Amherst where he graduated in 1824. He continued his studies at Harvard and at Yale. In 1844, Shepard was named Professor of Chemistry and Natural History at Amherst. A collection of minerals begun as a boy was enlarged and later given to Amherst. Professor Shepard described many new meteorites including two from New York State (Bethlehem in 1860 and Seneca Falls in 1853, see p. 110). His Treatise on Mineralogy was first published in 1832 with a second edition in 1844 and a third edition Vol. 1 in 1852, Vol. 2 in 1857. Several New York State minerals were described in the Treatise and illustrated by crystal drawings. Several new minerals found in New York State were described by Shepard. He died May 1, 1886.

Charles Henry Smyth, Jr. (Buddington–1938)

Charles Henry Smyth, Jr. was born in Oswego, New York in 1866 and died April 4, 1937. He became Professor of Geology at Hamilton

HENRY AUGUSTUS WARD, 1834–1906

College in 1891 and the following year he began field work in the Adirondack Mountains. From 1905 to 1934, Smyth was Professor of Geology at Princeton University. Among his students were W. M. Agar, D. H. Newland and A. F. Buddington, each of whom have made major contributions to the geology and mineralogy of the state. An iron sulfide was named smythite in 1957.

Henry Augustus Ward and Ward's Natural Science Establishment, Inc.
(Ward–1933, 1948; Lange–1975; Jensen–1977).

Henry Augustus Ward was born on March 9, 1834 in Rochester, New York seven weeks before the community became a city. At the age of three years, he collected his first specimen, a shiny pebble of banded gneiss that he found in a pile of stones near his home. This collecting instinct was a strong driving force throughout his entire life. After studying geology at Williams College, he became a pupil of the Swiss naturalist, Louis Agassiz, at Harvard College (now Harvard University). While at Cambridge, Henry became a close friend of Charles Wadsworth and joined him in 1854 to study at the famous School of Mines in Paris. Weekends and vacations afforded the two young men many opportunities to tour Europe and collect minerals and fossils. The trips even extended into Egypt and along the Nile. The growing collections of minerals and fossils encouraged Ward to continue to travel to museums in London and European cities in order to make sales and exchanges. In this way, the business enterprise which was to become Ward's Natural Science Establishment, Inc. was born.

In 1860, Henry A. Ward had returned to Rochester and was appointed Professor of Natural History at the University. Some 40,000 specimens of minerals, fossils and plaster casts of fossils had been collected during his European travels and had been shipped home. The news of this collection spread and soon requests began to come from colleges and museums for mineral and fossil specimens from European and other localities. By 1862, Ward's Natural Science Establishment, Inc. was firmly launched.

A great World's Fair was planned to be held in 1893 in Chicago. Ward made plans to exhibit and engaged 74 men to prepare the exhibition material. The 30 carloads that were sent to Chicago included a large collection of meteorites, minerals and fossils, a collection of replicas of gold nuggets, mounted skeletons and other biological materials. After the Fair was ended, the collection was acquired by Marshall Field for the Field Museum which is now the Chicago Natural History Museum.

In 1897, Ward married Mrs. Lydia Avery Coonley of Chicago and of Wyoming, New York. He had partly retired from active management of the firm and now had more time to make plans for new expeditions. Since about 1878, Henry Ward had become interested in meteorites. A steam driven saw and polishing equipment had been installed at the firm.

A campaign to acquire a great meteorite collection was launched. He thoroughly researched the available literature on known meteorites and engaged in voluminous worldwide correspondence. Then expeditions were launched. Ward's handled meteorites on a prodigious scale during the years 1894 to 1906. Examples of over 90% of the known meteorite falls at the time were secured. Probably more meteorites got into public and university museums via Ward's than from any other source, at least during the late 19th and early 20th centuries. Among the museums that received meteorite collections in the United States were the Field Museum, The American Museum of Natural History, Harvard, and the U.S. National Museum as well as museums in Paris, Vienna, London, and Mexico City. Ward was killed by an auto in Buffalo, N.Y. on July 4, 1906.

George Letchworth English joined Ward's as Head of its Mineral Department in 1913. Previously, Mr. English had been a successful mineral dealer in Philadelphia and New York and for ten years, he had prospected for monazite in the Carolinas. He retired in 1934.

In 1927, the University of Rochester acquired the Establishment and operated it as the Frank A. Ward Foundation of the University until 1934 when it returned to private ownership. In the spring of 1931, Dr. Dean L. Gamble became President of Ward's. He had developed new methods of biological preservations and soon revitalized the entire Biology Division. In 1947, an extensive series of color slides of minerals was introduced. This launched an Audiovisual Department that is now one of the major divisions of the company. William C. Gamble became president of Ward's in 1962.

Ward's Geology Division continues active acquisition of minerals and fossils from worldwide sources. New and modern teaching aids for the earth sciences have found wide popularity. Solo-Learn, a multimedia teaching aid designed for individual instruction, covers many titles in earth science, biology, and chemistry.

Henry A. Ward was the first American to take up the building of museum collections in a systematic and scientific manner. There was a great need for scientific materials (particularly in the field of the natural sciences) among schools, colleges and museums. Ward sensed these needs and spared no effort in world travel to obtain specimens of minerals, rocks, fossils and other natural history items to fill these needs. The phosphate mineral wardite was named after Henry A. Ward in 1896.

Herbert Percy Whitlock (Pough-1949)

Herbert Percy Whitlock was born July 31, 1868 and died 1948. He graduated from Columbia University in 1889 where he studied mineralogy and had been an assistant in the department. Two years later he joined the New York State Museum in Albany, becoming Mineralogist there in 1904. He became State Mineralogist in 1916 and continued in that position until 1918. At that time, he accepted an appointment as Curator and Chairman of the Department of Mineralogy at the American Museum of Natural History in New York City, positions that he held until his retirement in 1941. While at Albany, Mr. Whitlock was very active in mineralogical studies and published many articles. His list of New York mineral localities was published as New York State Museum Bulletin #70 in 1903. "Calcites of New York" was published in 1910 as a New York State Museum Memoir 13. The latter publication was notable for the magnificent crystal drawings of calcite from several localities in the state. A calcium magnesium phosphate was named whitlockite in 1941.

NATURAL SCIENCE ORGANIZATIONS

The histories of mineralogical and geological societies are very closely interwoven. Interest in the mineralogy of New York State is reported to have begun before the end of the 1700's. (Mitchill-1797; Beck-1842). Many societies were formed during the 1800's, three of which are in existence today: The Buffalo Society of Natural Sciences (1861) had a Geological Section soon after it was founded. The Rochester Academy of Science (1881) has a Mineral Section (1935) that has roots that were established in 1884. The New York Mineralogical Club was initiated in 1886.

THE BUFFALO SOCIETY OF NATURAL SCIENCES
(Riemann-1938; Hamlin-1938; Sparrow-1938)

A Young Men's Association founded in 1836 became the first principal center for organized cultural activities in Buffalo. The establishment of a library was their first concern. A Standing Committee on the Natural Sciences was appointed in 1847 and began to catalog and augment the collections of minerals, fossils, shells and pressed plants that had begun to accumulate in their possession. In 1861, a new association, The Buffalo Society of Natural Sciences was organized.

In 1865, the Society received the Charles Wadsworth cabinet of minerals and a Ward collection of casts of fossils. Donations from individuals and many other sources have continually augmented the research and exhibition collections of the Buffalo Museum of Science, which is operated by the Buffalo Society of Natural Sciences. During recent decades, the Mineral Department has acquired fine suites of minerals and gemstones, including superb specimens from recent world discoveries. Suites of local fossils have been presented to the Museum, including classic examples of pyrite-marcasite replacements of Devonian fossils. A suite of Herkimer "diamonds" from Herkimer County has been donated.

The Science Library of the Museum possesses nearly complete runs of important earth and life science periodicals from their early beginning. A book collection entitled "Milestones of Science," that has been assembled by the Museum, embraces first and early rare editions of books epochal in several fields of science. This is a collection of great works whose publication made revolutionary contributions to the advancement of science. The collection of Milestones of Science comprises one of the most complete collections of its kind in the world.

ROCHESTER ACADEMY OF SCIENCE—MINERAL SECTION
(Fairchild–1902)

An organizational meeting for a Microscopical Society was held in Rochester, N.Y. on January 13, 1879. Since many of its members had additional scientific interests, the organization was changed to The Rochester Academy of Science which became incorporated on May 14, 1881. From the time of its origin, the Academy was, for many years, the only scientific society in Rochester. Its declared purpose was to promote study and research on any aspect of the Natural Sciences in Western New York.

Herman LeRoy Fairchild was a leader of the Academy's activities in its early years. He was also instrumental in the formation of the Geological Society of America in 1884. Professor Fairchild thoroughly investigated the glacial and geological history of western New York. Many of his original articles on these subjects were published in the "Proceedings" of the Academy, which was first issued in 1890.

A Geological Section of the Academy was started in 1884. Increasing interest in minerals among its members caused the Geological Section of the Academy to become a Mineral Section in 1935. In support of the growing country-wide interest in gems and minerals, the Mineral Section became a Charter Member of the Eastern Federation of Mineralogical and Lapidary Societies, Inc. in early 1951. An annual mineral symposium started by the president of the Mineral Section in the spring of 1974, has developed a national interest.

THE NEW YORK MINERALOGICAL CLUB
(Levinson–1916)

The New York Mineralogical Club was instituted September 21, 1886 and formally organized April 1887. Professor D. S. Martin served as Chairman and George F. Kunz as Secretary of the newly formed organization. The object of the new club was to develop and maintain an interest in the study of the minerals occurring in the rocks of New York City. This area of interest was later expanded to include noted mineral localities near the city. The membership rolls of the Club include the names of many individuals who have made significant contributions to the mineralogy of New York State. Club members assembled a collection of the pegmatite and other minerals of New York City.

HOBBY GROUPS

Since 1930, more than 30 geological and mineralogical societies have sprung up in several communities in the state and on Long Island. Many of them are affiliated with the Eastern Federation of Mineralogical and Lapidary Societies, Inc. Various aspects of Mineralogy, Paleontology, the Lapidary Arts and Geology are included in club activities. Several colleges and universities in the state sponsor extra-curricular geology groups during the school year.

Professionals, students, and hobbyists alike belong to mineral clubs. Mineralogical studies by club members are often reported in scientific journals. Popular articles on minerals as well as current news items and events are listed in club newsletters and hobby magazines.

Mineral Magazines

Many of the first mineral magazines of this country were published in New York City. Dr. Archibald Bruce published the American Mineralogical Journal 1810-1814. This was the first journal in America devoted to Geological Sciences and was a milestone in the history of American science. It was also the predecessor to the American Journal of Science. (Greene-1958) The American Mineralogical Journal was reprinted by Hafner Publishing Co. (White-1958).

Arthur Chamberlain of New York City edited and published several popular magazines that were written for the collector:

Exchangers Monthly—November 1885 to November 1890.

Mineralogists Monthly—November 1890 to March 1893.

The Mineral Collector—March 1894 to February 1909.

THE AMERICAN MINERALOGIST (Phair-1969)

In 1916, several eminent mineralogists met in Albany, New York to discuss the formation of a mineralogical society that would be independent of the Geological Society of America (GSA). Three years later, The Mineralogical Society of America (MSA) was organized. H. P. Whitlock of the American Museum was one of the founding fathers of the new society.

The first issue of the American Mineralogist was issued in July, 1916 by a group of men who desired to distribute news of minerals and localities to a growing number of scientists and mineral collectors. The MSA chose this journal as the society's official publication. The great number of scientific reports in this journal on the minerals of the state is evidenced by references in the bibliography of this book (p. 180). Today, the articles in this journal are of a highly technical level.

ROCKS AND MINERALS MAGAZINE (Frondel and Montgomery-1951)

Peter Zodac was born in Peekskill, Westchester County, New York on September 24, 1894. For several years he served as an engineering inspector for the County Park Commission. An active mineral collector, he was encouraged by many friends to publish a mineral magazine for the beginning collector. The first issue of Rocks and Minerals appeared in September 1926. Since much of his financial support came from beginners rather than the advanced collector, the magazine was kept on the beginner's level. In the old days of mineral collecting, there was a close union of amateur and professional mineralogists and Zodac was able to obtain many articles of good professional level for his magazine. Zodac died on January 27, 1967. "Rocks and Minerals" is now published by Heldref Publications of Washington, D.C.

THE MINERALOGICAL RECORD

The first issue of the Mineralogical Record came off the press in the spring of 1970. This high quality magazine for the advanced amateur publishes many feature articles on outstanding minerals and their localities.

THE LAPIDARY JOURNAL

Published in San Diego, California, "The Lapidary Journal" was first issued 30 years ago. This high quality magazine for the amateur hobbyist is widely circulated. Articles on gem and ornamental minerals of the state have appeared on pages of the Journal.

Minerals of the Principal Rock Types of the State

MINERALS OF THE IGNEOUS ROCKS OF THE STATE

Albite
Allanite
Amphibole
  Hornblende
Andesine
Apatite
Beryl
Biotite
Chrysoberyl
Garnet
  Almandine
Ilmenite
Labradorite
Magnetite
Microcline
Monazite
Muscovite
Oligoclase
Olivine
Orthoclase

Perthite
Pyrite
Pyroxene
  Augite
  Enstatite
  Hypersthene
Quartz
  Milky
  Rose
  Rutilated
  Smoky
Rutile
Titanite (Sphene)
Tourmaline
  Schorl
Xenotime
Zircon
  Cyrtolite

The Minerals of the Pegmatites of the State

(Agar–1933; Frondel–1936; Buddington–1939; Rowley–1942a, 1942b, 1960, 1962; Jahns–1959; Tan–1966; Schuberth–1968)

Pegmatites are very coarse grained igneous rocks that occur as veins, dikes, sills, and lenses in other rocks. They are omnipresent in all different rocks of the Adirondack region, southeastern New York and Manhattan Island. Pegmatites vary greatly in size and in composition. They have abundant quartz that is usually milky or smoky, sometimes rose colored or clear. The presence of potash feldspar that usually occurs as perthite, has encouraged quarry operations in many of the larger pegmatites in years past. The common accessory mineral is mica (muscovite or biotite). Beryl has been found in New York, Saratoga and Westchester Counties. Rare earth minerals have been reported in Saratoga County and elsewhere. Uranium minerals are not abundant. Lithium minerals that are often found in many other

29

pegmatites in New England and elsewhere are nearly nonexistent. Pyrrhotite has been reported.

The pegmatites of upstate New York have been divided into four types (Tan–1966):

Southern Adirondacks: biotite pegmatites.

Eastern Adirondacks: biotite-muscovite and hornblende-biotite pegmatites.

Northwest Adirondacks: metamorphosed diopside-phlogopite pegmatites.

Southeastern New York (Bedford): muscovite-beryl pegmatites.

About 170 mineral species and varieties have been reported on Manhattan Island since 1798. They were discovered during excavations for the construction of highways, buildings, subways, bridges, water mains and utilities. Minerals have ranged from common quartz, feldspars and micas to rare crystals of xenotime. Faceted stones have been cut from gem quality beryl (aquamarine and golden beryl), garnet (spessartine), smoky quartz and tourmaline that were discovered in New York city excavations. (Chamberlin–1888; Manchester–1914; 1931; Schuberth–1968; Sinkankas–1959).

The ages of the Adirondack pegmatites have been reported at about 1020 to 1200 million years. (Marble–1943; Silver–1969) (See also pp. 31, 32, 46, 54, 178, 179.)

The Bedford Pegmatite—Westchester County

(Newland–1906; 1916; Lee–1928; Manchester–1931; Newland and Hartnagel–1932; Agar–1933; Tan–1966)

The production of feldspar was an important quarry industry in the state for several decades the early part of the 20th century. Pegmatites containing potash feldspar, usually microcline-perthite, were widely distributed in the Adirondacks and also south and southwest of Bedford village in Westchester County.

The Bedford quarries were opened in 1878. Altogether, eight mines and quarries were opened in the area. (Baylis, Bullock, Bueresch, Hobby, Kelt, Kinkel, McDonald, Speranza). The Baylis and the Kinkel (sometimes reported as Kinkle) quarries became a mecca for mineral collectors and a variety of minerals have been reported from them.

The potash feldspar, a perthitic microcline, occurred as crystals up to 5 feet in length, also as crystalline aggregates, and was suitable for pottery. Albite (cleavelandite) was common. It was not entirely free of quartz but was suitable for making enamel. Small albite crystals sometimes were found in vugs. The pegmatitic intergrowths of albite and quartz together with some microcline was used in the manufacture of glass and scouring soaps. Quartz was abundant. Massive milky quartz was shipped to potteries for making porcelains and was also used for a wood filler. The rose quartz was often of excellent color and shipments were made to Europe and the Orient for carving. Rose quartz from the Kinkel quarry was asterated, the asterism being caused by microscopic inclusions of rutile crystals which can be observed in thin section.

Greenish-yellow beryl was common and crystals up to a foot in length were found in the Kinkel quarry. Tourmaline was also abundant in the Bedford pegmatites. In 1928, a magnificent group of large black crystals was reconstructed from fragments. 32 crystals, each averaging 2 inches in diameter and from 8 to 18 inches in length were mounted in a radiating group.

Cyrtolite (an altered zircon) from the Baylis and Kinkel quarries was discovered to contain 5.5% of the element hafnium. The age of the Bedford pegmatites is reported to be about 360–380 million years (Agar–1933; Tan–1966).

Minerals reported from the Bedford pegmatites (Manchester–1931; Agar–1933):

Allanite

Almandite (Almandine)

Amphibole

  Hornblende

Apatite

Autunite

Beryl

  Aquamarine

  Golden

  Yellow

Biotite

Columbite

Cyrtolite—see Zircon

Feldspar

  Albite

    Cleavelandite

  Microcline

  Orthoclase

  Perthite

Graphite

Gummite

Ilmenite

  Menaccinite

Kaolinite

Limonite

Magnetite

Muscovite

Opal

  Hyalite

Pyrite

Pyrolusite (dendritic)

Pyroxene

Quartz

  Citrine

  Milky

  Rock Crystal

  Rose

  Rose (asterated)

  Smoky

Rutile

Titanite (sphene)

Torbernite

Tourmaline

  Green

  Black

*Uraconite

Uraninite (?)

Uranophane

*A discredited species

Washingtonite (= Hystatite = a
    mixture of ilmenite with
    hematite or magnetite)

Zircon
    Cyrtolite

The McLear Pegmatite—St. Lawrence County

(Shaub-1929, 1940; Yedlin-1940; Heinrich-1958; Tan-1966)

The McLear pegmatite near DeKalb Junction was discovered in 1907. It occurs as tabular masses in a series of metamorphosed limestones and quartzites of Grenville Age. The age of the McLear pegmatite is reported as 1,094 million years. Mining operations for feldspar (perthite) were continuous for about 25 years. Since then, the broken rock on the dumps has been used sporadically for highway construction.

The chief minerals are feldspar (perthite) and smoky quartz. Other minerals include actinolite, allanite, apatite, biotite, calcite, chlorite, danburite, diopside, kaolinite, magnetite, molybdenite, phlogopite, pyrite, pyrrhotite, rutile, serpentine, talc, thucholite, titanite (sphene), tourmaline, tremolite, and uraninite.

Minerals of the Sedimentary Rocks in the State

(Limestones, Shales, Conglomerates, and Sandstones):

Anhydrite
Aragonite
Barite
Calcite
Celestite
Dolomite
Goethite
Gypsum
   Massive selenite
Halite

Hematite
Limonite
Marcasite
Pyrite
Quartz
   Chalcedony
   Chert (flint)
Sphalerite
Strontianite
Sulfur

Herkimer "Diamonds"

(Vanuxem–1842; Cushing–1905a; Goldring–1931; Dake, Fleener, Wilson–1939; Newland and Vaughn–1942; Kay and Grossman–1952; Dunn and Fisher–1954; Fisher–1962; Tuttle–1973)

Herkimer "Diamonds" have been admired by man for more than two centuries. The shiny little crystals and fragments of quartz that washed out of hillsides intrigued the Indians. German emigrants (Palatines) began to settle along the Mohawk River Valley in the early 1700's. They, too, noticed the glass-like "little stones" that were uncovered as some lands were cultivated.

The expansion of commerce and industry in the State spurred the need for better ways of transportation from the Hudson River westward to Buffalo and Lake Erie. It was finally decided that canals would be the solution. The falls of the Mohawk River at Little Falls in Herkimer County were in the way of a canal. By 1796 a short canal with locks was completed to circumvent this obstacle. The canal and locks were later expanded and by 1825 the Erie Canal was completed all the way across the state.

While the canals were being built at Little Falls, excavations were made in the rock that contained the quartz crystals. When the canal basin was dredged in the mid 1940's, quantities of broken rock were dug up, piled along the river banks and later used for highway construction. During the construction of the canal and railroads at Little Falls, and the building of roads in Herkimer County, laborers found and sold many crystals. The crystal bonanzas near Middleville were more fully revealed when a new highway was built south of the town. At the present time there are several sites near Middleville in Herkimer County and near Stone Arabia in Montgomery County where collectors may go and, for a fee, collect "diamonds."

The fame of Herkimer "Diamonds" became world-wide. In 1842 Vanuxem reported that there was probably no locality in the world that produced more perfect or more beautiful quartz crystals than at Middleville. Some cavities were said to have yielded a half bushel of crystals. A collection of over 14,000 crystals and matrix specimens was exhibited at the Chicago World's Fair in 1893.

Herkimer "Diamond" (Syn: "Little Falls Diamond") is applied to the near perfect brilliant quartz crystals that occur in cavities of the Little Falls dolomite (dolostone) of Cambrian Age. The crystals are transparent and doubly terminated. Smoky quartz crystals are rare. It is reported that 100,000 tiny crystals weighed only one ounce. Crystals over 6 inches in length have been found. Small liquid inclusions are common and the liquid may contain a movable air bubble. When crystals that contain liquid occur near the frost line, low winter temperatures may cause the liquid to freeze and the crystal to fracture. The break often occurs along a poorly developed cleavage plane. A jet black hydrocarbon occurs as inclusions in the quartz crystals and as irregular masses up to one inch in size in the rock. Early mineralogists believed the black material to be a form of anthracite. It has been identified as anthraxolite (Dunn and Fisher–1954).

Quartz crystals may occur singly, as groups, or as druses in a rock cavity. Several crystals may be found in a large cavity along joint surfaces of the dolomite rock. The Little Falls dolomite (dolostone) is a gray crystalline rock of Cambrian Age with cherty layers at some horizons. It occurs in Herkimer and Montgomery Counties and also at Diamond Point and Diamond Island at the southern end of Lake George in Warren County.

Minerals of the Lockport Formation

(Eaton–1824; Giles–1920; Hawkins–1925, 1926; Jensen–1942; Awald–1958, 1969; Fisher–1959; Zenger–1965)

A region where sedimentary rocks predominate is seldom noted for fine mineral specimens. One exception is the Lockport formation of Middle Silurian age. Called the Niagara Limestone in early geological literature, it is made up of a series of magnesian limestones, or dolomites (called Lockport dolomite or dolostone in the literature) that are interbedded with limestone beds. The latter are frequently fossiliferous, containing corals, crinoid parts, brachiopods, etc.

The Lockport formation forms a conspicuous escarpment at Lewiston in Niagara County. This escarpment continues west from the Niagara River into Ontario, Canada where it is a dominant land feature south of Grimsby and at Hamilton. It is the cap rock at Niagara Falls and forms the upper crest of the Upper Falls of the Genesee River in Rochester. The formation extends nearly 200 miles eastward from the Niagara River. At Ilion, it becomes a series of shale layers and soon pinches out. The term Lockport dolostone has sometimes been used to distinguish the dolomitic rock layers from the mineral dolomite. The rock has been quarried in several localities and the crushed stone has been widely used in highway construction and in concrete.

Over 150 years ago, Amos Eaton described the Niagara limestone (Lockport formation) as possessing a peculiar fetid odor and abundant "geodes" containing crystals of "calc-spar," "zinc-blende," "fluorspar" and other minerals (Eaton–1824). Throughout its length, the dolomitic rock is dark grey to dark brownish-grey, massive and sometimes sugary. The upper layers contain rounded to irregular vugs that are often lined with dolomite crystals and may also contain crystals of calcite, celestite, fluorite, sphalerite, also crystalline anhydrite, clear selenite, and other minerals.

When the Erie Canal was dug west of the city of Lockport in Niagara County prior to 1824 and southwest of the city of Rochester in Monroe County prior to 1822, excavations were made in the Lockport formation. The broken rock that was piled along the Canal banks provided mineralogists with an introduction to the exceptional minerals that were present.

Minerals that occur in the vugs or in seams in the Lockport formation are:

Anhydrite.   Occurs as crystalline white to bluish-white masses often grading into gypsum. (common)

Barite.   Crystalline, white. (rare)

Calcite.   Occurs as white to golden yellow modified scalenohedral crystals up to 90 mm long. (abundant)

Celestite.   Occurs as white to pale sky-blue lath-like crystals, groups of crystals and crystalline masses sometimes embedded in clear gypsum (selenite). (common)

Dolomite.   Occurs as china-white to pinkish rhombohedrons, singly or in groups, sometimes partly coated with drusy calcite crystals or very tiny crystals of marcasite. (abundant)

Fluorite.   Occurs as sharp cubic crystals up to 65 mm on an edge, sometimes embedded in clear gypsum (selenite). Colors are shades of blue, rarely light green or yellow. Occasionally other crystal forms modify the cube. (common)

Galena. This occurs as fissure fillings in the massive dolomite rocks, rarely in small crystals. (not common)

Gypsum. Vugs frequently contain snow-white masses of gypsum that sometimes grade into anhydrite; also transparent masses (selenite) that may embed dolomite, fluorite, celestite, marcasite, etc. (common)

Marcasite. This occurs in some localities as dark, thin bladed, hair-like crystals seldom exceeding 3 mm on dolomite and calcite. The crystals have erroneously been reported in the past as acmite and rutile. (common)

Pyrite. This occurs as druses, sometimes as tiny crystals. (rare)

Quartz. Occurs as white druses, sugary masses and massive chert. (not common)

Sphalerite. Occurs as crystals and fissure fillings. The smaller crystals up to 6 mm are brilliant, light amber and translucent. Larger crystals and groups up to an inch are dark amber to reddish-brown and translucent to opaque and are sometimes coated with drusy calcite crystals. (common)

Sulfur. Pale yellow masses and crude crystals occur in cavities and seams. (rare)

Other mineral species that have been reported include chalcopyrite, magnesite, siderite, and strontianite.

The Hydrocarbons

The hydrocarbons present in the Lockport dolomite are responsible for the bituminous odor when the rock is broken. Dense black crusts coat fissures and partings in some of the rock layers. Gobs of grease-like material sometimes occur in vugs and may coat or infiltrate minerals present. The presence of hydrocarbon in the rock is sometimes evidenced by the fluorescence under long wave ultraviolet light of areas where fossils are present.

A geochemical study of muck soil and peat bogs overlying the Lockport dolomite near Manning, Orleans County has been reported. Excessive amounts of up to 16 percent of zinc in the soil had made areas of muck land commercially unproductive by the dwarfing of plants and the yellowing of leaves of such farm crops as spinach. It was concluded that the zinc in the soils were derived by ground water reactions on sphalerite in the underlying Lockport dolomite (dolostone). Concentrations of lead in the soils was derived by similar reactions on the galena in the underlying rock. Other metals found in the peat soils include strontium, vanadium, zirconium, phosphorus, boron, cobalt, zinc, lead, copper, nickel and barium. The concentration of these metals is greater in the peat soils than in the underlying mineralized soil (Cannon-1955; Goldschmidt-1937).

MINERALS OF THE METAMORPHIC ROCKS

Common minerals of the crystalline limestone (marbles) and the contact metamorphic calc-silicate rocks of the state are described (Kemp & Hollick-1894; Ries-1895; Agar-1921, 1923; Buddington-1934, 1939; Buddington & Whitcomb-1941; Ayres-1945; Cosminsky-1947).

Metamorphism produces mineralogical and structural changes in solid rock. (Turner & Verhoogen-1966). Contact metamorphism at or near the contacts of ancient sedimentary rocks and granitic intrusive rocks in many areas of the state has produced minerals that have had wide attraction and the attention of mineralogists for decades.

The principal regions of contact metamorphism occur in parts of St. Lawrence, Jefferson, Lewis, Essex and Orange (*) counties. The newly formed minerals occur as scattered individuals, or as aggregates in marble or calc-silicate rocks at varying distances from the contact with the igneous rocks.

The following minerals have been reported. Included are examples from classic and type localities for several minerals.

Amphibole	Pyroxene
Actinolite	Diopside
Edenite**	Enstatite
Tremolite	Quartz
Apatite	Rutile
Calcite	Scapolite
Chondrodite	Serendibite
Clinochlore	Serpentine
Dolomite	Spinel
Epidote	Talc
Garnet	Titanite (sphene)
Grossular	Vesuvianite (idocrase)
Graphite	Warwickite**
Phlogopite	Wollastonite
Pyrite	

*Orange County was a very popular collecting area during the early and middle 19th centuries.

**The type localities for these minerals are in Orange County.

Minerals found in the gneisses of the State include:

Albite	Hematite
Allanite	Kyanite
Amphibole	Magnetite
Hornblende	Muscovite
Apatite	Pyrite
Biotite	Pyroxene
Epidote	Augite
Feldspar	Hypersthene
Garnet	Quartz
Almandine	Sillimanite
Andradite	Zircon
Graphite	

Minerals found in the schists of the State include:

Amphibole	Kyanite
Actinolite	Monazite
Tremolite	Muscovite
Biotite	Quartz
Chlorite	Sillimanite
Garnet	Staurolite
Almandine	Tourmaline

Some Mines
of the State
and Their Minerals

THE IRON MINES

Many outstanding minerals have been reported from the iron mines of the state. During the 19th century and the early 1900's, some of these mines have been the source of minerals that have captivated the world wide attention of mineralogists. Included in such a list are chondrodite and the associated minerals from the Tilly Foster mine at Brewster in Putnam County and millerite from the Sterling hematite mine at Antwerp in Jefferson County.

MAGNETITE MINES

Magnetite has long been an important ore mineral in both the Adirondack region and the Hudson Highlands. Some of the earliest discoveries were made by surveyors when their magnetized compass needles were affected by masses of magnetite in the rocks.

THE ADIRONDACK MAGNETITE MINES

(Emmons–1838; Beck–1842; Newland–1919; Newland and Kemp–1908)

Adirondack magnetites were worked prior to 1800. The occurrence of ore in the region is indicated on the early maps made during the French occupation of the Champlain Valley. Several of the magnetite ore bodies occur in the Mineville area. The first mine was opened about 1785. Lovers Hole, a pit in the Barton Hill mines north of Mineville, contained extremely rich ore. This was the source of excellent modified octahedral crystals of magnetite up to 3 cm. in size, first obtained about 1887–1888.

The major magnetite deposits that have been prospected and mined in the Adirondacks are immense lenticular or tabular masses, usually very irregular in shape, that occur in the rocks of the area. Nearly all of these rocks are metamorphic and include granitic and other gneisses, meta-anorthosite, etc. (Newland and Kemp–1908; Buddington–1939; Broughton, Fisher, Isachsen and Rickard–1966).

The magnetites of the Adirondacks have been classified as titaniferous and non-titaniferous based on their titanium content due to the presence of ilmenite. Even the non-titaniferous magnetite ores are reported to contain a small percentage of titanium that is believed due to omnipresent titanite (sphene) which is easily removed during milling operations.

Many interesting minerals occur with magnetite and in the rocks in which it occurs. Allanite is abundant in the Mineville district of Essex County and was reported to have occurred in tabular crystals up to the size of one's hand. (Kemp–1897; Kemp and Ruedemann–1910; Newland–1935). The age of an allanite from a pegmatite at the summit of Whiteface Mountain was calculated to be about 1,200 million years old (Marble–1943).

Apatite is an accessory mineral in nearly all of the rocks associated with the Adirondack magnetite deposits. At Lyon Mountain in Clinton County, small bright transparent crystals up to 6mm were found (Whitlock–1907). A reddish-brown, rare earth-bearing apatite occurs with the magnetite at Mineville in Essex County (McKeown and Klemic–1956).

Martite is hematite that is pseudomorphous after magnetite. It is black, only weakly magnetic and is abundant at many localities in the Adirondacks. The lack of its early recognition by mine companies often delayed the successful processing of the ore.

Lyon Mountain

(Whitlock–1907; Buddington–1939; Gallagher–1937)

Numerous miarolithic cavities up to 3 feet by 4 feet by 1 foot and larger were discovered in the granite of the magnetite deposits at Lyon Mountain in Clinton County. Minerals that have been found in the cavities and in the rocks include:

Albite	Molybdenite
Amphibole	Orthoclase
Asbestos (Byssolite)	Perthite
Hastingsite	Pyrite
Hornblende	Pyroxene
Apatite	Aegirine–Augite
Biotite	Augite
Calcite	Quartz
Chlorite	Scapolite (wernerite)
Epidote	Stilbite
Hematite	Titanite (sphene)
Ilmenite	Wernerite
Magnetite	Zircon

Many of these minerals occurred as small, sharp crystals. The larger crystals of hornblende, microcline-perthite, orthoclase, and quartz were commonly etched and corroded.

Lake Sanford Titaniferous Magnetite

(Emmons–1842; Kemp–1899; Newland–1908)

A group of prospectors searching for silver in 1826 discovered magnetite in the Lake Sanford area of Essex County. The magnetite ore contains abundant ilmenite and its presence used to create economic problems in processing the ore. Mining was sporadic until May, 1941. Shortages of imported titanium ore during World War II spurred active development of the titaniferous magnetite mine at Lake Sanford. Ilmenite is now the chief domestic ore of titanium metal. The ore occurs chiefly in anorthosite and gabbro. The following minerals have been reported:

Amphibole
  Hornblende
Apatite
Biotite
Chlorite
Epidote
Garnet
Ilmenite
  Leucoxene
Magnetite
Plagioclase
  Andesine
  Labradorite

Pyrite
Pyroxene
  Augite
  Diallage
  Hypersthene
Pyrrhotite
Scapolite
  Dipyre
Spinel

MAGNETITE MINES OF SOUTHEASTERN NEW YORK

Mines of the Highlands

(Beck–1842; Newland–1919; Colony–1921; Dahlberg–1976)

Magnetite is a very common mineral in the crystalline rocks of the Highlands of southeastern New York. Large deposits of commercial grade were discovered as early as 1740. The Stirling Mine in southern Orange County was discovered in 1750. The Forest of Dean Mine near West Point was opened in 1756. Iron produced from the magnetite ore was used to forge a chain which was stretched across the Hudson River from West Point to Constitution Island to halt the northward advance of the British during the Revolutionary War. More than a dozen magnetite mines were subsequently developed in Orange and Putnam Counties. None has been worked for many years.

The Tilly Foster Magnetite Mine Near Brewster, Putnam County

(Kunz–1892; Koeberlin–1909; Colony–1921; Newland and Hartnagel–1936; Trainer–1938, 1940, 1941, 1942, 1943; Prucha–1956; Nuwer–1971)

Tilly Foster is the name of a farmer who was born in Carmel, New York, April 18, 1793. The first mining of iron ore on the Foster property is reported to have taken place in 1810. The mine was named the Tilly Foster Mine in 1860. A rock fall at the mine in 1895 claimed over a dozen lives and the mine was officially closed in 1897.

In the 1890's, magnificent crystals of chondrodite and of titanite were found from which small gems were cut. Exceptional crystals of clinochlore were also found. The Tilly Foster Mine became established as a noted mineral locality. The ore consisted of massive magnetite intergrown with massive chondrodite. Magnetite crystals were also discovered associated with dolomite, chondrodite, and clinochlore. The magnetite crystals were dodecahedral and some were an inch in diameter.

During the 1920's and 1930's the rock piles of the mine were the mecca for mineral collectors. Many good mineral specimens were collected then and new finds were reported. Chondrodite, magnetite and clinochlore were still abundant. Serpentine in several forms including interesting pseudomorphs of serpentine after other minerals were reported (Frondel–1935A; Trainer–1938, 1940, 1941, 1943).

In the 1940's and early 1950's the mine became a site for producing crushed stone utilized by local road construction companies. Today excellent specimens of minerals from the Tilly Foster Mine repose in many museums throughout the world as well as in private collections.

The following minerals have been reported from the Tilly Foster Mine:

Albite	*Brucite
Amphibole	*Calcite
Actinolite	Chalcopyrite
Asbestos	**Chondrodite
Byssolite	Chrysocolla
Hornblende	**Clinochlore
Pargasite	Clinohumite
Riebeckite	Datolite
Crocidolite	*Dolomite
Tremolite	*Enstatite
Ankerite	Bronzite
Apatite	Fluorite
Apophyllite	Garnet
Arsenopyrite	Gypsum
Autunite	Hematite
Barite	Heulandite
Biotite	Hisingerite

*Common
**Very common. Some exceptional museum specimens were reported.

Humite
Hydromagnesite
Hydrotalcite
Ilmenite
Kaolin
Laumontite
Limonite
Magnesite
**Magnetite
Malachite
Marcasite
*Microcline
Molybdenite
Muscovite
Natrolite
Oligoclase
Olivine
Opal
Phlogopite
Prochlorite
Pyrite
Pyrolusite
Pyroxene
  Augite
* Diopside
    Coccolite

Diallage
Pyrrhotite
Quartz
* Milky
  Rose
  Smoky
Scapolite
Dipyre
*Serpentine
  Antigorite
    (Picrolite)
  Chrysotile
    (Marmolite)
Serpentine pseudomorph after
  Chondrodite, Clinochlore,
  Dolomite, Enstatite, Horn-
  blende, Periclase
Siderite
Spinel
Stilbite
Talc
Thomsonite
**Titanite (Sphene)
Tourmaline
Vermiculite
Zircon

Other minerals and other serpentine pseudomorphs have been reported but the mineral names that were used are now obsolete.

HEMATITE MINES

Hematite, ground and probably mixed with oil or grease was used as a mineral pigment for personal ornamentation by the Seneca Indians (Ritchie–1954).

There were two principal districts in the state where hematite was mined for iron ore but mining operations ceased many years ago.

The Hematite of Jefferson and St. Lawrence Counties

(Hough–1850; Newland–1919; Buddington–1934)

Before the turn of the 19th century, hematite was mined in a narrow belt about 30 miles long from between Keene and Antwerp in

Jefferson County, northeastward to Herman in St. Lawrence County. The hematite occurs in a gneiss belt beneath the Potsdam sandstone and was generally massive and red, though metallic and specular hematite was occasionally encountered. Some of the red hematite was used as a pigment for painting red barns. The first blast furnace was built near Rossie in 1813. The mine openings and shafts are now filled with water.

Sterling Mine, Near Antwerp, Jefferson County

The Sterling hematite mine was opened in 1836 about 2¾ miles north of Antwerp. The hematite included soft massive red, hard steel-gray and specular types. Botryoidal forms were present and tiny black crystals up to 1mm in size often lined vugs in the omnipresent quartz. Slender to capillary millerite crystals were first discovered in 1848. The crystals often occurred in radiating groups and the mine is a classic locality for the mineral. Velvety coatings of stilpnomelane and small crystals of ankerite and quartz also occur in the quartz vugs. (See also under hematite and millerite pp. 104, 122. The last operations of the mine were between 1904–1912.

The Clinton Hematites

(Newland and Hartnagel–1908; Newland–1909, 1919)

The Clinton iron ores of Silurian age occur in a single belt of inter-bedded shales, limestones and sandstones extending from the area around Clinton in Oneida County westward to the Niagara River and beyond. The strata dip to the south. Since the hematite layers were thin (6 inches to at most 6 feet near Clinton) and diminished eastward, extensive mining has not been economic. The Clinton hematite occurs in two types. The oolitic hematite is composed of oolites up to 2 mm in diameter. The fossiliferous hematite is composed of calcareous fossils that have been entirely or completely replaced by hematite. The fossils represent a dwarf fauna, mostly bryozoa, crinoids and brachiopods. By the 1930's, mining the hematite as an iron ore had ceased though a small amount was used for red paint.

Hematite Mines Near Ontario, Wayne County

(Cooper–1957)

The first discovery of hematite ore in Ontario was made in 1811 by a Mr. Knickerbocker while digging a pit to water his cattle. Mining began soon afterwards. By 1815, a furnace and a forge were in operation producing about 400 pounds of iron a day. Since the region was thickly forested, wood was a convenient and inexpensive fuel.

Charcoal was made by burning chopped logs in pits with dirt used to cover the logs. In 1825 a furnace was built with a capacity of three or four tons of iron a day. The furnace was enlarged several times with the walls of the plant being constructed of cobbles from the shore of Lake Ontario, and fieldstone. In 1875 the plant was destroyed by fire and was not rebuilt.

LEAD-ZINC MINES

Rossie Lead Mines

(Emmons-1842; Durant & Pierce-1878; Whitlock-1903, 1910a; Buddington-1934)

Indian traditions led early prospectors to the Rossie area northwest of Gouverneur where it is reported that lead had been found in the ashes of a log fire. Galena-bearing calcite veins were discovered in granite gneiss and mining was started in 1836. Several mines were opened and worked intermittently until 1868 when all the mines were closed. A tall stone chimney still stands at one of the mine sites two miles south of Rossie village.

Numerous calcite crystals occurred in water filled cavities of the mines. Attaining a diameter of 10cm and more, the highly modified rhombohedral crystals were often twinned on (0001). The crystals were clear (Iceland Spar) to pale lilac in color. Large cubic crystals of galena were occasionally found. Also reported were anglesite, celestite, cerussite, chalcopyrite, fluorite and pyrite.

The Mines of Shawangunk Mountain in Orange, Sullivan and Ulster Counties

(Whitlock-1903; Newland-1919; Ingham-1940; Heusser-1977)

The lead and zinc mines of southeastern New York are among the earliest ones worked for these metals in the country. Tradition has it that the ores were smelted by Indians and hunters to make bullets. The Ellenville Mine was opened as early as 1820, and worked intermittently until 1917.

The (lead and zinc) ores occur in the Shawangunk conglomerate (grit) of Silurian age. Sphalerite is the most abundant ore mineral. Galena was reported to have been very abundant in the early mining activities. Silver was reported at 2.25 oz. per ton.

Chalcopyrite was abundant at the Ellenville Mine where it formed crystal aggregates in vugs with vein quartz. Clear prismatic quartz crystals lined vugs at the Ellenville Mine. Occasional small brilliant crystals of brookite occurred with the quartz crystals. Pyrite was also present.

The Balmat-Edwards Zinc District of St. Lawrence County

(Newland–1916, 1919; Cushing and Newland–1925; Pough–1940; Brown–1932, 1936a, 1936b, 1947, 1959; Bateman–1950; Brown and Engel–1956; Doe–1960, 1962; Engel–1962; Lea and Dill–1968; Lessing and Grout–1969; Dill–1976; Hogarth–1977)

The presence of sphalerite and galena in the Balmat–Edwards area was recognized as early as 1838. Serious prospecting did not begin until 1903 when workmen uncovered a sizeable lead-zinc vein while quarrying for road material.

Actual mining at Edwards began in 1915 and the mine at Balmat opened in 1930. Both mines have continuously produced economic quantities of lead and zinc ore, as well as small amounts of recoverable silver. The ore occurs in a series of dolomites and silicated units of the Precambrian Grenville.

The mineralogy of the Balmat–Edwards zinc deposits is unique. The age of the mineralization is reported to be 1050± 100 million years (Brown and Kulp–1957; Doe–1960).

Amphibole
  Actinolite
  Anthophyllite
  Pargasite
  Tremolite
    Chromian tremolite
    Mountain Leather
    Hexagonite
Anhydrite
Apatite
Arsenopyrite
Barite
Calcite
Celestite
Chalcopyrite
Chlorite
Dolomite
Feldspar
  Oligoclase
  Orthoclase
Galena
Garnet
  Andradite
  Grossular

Geocronite
Goethite
Greenockite
Guitermanite
Gypsum
Halite
Haüynite
Hematite
Hydrozincite
Ilvaite
Jordanite
Limonite
Magnetite
Marcasite
Mica
  Biotite
  Phlogopite
Orpiment
Pyrite
Pyrargyrite-Proustite
Pyroxene
  Diopside
Pyrrhotite
Quartz

Realgar
Rhodonite
Scapolite
  Dipyre
Serpentine
Silver
Sphalerite
Talc
Tennantite
Tetrahedrite
Tourmaline
Willemite
Wurtzite

GARNET AND TALC MINES

The Garnet Mine of Gore Mountain, Warren County

(Miller-1913, 1914; Krieger-1937; Shaub-1949; Levin-1950)

The world's largest garnet mine is located in the scenic mountain country along the southern fringe of the Adirondack Mountains high peaks area. It is situated about 2/3rds of a mile north of the summit of Gore Mountain, and about 3 miles west of North Creek. Mining operations have been carried on irregularly since 1882, and continuously since 1924.

The garnet occurs as large masses in a dark gray metagabbro. Large crude dodecahedral crystals up to a foot in diameter and irregular masses three feet in diameter have been reported. Nearly every garnet is enclosed by a wide rim of hornblende. Glassy oligoclase and gray hypersthene occur in both garnet and its hornblende envelope. The quarry walls are spectacular since the dark red garnets, surrounded by black hornblende rim, are scattered through the gray metagabbro.

While most of the garnet from Gore Mountain is thoroughly shattered, small clear fragments of dark red color have been cut and garnet has been chosen the gem mineral of New York State. It is about 85 to 65% pyralmandite and 15 to 35% lime garnet (Levin-1950).

The Talc Mines of St. Lawrence County

(Cushing and Newland-1925; Engel-1949, 1962a; Elberty and Lessing-1971)

Talc has been one of the major economic minerals of the state for a century. The first commercial talc mine was opened at Talcville in 1878. The productive talc area occurs in a belt of Grenville Marble in the southeastern portion of the Gouverneur quadrangle. The area extends from Sylvia Lake in the Town of Fowler into and across the town of Edwards. The talc occurs in lenses or sheets that are often intricately contorted. The talc units are presumed to have been formed as a result of alteration of an original dolomitic limestone. Pure talc from this area is white and has a pearly luster. Fibrous tremolite is universally present, associated with and included in the talc.

Minerals reported from talc mines include:

Amphibole	Tirodite
Anthophyllite	Tremolite
Chromian Tremolite	Anhydrite
Hexagonite	Apatite
Mountain Leather	Braunite

Calcite
Chlorite
Dolomite
Groutite
Potash feldspar
Mica
  Biotite
  Phlogopite
Pyrite

Pyroxene
  Diopside
Quartz
Serpentine
Talc
Titanite (sphene)
Tourmaline
  Uvite

THE MINERALS OF THE GLACIAL DRIFT OF WESTERN NEW YORK STATE

(Flint–1957; Holmes–1952, 1960; Connally–1960; Milner–1962; Broughton et. al. 1966).

Glacial drift is a general term applied to all rock material (clay, sand, gravel, cobbles and boulders) transported by a glacier. Almost all of New York State was buried beneath the ice cap of the Laurentide Ice sheet that originated in Labrador and northern Quebec. The uplands of Allegheny State Park, on the western part of the New York-Pennsylvania border, escaped glaciation.

The heavy minerals that are present in the sand-size fractions of the glacial drift can be considered as representative of the minerals also present in rock fragments of the drift. Heavy minerals* are those having a specific gravity greater than 2.8 and have been reported from glacial till and moraines in the western part of the state.

The following heavy minerals have been reported:

Common minerals
  Garnet
  Hornblende
  Hypersthene
  Monoclinic pyroxenes
    Augite
    Diopside
Opaque minerals
  Magnetite
  Hematite
  Limonite

Less common minerals
  Apatite
  Chlorite
  Tremolite–Actinolite
Trace
  Zircon
  Sillimanite
  Titanite (sphene)
  Tourmaline
  Rutile
  Epidote
  Monazite

*Minerals that have a specific gravity of less than 2.8 include: Beryl, calcite, chlorite, feldspars, graphite, mica, quartz, scapolite, talc, the zeolites.

BEACH SANDS—LAKE ONTARIO

(Coch–1961)

A study of the beach sands of the south shore of Lake Ontario reported the presence of minerals that were derived chiefly from igneous and metamorphic rocks of the Adirondacks and of the Grenville series of rocks in Ontario. The minerals that have been listed include: actinolite, aegirine, andalusite, apatite, augite, calcite, corundum, epidote, garnet*, hornblende*, hypersthene*, kyanite, monazite, opaques*, rutile, staurolite, titanite (sphene), topaz, tourmaline, tremolite, zircon.

*Common

THE GEM AND ORNAMENTAL MINERALS OF THE STATE

(Manchester–1931; Kraus and Slawson–1947; Schlegel–1957; Sinkankas–1951, 1959)

The most important qualities of a *precious gem* are beauty, durability and rarity. For the most part, they are also transparent. *Semi-precious gemstones* possess only one or two of these qualities.

The beauty of a gemstone is determined by personal taste. Durability depends on hardness and lack of ready cleavage. Diamond, ruby, sapphire and emerald are considered precious gems. No confirmed reports of these minerals have been made in the state.

Ornamental stones are those from which decorative objects are fashioned. The latter include spheres, bookends, table tops, pan sets, mosaics, carvings, and building interiors.

The following are some of the minerals of the state that have been used for gems and ornamental purposes.

Amphibole
  Hexagonite
Beryl
  Aquamarine
  Golden Beryl
Calcite
Chondrodite
Feldspar
  Albite (Peristerite)
  Andesine-Labradorite series
  Microcline (Amazonite)
  Oligoclase (Sunstone)
Fluorite

Garnet
  Almandine
  Gore Mt. Garnet (See pp. 47, 93)
  Spessartine
Gypsum
Haüynite-Lapis Lazuli
Pyrite
Pyroxene
  Diopside
Quartz
  Citrine
  Clear Rock Crystal
  Jasper

Rose
Smoky
Sphalerite
Talc
  Steatite

Titanite (Sphene)
Tourmaline
Zircon

Rocks are chiefly composed of two or more minerals. The following are some of the rocks in the state that have been used for architectural purposes and monuments (Newland–1916; Richardson–1917; Fairchild and Warner–1933).

Anorthosite
Diabase
Gabbro
Gneiss
Granite
Limestone

Marble
Quartzite
Sandstone
Serpentine
Slate
Syenite

The following elements and their abbreviations are used in this book.

Aluminum	Al	Manganese	Mn
Antimony	Sb	Mercury	Hg
Arsenic	As	Molybdenum	Mo
Barium	Ba	Nickel	Ni
Beryllium	Be	Niobium	Nb
Bismuth	Bi	Oxygen	O
Boron	B	Phosphorus	P
Cadmium	Cd	Platinum	Pt
Calcium	Ca	Potassium	K
Carbon	C	Silicon	Si
Cerium	Ce	Silver	Ag
Chlorine	Cl	Sodium	Na
Chromium	Cr	Strontium	Sr
Cobalt	Co	Sulfur	S
Copper	Cu	Tantalum	Ta
Fluorine	F	Thorium	Th
Gold	Au	Tin	Sn
Hafnium	Hf	Titanium	Ti
Hydrogen	H	Uranium	U
Iron	Fe	Vanadium	V
Lanthanum	La	Yttrium	Y
Lead	Pb	Zinc	Zn
Lithium	Li	Zirconium	Zr
Magnesium	Mg		

Descriptive Mineralogy — The Minerals

Achroite — See Tourmaline.
Acmite — See Pyroxene
Actinolite — See Amphibole.
Aegirine — See Pyroxene.
Agate — See Quartz.
Albite — See Plagioclase.

Albite, twin crystal   near Warrensburg, Warren Co.

ALLANITE $(Ce, Ca, Y)_2 (Al, Fe)_3 (SiO_4)_3 (OH)$ rare earth calcium aluminum iron silicate hydroxide
    Syn. Orthite   Epidote Group   Monoclinic

Allanite is a common accessory constituent of many granites, pegmatites and gneisses. It occurs as grains, masses and flat tabular crystals. It contains rare earths. Small amounts of thorium (Th) and Uranium (U) are usually present. Highly radioactive allanite has been mistaken for uraninite.

Dutchess Co. Lustrous black crystals were reported in the pegmatite at Shaft #7 of the Delaware Aqueduct (Zodac-1941).

Essex Co. Reported at a pegmatite quarry near Crown Point. Some crystals were very large (Rowley-1962, 1963; Tan-1966).

Exceptionally large allanite crystals with secondary lanthanite were reported at the "Sanford Bed", Mineville (Blake-1858; Kemp and Ruedemann-1910).

The rare earth content of allanites at Essexville and Whiteface Mt. is reported (Frondel, J.-1964). Radial fracturing in feldspar and fine grained quartz occurs adjacent to allanite crystals at Whiteface Mtn. (Shaub-1951). The age of allanite in pegmatite veins at the summit of Whiteface Mtn. is about 1,200 million years (Marble-1943). Radioactivity (Newland-1935).

Lewis Co. Massive allanite occurs with quartz in a pegmatite east of Watson (Jensen and Wishart-1956).

New York Co. Orthite is reported (Manchester-1931).

Orange Co. Small crystals and masses of allanite are abundant in the granite of Mount Adam (Kemp and Hollick-1894; Cosminsky-1947). Rare earth content reported (Frondel, J.-1964).

St. Lawrence Co. McLear pegmatite (Shaub-1929).

Saratoga Co. Present in pegmatites (Tan-1966).

Warren Co. Crystals near Schroon Lake that were paper-thin to ⅛" thick and up to 3 inches long were reported. (Rowley-1957).

Westchester Co. Present at the Kinkel quarry, Bedford (Tan-1966).

Almandine — See Garnet.

ALUNOGEN $Al_2 (SO_4)_3 \cdot 18 H_2O$ Triclinic

Alunogen occurs as incrustations or coatings due to decomposition of pyritiferous or marcasite-bearing rocks.

Tompkins Co. Near Portland Point, 6 miles north of Ithaca, white to yellow, slightly botryoidal masses of finely fibrous alunogen occur on the Moscow and Genesee (Devonian) shales with epsomite, melanterite, etc. (Martens-1925).

Amazonite — See Microcline.

Amethyst — See Quartz.

AMPHIBOLE   A group of minerals with a general formula A_2 B_5 (Si, Al)$_8$ O_{22} (OH, F)$_2$ Monoclinic or orthorhombic
   A= Na, Ca, K
   B= Mg, Fe'', Fe''', Ti, Al, Li, Mn

Several members and varieties of the amphibole group occur in New York state. Hornblende and the actinolite-tremolite series are most common.

Amphibole, Uralite   Pierrepont, St. Lawrence Co.

Actinolite Ca_2 (Mg, Fe)$_5$ Si$_8$ O_{22} (OH)$_2$ calcium magnesium iron silicate hydroxide

Tremolite Ca_2 Mg$_5$ Si$_8$ O_{22} (OH)$_2$ calcium magnesium silicate hydroxide

Actinolite and Tremolite constitute a calcium-magnesium-iron series of monoclinic amphiboles in which actinolite has a significant and variable iron content. The color ranges from green to white as the iron content decreases. An asbestiform actinolite is called byssolite. Tremolite is the iron-free end member, is white in color, and is sometimes asbestiform; a felted aggregate of tremolite fibers is called mountain leather.

   Hexagonite is a lilac to reddish-purple colored tremolite that owes its color to the presence of manganese. It is common at the talc mines of St. Lawrence County. Members of the actinolite-tremolite series are very common in St. Lawrence County where they have formed as a result of metamorphism of impure limestones, shales, crystalline schists, etc. Chromian tremolite is a bright green type that may contain up to 2% $Cr_2 O_3$.

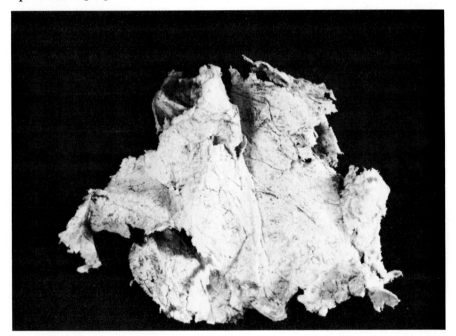

Amphibole, Tremolite (Mountain Leather)   Balmat, St. Lawrence Co.

Anthophyllite $(Mg, Fe)_7 Si_8 O_{22} (OH)_2$ magnesium iron silicate hydroxide

This orthorhombic member of the amphibole group occurs in metamorphic rocks. It is usually brownish-gray in color.

Edenite $Na Ca_2 Mg_5 (Al Si_7) O_{22} (OH)_2$

This is a light colored member of the hornblende series that is named from the type locality at Edenville in Orange County.

Glaucophane $Na_2 (Mg, Fe)_3 Al_2 Si_8 O_{22} (OH)_2$

Hastingsite $Na Ca_2 (Fe, Mg, Al)_5 (Al_2 Si_6) O_{22} (OH)_2$

Hornblende $(Ca Na)_{2-3} (Mg, Fe'', Fe''', Al)_5 (Al, Si)_8 O_{22} (OH)_2$ calcium sodium magnesium iron aluminum silicate hydroxide

Hornblende is a very common member of the amphibole group. It occurs in granites, syenites, gabbros, amphibolites, gneisses, schists, etc. The color may be black, dark brown or dark green.

Hudsonite is listed as a variety of hastingsite by Hey (1955).

Pargasite   Na Ca Mg$_4$ Al (Al, Si)$_8$ O$_{22}$ (OH)$_2$ is present in some metamorphosed rocks.

Riebeckite   Na$_2$ (Fe″, Mg, Fe‴)$_5$ Si$_8$ O$_{22}$ (OH)$_2$ sodium iron silicate hydroxide

The blue asbestiform variety, crocidolite has been reported.

Tirodite   (Mg, Mn)$_7$ Si$_8$ O$_{22}$ (OH)$_2$

This manganese-bearing amphibole was once described as a manganoan cummingtonite.

Tschermakite   Ca$_2$ Mg$_3$ (Al, Fe)$_2$ (Al$_2$ Si$_6$) O$_{22}$ (OH, F)$_2$

Uralite — An amphibole pseudomorphous after pyroxene such as augite.

Literature references for the following amphiboles in New York State are given (Leake-1968):
  Alumino-tschermakitic hornblende
  Edenitic hornblende
  Ferro edenitic hornblende
  Feroan-pargasitic hornblende
  Ferro-tschermakitic hornblende
  Hastingsite
  Sodic hastingsite
  Titaniferous hastingsite
  Sodic ferron pargastic hornblende
  Sodic potassic-ferri-ferroan pargasitic hornblende
  Titaniferous-ferroan-pargasitic hornblende
  Titaniferous ferro-tschermakitic hornblende
  Titaniferous-magnesium-hastingitic hornblende
  Tschermakitic hornblende
  Titaniferous-ferroan pargasite
  Tschermakite
  Ferro tschermakite
  Titaniferous tschermakite

Identification: Actinolite, asbestos, crocidolite, hexagonite, hornblende, and tremolite can be reasonably well identified by the amateur with the aid of a good mineral text. Other varieties and sub-varieties of amphiboles can best be identified by combinations of optical properties, chemical analyses, spectrographic analyses, densities and unit cell structure.

Clinton Co. Large crystals of hastingsite and hornblende, up to a foot in length and usually etched, were found in the Chateaugay iron mines at Lyon Mountain (Whitlock-1907); Gallagher-1937); byssolite is also reported (Whitlock-1907).

Dutchess Co. Actinolite and hornblende; also mountain leather in a sheet 4 feet long by 5 feet wide and ½ inch thick are reported on the dumps from shaft #7, Delaware aqueduct (Zodac-1941).

Essex Co. Asbestos, actinolite and hornblende were reported near Port Henry (Beck-1842); hornblende was reported near Crown Point (Tan-1966).

Lewis Co. Hastingsite (femag-hastingsite) was reported in granite, syenite and gneiss (Buddington and Leonard-1953).

New York Co. Hornblende is a common constituent of the Fordham gneiss; a hornblende schist is sometimes interbedded with the Manhattan schist (Agar-1933; Schuberth-1968). Thin flexible sheets of mountain leather and tremolite in columnar to fibrous masses with silky luster occur in the Inwood crystalline limestone (Manchester-1931).

Orange Co. Gray to brownish-gray edenite is reported near the type locality at Edenville (Beck-1842; Buerger-1927) and at the Atlas quarry (Cosminsky-1947). Nearly pure glaucophane formed part of the northwest wall of the O'Neil Mine (Colony-1921).

Hastingsite (Hudsonite) is reported at Cornwall (Weidman-1903).

Hornblende is reported at the Atlas quarry (Cosminsky-1947); also near Monroe (Ayres-1945).

Hudsonite is reported at Cornwall (Weidman-1903).

Pargasite occurs at Edenville (Buerger-1927)

Tremolite is found in white limestone at the Atlas quarry. (Cosminsky-1947).

Putnam Co. The following are reported at the Tilly Foster Mine at Brewster (Trainer-1938, 1941, 1942):

Actinolite as curved crystals and as fibrous byssolite.

Hornblende occurred as large cleavable black to dark green masses and small crystals.

Riebeckite (Crocidolite) was reported as lavender blue fibers on gneiss.

Tremolite occurred as grayish-green crystalline and as matted fibers.

Richmond Co. Anthophyllite is reported in serpentine on Staten Island (Okulewicz-1977).

Amphibole, Tremolite (Hexagonite) near Fowler,
St. Lawrence Co.

St. Lawrence Co. Actinolite and pyrite surrounded a haüynite mass at Edwards Mine (Lessing & Grout-1971). Fine crystals of actinolite occur at Colton and West Pierrepont (Alverson-1975, et al). Actinolite crystals occur with titanite in quartz at McLear pegmatite (Shaub-1929; Leake-1968).

Anthophyllite is reported at the Jayville magnetite deposit (Leonard-1951; Leonard & Vlisidis-1960); with tremolite in schist at Edwards (Rabbitt-1948); tremolite altering to anthophyllite is reported at Balmat zinc mines (Brown & Engel-1956).

Hastingsite, ferro hastingsite and femaghastingsite are reported in hornblende granite and hornblende granite gneiss (Buddington & Leonard-1953).

Hornblende occurs in granite and gneiss (see hastingsite above); also in pegmatites.

Pargasite is present in amphibolite (Buddington & Leonard-1953); also with haüynite at Edwards (Hogarth-1977).

Tirodite. Light pink fibrous masses of tirodite that often contain bladed tirodite crystals up to 3 inches long are reported at the International Talc Co. Mine, Talcville (Segeler-1961).

Tremolite is very common. Some of the finest tremolite specimens in the world have come from St. Lawrence Co. Excellent coarse crystalline aggregates, occasionally crystalized, occur with brown tourmaline and scapolite on the Dale Bush farm near Richville.

Fibrous to crystalline tremolite is abundant at all of the talc mines in the Fowler-Balmat area. Presence of manganese causes some tremolite to fluoresce various shades of red to orange under long wave ultra violet light. Hexagonite is common at the talc mines (Newland-1919; Whitlock-1903; Engel and Engel-1953). Good crystals of tremolite are reported near Colton and West Pierrepont (Alverson-1975; VanDiver-1977). Chromian-tremolite is reported at the talc mines. Mountain leather has been found at Balmat (Robinson, Alverson-1975).

Uralite. Crystals of uralite occur at the Pierrepont black tourmaline locality (Jensen-p.o.; Robinson-1971; VanDiver-1977).

Warren Co. Hornblende is a constituent of the metagabbro and occurs in the black rims around garnet at the Gore Mtn. garnet mine and elsewhere (Miller-1914; Shaub-1949; Levin-1950).

Westchester Co. Hornblende is a constituent of the country rock adjacent to the emery mines at Peekskill and also is present in the Cortlandt complex; also Kinkel quarry, Bedford (Tan-1966); mountain leather was occasionally found in the Inwood limestone (Manchester-1931).

ANALCIME Na Al Si$_2$ O$_6$•2 H$_2$O sodium aluminum silicate hydrate Cubic

Small crystals are reported in crevices in gneiss, etc.

New York Co. (Manchester-1931).

Westchester Co. near Peekskill (Phillips-1924).

ANATASE Ti O_2 titanium oxide Tetragonal

Trimorphous with brookite and rutile.

Essex Co. A yellowish crystalline substance enclosed in titanite at New-comb is listed as zanthitone (=xanthitane?) (Nason-1888).

St. Lawrence Co., etc. A soft, friable, yellow earthy material found as alteration of sphene may be xanthitane which is identical with anatase. (Palache, Berman, Frondel-1944).

ANDALUSITE Al_2 Si O_5 aluminum silicate Orthorhombic

Trimorphous with kyanite and sillimanite.

   Andalusite is rare in New York state and has only been reported in thin section study.

New York Co. Andalusite occurs with dumortierite (Schaller-1905).

Westchester Co. Reported in the wall rock of emery deposits in Cortlandt Twp. (Friedman-1956); also was found in excavations in pegmatite in New York City (Schaller-1905).

Andesine — See Plagioclase

Andradite — See Garnet

ANGLESITE Pb SO_4 lead sulfate Orthorhombic

Anglesite occurs sparingly in New York state as an oxidation of galena.

St. Lawrence Co. Reported at Old Rossie lead mines as a coating on galena (Whitlock-1903).

Westchester Co. Reported at an old copper mine at Sparta (Manchester-1931).

ANHYDRITE Ca SO_4 calcium sulfate Orthorhombic

Anhydrite is commonly associated with the deposits of rock gypsum which are interbedded with shales and shaly limestones of Salina Age that occur in a wide band from northwestern Erie Co. eastward to Oneida Co. and beyond. There are few outcrops (Newland-1929).

   Grains of anhydrite occur occasionally in the Silurian salt beds which underly the rock gypsum (Alling-1928).

Also:

Clinton Co. Anhydrite was found intergrown with magnetite at Lyon Mountain (Zimmer-1947).

Erie & Niagara Co. White to bluish-white crystalline masses of anhydrite are often associated with gypsum in cavities of the Lockport dolomite (dolostone) (Awald-1958).

Anhydrite   Rochester, Monroe Co.

Monroe Co. White to bluish-white crystalline anhydrite often grades into massive gypsum in cavities of Lockport dolomite (dolostone) (Jensen-1942).

St. Lawrence Co. Crystalline white, and gray to lavender anhydrite was reported to be associated with zinc ore at Edwards. (Brown-1932; Lea and Dill-1968).

ANKERITE Ca (Fe, Mg, Mn) $(CO_3)_2$ calcium iron magnesium carbonate Trigonal

Jefferson Co. Fine quality small and medium sized rhombohedral ankerite crystals, light to dark brown in color occur with hematite, quartz, stilpnomelane, etc. in vugs in the hematite ore at the Old Sterling iron mine at Antwerp (Buddington-1934).

Putnam Co. Reported at the Tilly Foster Mine, Brewster. (Trainer-1941).

ANORTHOCLASE (Na, K) Al Si_3 O_8 Triclinic

Feldspar group. A sodium rich microcline.

St. Lawrence Co. Occurs in a pegmatite at Fine where it was observed in thin section.

Anthophyllite — See Amphibole

Antigorite — See Serpentine

APATITE   A group name   Hexagonal

The following members of the apatite group have been reported in the state.

Fluorapatite Ca_5 $(PO_4)_3$ F calcium phosphate fluoride

This is the most common apatite. It is present as an accessory rock-forming mineral in many types of rocks including titaniferous magnetites though its presence may only be noted microscopically (in thin section). Fluorapatite is very common in metamorphosed rocks, especially crystalline limestones (e.g. Grenville of the Adirondack region) where it often occurs as large crystals and is frequently associated with phlogopite, pyroxene, sphene, etc.

Carbonate-fluorapatite (Collophane) This member of the apatite group contains large amounts of CO_2. It is present in black phosphate pebbles and steinkerns that occur in a thin bed of Middle Devonian calcareous shales in western New York (northwest Erie Co. eastward as far as Cayuga Co.) (Baird-1975). It also occurs in other Silurian and Devonian rocks of western New York (Alling-1946; Jensen-P.O.). Eupyrchroite is a carbonate-fluorapatite and was one of the earliest minerals listed in the state (Emmons-1838).

Manganoan fluorapatite. This name has been applied to a fluorapatite containing a small amount of manganese. It is dark blue-green and fluoresces yellow-orange.

Clinton Co. Chateaugay iron mines, Lyon Mountain. Small bright apatite crystals, transparent and light yellowish-green to bluish-green occur up to 6 mm (Whitlock-1907).

Dutchess Co. Tiny blue crystals were found in white calcite during excavations for Shaft #7, Delaware Aqueduct (Zodac-1941).

Essex Co. Apatite is reported in a pegmatite near Crown Point (Rowley-1962; Tan-1966). Pale grayish-green fibrous crusts of carbonate apatite (eupyrchroite) occurred in gneiss contact south of Hammondsville (Emmons-1838; Beck-1842; Whitlock-1903; Newland-1906, 1919). At Lake Sanford, apatite is widely disseminated as grains and occasionally as crystals in pyroxenes and ore minerals (Stephenson-1945).

A reddish-brown to white rare earth-bearing apatite was present in the magnetite ore at Mineville (McKeown and Klemic-1956). Perfect apatite crystals were noted in a section of the ore (Beck-1842). Small translucent blue apatite was reported at Newcomb (Nason-1888). Sharp olive to yellow-green crystals of apatite were found in a pyrrhotite vein near New Russia (Rowley-1967). White, yellow and green apatite were associated with vesuvianite at Olmsteadville (Rowley-1948).

Apatite–Carbonate fluorapatite (Eupyrchroite)   Crown Point, Essex Co.

Jefferson Co. & Lewis Co. Fine large apatite crystals were reported (Beck-1842).

Monroe Co. Collophane (carbonate-fluorapatite) was noted (Alling-1946).

New York Co. (Manchester-1931).

Onondaga Co. Minor amounts of apatite were observed in peridotite (Maynard–Ploger-1946).

Orange Co. Yellow to blue and green apatite crystals were reported in calcite, etc. (Beck-1942; Cosminsky-1947). Reported near Greenwood Lake (Ries-1895).

Putnam Co. Tilly Foster Mine. Green apatite was associated with magnetite, etc. (Trainer-1938). Gray-green to brownish crystals up to 2″ long occurred in pyrrhotite at Anthony's Nose pyrrhotite mine (Zodac-1933).

St. Lawrence Co. A 12 inch apatite crystal weighing 18 pounds was reported by Durant & Paige (1878). Terminated gray-green crystals up to 3½ inches in length occurred in salmon calcite with large phlogopite crystals, scapolite and pyroxene near Pyrites (Agar-1921; Alverson-1975).

Small bright blue apatite crystals occur in talc at Talcville. Gray-green crystals up to 1¼ inch in diameter occur with calcite, pyroxene, etc. near Fine (Jensen-1955). Well formed crystals, some quite large, have been noted in many areas near Hammond, Rossie and Russell (Agar-1921).

Saratoga Co. In pegmatite at Batchellerville (Tan-1966). Manganoan fluorapatite was reported at Overlook (Lapham-1955).

Warren Co. Apatite is present in the garnet-bearing rock at Gore Mtn. (Shaub-1949).

Westchester Co. Apatite is present in pegmatite at Bedford, etc. (Agar-1933; Tan-1966).

Antigorite — See Serpentine

APOPHYLLITE   K Ca$_4$ Si$_8$ O$_{20}$ (F, OH)•8 H$_2$O potassium calcium silicate fluoride hydroxide hydrate   Tetragonal

New York Co. Found in narrow veins in gneiss (Manchester-1931).

Putnam Co. Tilly Foster Mine. White or colorless crystals were seen in gneiss. (Trainer-1938, 1942)

Warren Co. Tiny crystals were found in cavities near epidote veins in gabbro, associated with chabazite, datolite and heulandite (Rowley-1957).

Aquamarine — See Beryl

ARAGONITE   Ca CO$_3$ calcium carbonate   Orthorhombic

Aragonite is polymorphous with calcite. It is not as abundant and is sometimes found as coralloidal aggregates (Flos ferri).

Albany Co. Reported as small acicular crystals and grayish-brown reniform masses in Albany crushed stone quarry (Rocks & Minerals-1956, p. 21).

Dutchess Co. White incrustations on rock were found at Shaft #7, Delaware Aqueduct (Zodac-1941).

Essex Co. Flos ferri was seen covering calcite at Olmsteadville (Rowley-1948).

Lewis Co. Coating on calcite crystals at Sterlingbush (Gardner-1920).

New York Co. Short stalactitic (Manchester-1931, plate No. 36).

Orange Co. Grayish to brown crusts of aragonite occur on limestone at the Atlas quarry (Zodac-1940).

Putnam Co. Tilly Foster Mine at Brewster. Grayish-white aragonite incrustations were reported on bronzite and magnetite; also gray crystals on serpentine and radiating groups on magnetite (Trainer-1938).

St. Lawrence Co. White globular masses of aragonite were reported in cavities of iron ore at the Kearney Mine (Durant & Paige-1878).

Saratoga Co. Aragonite occurs as a secondary coating on calcite at the Gailor Quarry (Rowley-1951).

ARSENOPYRITE Fe As S iron arsenic sulfate   Monoclinic, pseudo orthorhombic

Dutchess Co. Reported as small grains in gneiss.

Essex Co. Arsenopyrite is reported to be rare near Mineville (Kemp & Ruedemann-1910) Masses occur in hornblende at Lewis, near Keeseville (Palache, Berman, Frondel-1944).

Orange Co. Reported at the Atlas limestone quarry (Cosminsky-1947).

Putnam Co. Arsenopyrite occurred in a vein with pyrite intersecting gneiss in a mine that was operated 1906–1907 near Pine Pond, northwest of Carmel (Newland-1919); it was scarce at the Tilly Foster Mine at Brewster but a flattened group of twinned crystals was reported (Trainer-1938).

Warren Co. Arsenopyrite was reported as silver-white films, coating epidote, hornblende and also granular in diorite (Rowley-1957).

ARTINITE Mg_2 (CO_3) $(OH)_2 \cdot 3$ H_2O magnesium carbonate hydroxide hydrate   Monoclinic

Artinite occurs on or in serpentinized ultrabasic rocks.

Richmond Co. Staten Island. Crusts of delicate white needles of artinite up to 3 mm. long and botryoidal aggregates were associated with hydromagnesite on serpentine (Reasenberg-1968). Artinite was reported in serpentinized harzburgite-dunite on Staten Island (Okulewicz-1977).

Asbestos — See Amphibole, Serpentine

Augite — See Pyroxene

AUTUNITE Ca $(UO_2)_2$ $(PO_4)_2 \cdot 10$-12 H_2O Tetragonal

Autunite is a secondary uranium mineral and is fluorescent. Most autunite rapidly alters to meta-autunite when placed in a collection and exposed to a warm, dry atmosphere.

Fulton Co. Observed in a pegmatite prospect near Mayfield (Tan-1966).

Putnam Co. Observed as yellow scales on gneiss at the Tilly Foster Mine at Brewster (Trainer-1938).

Artinite with Hydromagnesite Staten Island, Richmond Co.
(Photo by Julian Reasenberg)

Westchester Co. Autunite was observed as tiny tabular plates on feldspar and on muscovite at Bedford (Luquer-1896; Manchester-1931; Agar-1933; Tan-1966).

AXINITE Ca_2 (Fe", Mn) Al_2 B Si_4 O_{15} OH calcium manganese iron aluminum borosilicate Triclinic

Dutchess Co. Axinite was found in the South Tunnel, Aqueduct Shaft #7, near Fishkill as crystalline masses and small brilliant crystals in calcite-filled vugs in pegmatite approximately 300 feet below sea level (Rocks and Minerals-1940, p. 346).

AZURITE Cu_3 $(CO_3)_2$ $(OH)_2$ copper carbonate hydroxide Monoclinic

Jefferson Co. Reported at Muscalonge Lake (Hough-1854).

Niagara Co. Blue encrustations of azurite occurred on sandstone with malachite and chrysocolla (Awald-1958).

St. Lawrence Co. Reported at the Benson Mines (Robinson & Alverson-1971; Van Diver-1977).

Sullivan Co. Tiny azurite crystals occurred on fractures in flagstone at Kenoza Lake (Yedlin-1976).

Westchester Co. Azurite was reported as incrustations on mica schist at Old Copper Mine, Sparta (Manchester-1931) and at the Orchard Hill shaft of the Delaware Aqueduct (Waite-1940).

BABINGTONITE Ca_2 (Fe″, Mn) Fe‴ Si_5 O_{14} (OH) calcium iron manganese silicate hydroxide   Triclinic

St. Lawrence Co. Said to occur as coating on feldspar crystals at Gouverneur (Beck-1842).

BARITE   Ba SO_4 barium sulfate   Syn. Barytes   Orthorhombic

Barite is the most common barium mineral. It occurs in some sedimentary rocks and in some lead and zinc deposits.

Columbia Co. White, massive at Ancram lead mines (Beck-1842).

Herkimer Co. Yellowish-white lamellar barite was reported near Little Falls. (Beck-1842).

Jefferson Co. Massive banded barite with few crystals occurred in veins in Trenton limestone at Pillar Point, north of Sacketts Harbor. Masses 2 to 3 feet long and a foot or more thick were obtained during mining operations about 1840. (Newland-1919; Gosse-1968).

Monroe Co. & Niagara Co. White to bluish-white barite is reported on celestite crystals, also crystalline in the Lockport dolomite (Niagara limestone) of western New York (Giles-1920).

Putnam Co. Small yellow barite crystals occurred in stalactitic dolomite in massive chondrodite (Trainer-1941).

St. Lawrence Co. Tabular crystals of barite have been found near De-Kalb, Fowler, Rossie, etc. (Beck-1842). Large crystals and crystalline masses have been reported in the St. Joe Mineral Corp. mines at Balmat and Edwards.

Schoharie Co. Gray-white barite occurred with strontianite near Schoharie (Palache, Berman, Frondel-1951).

Baryte — See Barite

Barytocelestite — See Celestite

BASTNAESITE   (Ce, La) (CO_3) F Hexagonal

Essex Co. Small amounts were found in the rare earth-bearing apatite associated with magnetite at Mineville (McKeown and Klemic-1956).

BERTRANDITE Be_4 Si_2 O_7 $(OH)_2$ beryllium silicate hydroxide Orthorhombic

Westchester Co. Minute colorless crystals under 0.5 mm. were found in contact with greenish-yellow beryl at Baylis quarry, Bedford (Pough-1936).

BERYL $Be_3 Al_2 Si_6 O_{18}$ beryllium aluminum silicate   Hexagonal

Beryl is the most common beryllium mineral. It occurs in pegmatites, etc. but it is not common in New York state.

New York Co. Beryl crystals were reported in pegmatites; also gem quality aquamarine and golden beryl from which faceted stones were cut (Manchester-1931).

Saratoga Co. Quarries in pegmatites at Batchellerville were famous for large beryl crystals, one reported to be 27 inches long and 10 inches in diameter. Gemmy aquamarine was found (Newland & Hartnagel-1932; Tan-1966; Rowley-1976).

Westchester Co. Beryl was common at the Baylis and Kinkel quarries, Bedford. Large, well formed greenish-yellow crystals exceeding 1 foot in length were found at the Kinkel quarry in 1962–63. Aquamarine and golden beryl were reported (Agar-1933; Tan-1966).

BETA-URANOPHANE $Ca (UO_2)_2 Si_2 O_7 \cdot 6 H_2O$ calcium uranyl silicate hydrate   Monoclinic
    syn. Beta-uranotile

Essex Co. Reported in pegmatite, near Crown Point Center. Very sharp, lemon-yellow transparent terminated crystals occurred as radiating aggregates in uranophane (Rowley-1962).

Westchester Co. (Frondel-1958) A greenish-yellow mineral found at Bedford was originally thought to be schroeckingerite but is beta-uranophane. (See under Schroeckingerite).

BIOTITE $K (Mg, Fe)_3 (Al, Fe) Si_3 O_{10} (OH, F)_2$ potassium magnesium iron aluminosilicate hydroxide   Monoclinic   Mica group

Biotite is a very common rock-forming mineral and its occurrences in New York State are too numerous to list in this publication. It occurs in many igneous rocks, especially granites and pegmatites and it is a common constituent of metamorphic rocks, especially gneisses and schists.

Clinton Co. Distinct crystals were reported in calcite at Lyon Mountain (Whitlock-1907).

Essex Co. Large books of reddish-brown biotite have been reported at an old pegmatite quarry near Crown Point Center. Some of the biotite is chloritized (Rowley-1962; Tan-1966).

Braunite and Tremolite (Hexagonite)   near Fowler, St. Lawrence Co.

New York Co. Biotite is a constituent of the Fordham gneiss (Schuberth-1968).

Orange Co. Crystals of biotite up to 4 inches thick and associated with magnetite were reported at the Rich Mine near Monroe (Ayres-1945).

Putnam Co. Tilly Foster Mine. A common constituent of schist and gneiss with occasional crystals (Trainer-1938).

Saratoga Co. Biotite sheets over 18″ in diameter were reported near Overlook (Rowley-1942a; Tan-1966).

Warren Co. Biotite is a constituent of the garnet rock at Gore Mtn., garnet mine (Shaub-1949).

Westchester Co. Abundant at Bedford quarries (Agar-1933; Tan-1966).

BISMITE $Bi_2 O_3$ bismuth oxide   Monoclinic

Westchester Co. Reported at Baylis quarry, Bedford (Januzzi-1959).

BISMUTHINITE Bi$_2$ S$_3$ bismuth sulfide Orthorhombic

Westchester Co. At the Baylis and Kinkel quarries, Bedford. Blue-gray grains of bismuthinite were disseminated with mica and quartz (Black-1948; Tan-1966).

Boltonite — See Forsterite

BORNITE Cu$_5$ Fe S$_4$ copper iron sulfide Cubic

Essex Co. Bornite was closely associated with chalcopyrite and pyrrhotite in a pegmatite near Crown Point Center (Rowley-1962; Tan-1966).

Orange Co. Atlas quarry (Cosminsky-1947).

St. Lawrence Co. Bornite is reported at the Benson Mines (Robinson and Alverson-1971). Scattered flecks and small grains of bornite are reported at the Parish magnetite district (Leonard-1951). Reported in Balmat-Edwards district (Lea and Dill-1968).

BOURNONITE Pb Cu Sb S$_3$ lead copper antimony sulfide Orthorhombic

New York Co. Reported at Fourth Ave. & 80th St. (Chamberlain-1888).

BRAUNITE 3 Mn$_2$ O$_3$•Mn Si O$_3$ Tetragonal

St. Lawrence Co. Braunite was found between diopside and dolomite layers in the hanging wall of a fault at the Gouverneur Talc Co. mine (Stockman-1975).

Bronzite — See Enstatite

BROOKITE Ti O$_2$ titanium oxide Orthorhombic
Trimorphous with rutile and anatase.

Albany Co. Brookite was reported near Meadowdale and Indian Ladder (Palache, Berman, Frondel-1944).

Ulster Co. Small crystals of brookite occurred on quartz at the Ellenville lead mine (Frondel, Newhouse and Jarrell-1942).

BRUCITE Mg (OH)$_2$ magnesium hydroxide Hexagonal

Putnam Co. Tilly Foster Mine, Brewster. Fine crystals and foliated masses were found associated with chondrodite and clinochlore; also pseudomorphs after dolomite (Trainer-1938, 1939).

Byssolite — See Amphibole — Actinolite

Bytownite — See Plagioclase

CACOXENITE $Fe_9 (PO_4)_4 (OH)_{15} \cdot 18 H_2O$ iron phosphate hydroxide hydrate   Hexagonal

Jefferson Co. Reported on earthy hematite at Antwerp (Beck-1842; Dana, J.D-1892; Palache-Berman-Frondel-1951).

CALCITE $Ca CO_3$ calcium carbonate   Trigonal

Calcite is an important rock-forming mineral in many rocks of sedimentary origin and their metamorphic equivalents. It often is the dominent and almost pure constituent of limestones and marbles. It is present in many shales and may occur as cementing material in other sedimentary rocks. The crystalline limestones (marbles) of northern and southeastern New York may contain both calcite and dolomite.

Calcite is also deposited from meteoric lime-bearing water in a variety of forms including travertine and calc-tufa from springs and streams; it forms stalactites and stalagmites in limestone caves; and it

Calcite-Calcareous Tufa showing leaf molds   Mumford, Monroe Co.

is the principal petrifying material of fossil corals, fossil algae (crypto-zoon) and fossil mollusks (clams, snails, etc.). Travertine (calc-tufa) is of common occurrence in localities where lime is deposited by springs. It often contains impressions of leaves and other vegetable matter. At Saratoga Springs in Saratoga Co., large travertine terraces have been built up near the "geysers." At Mumford in Monroe County, thick travertine deposits have been used as a source of building stone.

Calcite is a mineral species whose crystals present a remarkable variety of crystal forms and combinations. "Calcites of New York" by Dr. H. P. Whitlock (N.Y. State Mus. Memoir 13-1910) is a classic treatise on many of the outstanding crystallized calcites from New York state localities. It is superbly illustrated with line drawings.

Calcite localities are too numerous to mention here. The listed occurrences are therefore restricted to localities from which good specimens have been reported. A fairly extensive list of calcite localities has been given by Whitlock (1903, 1910).

Albany Co. Crystals in Cobleskill limestone at South Bethlehem (Whitlock-1910a).

Cayuga Co. Small calcite crystals were reported in the Onondaga limestone at Union Springs (Whitlock-1910a).

Clinton Co. Calcite crystals of several different types were found in upper levels of Chateaugay iron mines at Lyon Mountain; also at Arnold Hill (Whitlock-1907–1910a).

Columbia Co. Small calcite crystals occur in veins in the Becraft limestone at Hudson (Whitlock-1910a).

Essex Co. Calcite crystals reported at Mineville, Crown Point and Chilson Lake (Whitlock-1910a). It is a constituent of Grenville crystalline limestone (Shaub-1953).

Greene Co. Reported at New Baltimore; also Austin's Glen near Catskill (Whitlock-1910a).

Herkimer Co. Calcite crystals are sometimes associated with "Herkimer diamonds".

Jefferson Co. Reported at the Sterling mine, near Antwerp (Whitlock-1910a) near Oxbow (Nason-1888), and near Natural Bridge (Slocum-1948).

Lewis Co. Sterlingbush, near Natural Bridge. In 1906, 14 tons of large violet to lavender crystals were discovered in an operating quarry in dolomitic limestone. The chamber of the cave was 4 meters wide, 2.5 meters high and extended 15 meters. Penetration twins were found and some crystals were partly coated with secondary aragonite. The cause of the color is ascribed to presence of manganese and also traces of neodymium (Whitlock-1910a; Gardner-1920). In a quarry about 0.5 mile north of Natural Bridge, large solution cavities contained calcite crystals up to 10 cm. long (Agar-1921).

Madison Co. North of Chittenango Falls, small double terminated scalenohedral crystals, clear to pale yellow, sometimes twinned on "c", are associated with celestite (Jensen-P.O; Thibault-1935).

Monroe Co. Penfield, etc. Fine gray, white to golden scalenohedral crystals up to 4 inches long associated with crystallized dolomite, etc. occur in cavities in the Lockport dolomite (dolostone) (Jensen-1942) (See pp. 35, 36).

Niagara Co. Excellent quality, light gray to golden yellow "dogtooth" crystals are in cavities in the Lockport formation at Lockport, etc. (Awald-1958).

Calcite crystal group   Penfield, Monroe Co.

Onondaga Co. Small calcite crystals were found on Silurian limestone near Fayetteville (Whitlock-1910).

Ontario Co. and Yates Co. Partly crystallized calcite veins occur in septaria north of Vine Valley, also in Bristol Valley area (Jensen-1954).

Orange Co. Pink to salmon calcite is reported near Twin Lakes (Two Ponds) (Pegau and Bates-1941; Ayres-1945).

Putnam Co. Tilly Foster Mine at Brewster. Salmon to white calcite cleavages, also yellow columnar, fluorescent (Trainer-1938, 1939, 1942).

Saratoga Co. Gailor quarry at Saratoga Springs. Small colorless to light yellow "dogtooth" crystals were associated with quartz crystals in cavities in dolomite (Rowley-1951). The mound of calcareous tufa at High Spring, Saratoga was known as early as 1767 (Kemp-1912).

St. Lawrence Co. Calcite, occasionally dolomitic, is the chief constituent of the Grenville marble.

The lead mines 2 miles southwest of the village of Rossie were the source of exceptionally fine calcite crystals between 1835 and 1840. The clear to white crystals were highly modified rhombohedrons and scale-

Calcite cleavage, shows twinning lines   near Fine, St. Lawrence Co.

nohedrons, many being superbly twinned. A few crystals were light lilac in color. Crystals up to 18 inches in size were reported. The crystals were associated with galena (Beck-1842; Nason-1888; Whitlock-1910a) (See also p. 45).

Salmon calcite containing large crystals of phlogopite occurs at the old mica pits near Pyrites (Agar-1921; Jensen-P.O.). Calcite at Balmat is reported to show traces of barium, magnesium, manganese, lead and strontium (Doe-1962).

Schoharie Co. Stalactites and stalagmites are abundant at Howe Caverns, Ball's Cave, etc. (Grabau-1906; Whitnall-1930; Thurston-1942). Calcite crystals were reported in the Rondout limestone (Whitlock-1910a).

Ulster Co. Unique calcite crystals were reported to occur at Rondout (Whitlock-1910).

Westchester Co. Groups of large tabular crystals, some coated with drusy quartz were found at the pyrite mines on Anthony's Nose (Dana, J.D.-1892 p. 270).

Yates Co. See under Ontario County.

Carbonate fluorapatite — See Apatite

Calcite, clear cleavage   near Balmat, St. Lawrence Co.

CARNALLITE K Mg Cl$_3$•6 H$_2$O potassium magnesium chloride hydrate   Orthorhombic

Grains of carnallite occur with anhydrite, etc. in halite beds (Alling-1928).

Calcite, twin crystal   Rossie, St. Lawrence Co.

CELESTITE (Celestine)   Sr SO$_4$ strontium sulfate   Orthorhombic

Crystalline masses and occasional excellent crystals of celestite are found in cavities in sedimentary rocks. Barytocelestite contains barium in substitution for strontium.

Cayuga Co. Thin radial blades of celestite occurs in limestone at Owasco Creek, near Auburn (Whitlock-1903).

Herkimer Co. Fibrous, bluish to white celestite is reported in limestone near Starkville (Whitlock-1903).

Jefferson Co. White crystalline celestite occurs in limestone near Theresa (Whitlock-1903).

Madison Co. Choice, well developed tabular light blue celestite crystals up to 1½ inch long, prismatic crystals up to 1 inch long and fibrous veins about ½ inch thick occur in vugs in limestone northwest of Chittenango Falls (Thibault-1935).

Celestite crystals   Penfield, Monroe Co.

Monroe Co. Celestite is present in cavities in the Lockport dolomite (dolostone). It occurs as fibrous to lamellar masses or as crystals up to 6 inches long. The clear to light blue crystals are often well terminated and may be embedded in clear selenite (Jensen-1942) (See also p. 35).

Niagara Co. Celestite is present in cavities in the Lockport dolomite (dolostone) as white to gray crystalline masses. Terminated crystals are rare (Awald-1958).

Oneida Co. Celestite is reported to occur in cavities in the Lockport dolomite (dolostone) near Sherrill as fibrous masses and crystals up to 2½ inches long (Monahan-1928).

St. Lawrence Co. Small to large celestite crystals of delicate blue color have been found at the Rossie lead mine (Beck-1842). Radiating groups of white celestite crystals are found at Balmat (Robinson-1971).

Schoharie Co. Gray-blue tabular crystals occur in cavities in waterlime (Grabau-1906). There is an unconfirmed report of the occurrence of barytocelestite in the Rondout limestone east of Schoharie Village (Newland-1919).

CERITE $(Ce, Ca)_9 (Mg, Fe) Si_7 (O, OH, F)_{28}$ Trigonal

Saratoga Co. Found near Gordon Creek at Batchellerville (Tan-1966).

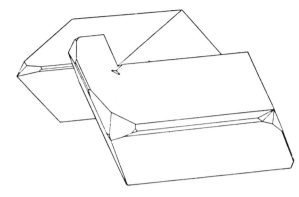

Calcite from Rossie
Twin crystal
St. Lawrence Co., N.Y.

Calcite from Rondout
Rhombohedral–scalenohedral habit.
Ulster Co., N.Y.

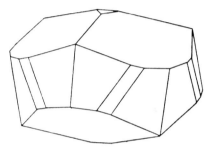

Crystal drawings of calcite by Dr. H. P. Whitlock
from N. Y. State Museum Memoir 13, 1910

CERUSSITE   Pb CO_3 lead carbonate   Orthorhombic

St. Lawrence Co. Rare at the Rossie lead mines (Beck-1842).

Saratoga Co. Reported at Gailor quarry, Saratoga Springs (Rowley-1951).

Westchester Co. Small prismatic cerussite crystals were reported at an old lead mine south of Sing Sing (Torrey-1848). It is reported in an old copper mine at Sparta (Whitlock-1903).

CHABAZITE   Ca $(Al_2 Si_4)$ $O_{12}•6$ H_2O calcium aluminosilicate hydrate   Trigonal   Zeolite group

Bronx Co. Found in narrow veins in gneiss at subway excavation (Manchester-1931).

Warren Co. Microscopic chabazite crystals were observed in diorite near Schroon Lake (Rowley-1957).

Chalcedony — See Quartz

Celestite, fibrous   near Chittenango Falls, Madison Co.

CHALCOCITE $Cu_2 S$ copper sulfide   Monoclinic

Columbia Co. Chalcocite has been reported with galena near Canaan (Whitlock-1903).

Dutchess Co. Near Smithfield (Beck-1842).

St. Lawrence Co. Chalcocite is reported with bornite, etc. in the Parish District (Leonard-1951).

CHALCOPYRITE $Cu Fe S_2$ copper iron sulfide   Tetragonal

This is an important copper ore mineral but only a few occurrences have been reported in the state.

Essex Co. Chalcopyrite is reported associated with pyrrhotite in pegmatite near Crown Point Center (Rowley-1962; Tan-1966).

Herkimer Co. In gneiss at Salisbury (Whitlock-1903).

Jefferson Co. Chalcopyrite was present in copper prospects opened in 1934–35 on the Robinson farm near Oxbow (Anderson-1947).

Monroe Co. Noted in Reynales limestone (Hall-1843).

Orange Co. Tiny crystals of chalcopyrite were reported in calcite at the Atlas limestone quarry near Pine Island (Cominsky-1947).

Putnam Co. Small masses of chalcopyrite are reported in pyrrhotite and also in gneiss at the Tilly Foster mine (Trainer-1938).

St. Lawrence Co. At a copper mine near Canton about 1846 (Durant and Paige-1898). A small amount of chalcopyrite was present in gangue of galena veins at Rossie (Buddington-1934). Chalcopyrite is listed at the Benson Mines (Robinson and Alverson-1971), and is present at the Balmat-Edwards district (Lea and Dill-1968).

Ulster Co. Chalcopyrite crystals occur with quartz crystals at Ellenville lead mine (Whitlock-1903).

Warren Co. Masses with epidote are reported (Rowley-1957).

Westchester Co. Chalcopyrite was reported at Old Copper Mine, Sparta (Manchester-1931).

Chamosite — See Chlorite

Chert — See Quartz

Chromian tremolite — See Amphibole

CHLORITE   A group name.
(Foster-1962; Strunz-1970; Fleischer-1975)
The members of the chlorite group are soft (hardness 2–2½), usually green and resemble micas. They occur as foliated masses, aggregates of fine scales and tabular pseudohexagonal crystals. Chlorites form as the result of the alteration of ferrimagnesium silicates such as amphiboles, biotite and pyroxenes. They occur in metamorphic rocks (slates, schists, etc.) and may be present in igneous rocks where ferrimagnesium silicates have been altered. The following chlorites have been reported in the state:
Chamosite $(Fe'', Mg, Fe''')_5 Al (Si_3 Al) O_{10} (OH, O)_8$
Clinochlore $(Mg, Fe'')_5 Al (Si, Al)_4 O_{10} (OH)_8$
Leuchtenbergite — a variety of Clinochlore
Ripidolite — is intermediate between clinochlore and chamosite.

Jefferson Co. Chlorite occurs as fine grained aggregates replacing biotite, feldspar, hornblende, etc. at pyrite prospects (Prucha-1957).

Monroe Co. Chamosite was noted in thin section of Furnaceville hematite (Alling-1946).

Oneida Co. Chamosite is present as oolites above and below oolitic hematite; a one inch band was noted at Lairdsville (Dale-1953).

Orange Co. Leuchtenbergite was reported at Amity (Dana, J.D.-1892).

Putnam Co. Scaly green aggregates and good tabular crystals of clinoch-

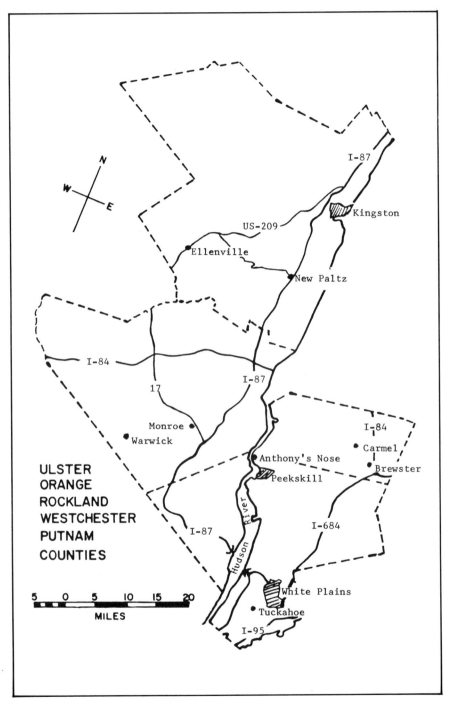

ULSTER
ORANGE
ROCKLAND
WESTCHESTER
PUTNAM
COUNTIES

lore were reported at the Tilly Foster magnetite mine (Manchester-1931; Trainer-1938). Ripidolite is associated with chondrodite at Mahopac iron mines (Gillson-1926).

St. Lawrence Co. A dark green to nearly black highly chloritized rock reported at Balmat zinc mine (Brown-1936a). Talc-chlorite-serpentine is listed at the McLear pegmatite (Shaub-1929). Chlorite is reported at pyrite prospects (See Jefferson Co. above).

CHLORITOID $(Fe, Mn)_2 Al_4 Si_2 O_{10} (OH)_4$ iron aluminum silicate hydroxide   Monoclinic

Dutchess Co. Clove quadrangle. Specks up to ¼″ diameter in phyllitic schist (Barth and Balk-1934).

CHONDRODITE $(Mg, Fe)_3 (Si O_4) (OH, F)_2$ magnesium iron silicate hydroxide fluoride   Monoclinic   Humite group

Essex Co. Yellow grains of chondrodite were observed in white crystalline limestone west of North River (Jensen-P.O. 1970).

Orange Co. Chondrodite is abundant as yellow grains disseminated in crystalline limestone at the Atlas limestone quarry. Larger red-brown grains may be norbergite (Cosminsky-1947). Chondrodite was also reported 5 miles west of Bear Mountain near upper Twin Lakes (Pegau and Bates-1941).

Putnam Co. At the Mahopac iron mine, 7 miles southwest of Tilly Foster Mine, golden brown crystals of chondrodite occur in white marble; deep red chondrodite with magnetite, etc. was reported (Gillson-1926).

Chondrodite was the finest mineral from the Tilly Foster mine near Brewster. Deep cinnamon-red crystals with brilliant luster, some of gem quality, as well as amber-brown and grayish-brown crystals occurred up to 1 inch in width. Massive chondrodite was the principal gangue mineral of the magnetite ore. The best crystals were found in 1891–1892. Serpentine pseudomorphs after chondrodite crystals were also reported (Breidenbaugh-1873; Dana, J.D.-1875; Trainer-1938; Sinkankas-1959) (See also pp. 41, 42, 43).

St. Lawrence Co. Yellow rounded grains of chondrodite are abundant in some of crystalline limestone near Oxbow and Yellow Lake (Buddington-1934) also near Somerville (Agar-1921).

CHROMITE $Fe Cr_2 O_4$ iron chromium oxide   Cubic   Spinel group

Onondaga Co. Small grains were noted in thin section of peridotite at Syracuse (Maynard and Ploger-1946).

Richmond Co. & Westchester Co. Small grains occur in serpentine at several localities (Newland-1901, 1919).

Tompkins Co. Reported in peridotite dikes near Ithaca (Martens-1924).

CHRYSOBERYL Be Al_2 O_4 beryllium aluminum oxide   Orthorhombic

New York Co. A light yellow crystal 8 × 10 × 14 mm. was found in pegmatite at an excavation at 88th and Amsterdam Ave; a large crystal fragment 8 × 25 mm. was found in quarry at 93rd and Riverside Park (Levinson-1901).

Saratoga Co. Yellowish-green tabular twinned chrysoberyl crystals up to 4 cm. long were found in a pegmatite at Greenfield, north of Saratoga Springs. First reported in 1822 (Steel-1822; Whitlock-1903; Navias & Ostrom-1951).

CHRYSOCOLLA $(Cu, Al)_2$ H_2 Si_2 O_5 $(OH)_4 \cdot n$ H_2O copper silicate hydroxide   Monoclinic

Niagara Co. Rare as spots on sandstone with azurite and malachite at Lewiston (Awald-1958).

Putnam Co. Stains on bronzite rock were noted at Tilly Foster Mine (Trainer-1938).

Rockland Co. Masses on rock near Nyack (Buyce-1976).

Warren Co. Microscopic porcelain-like masses in epidote were reported near Schroon Lake (Rowley-1957).

Chrysotile — See Serpentine

Citrine — See Quartz

Clays — See Illite, Kaolinite, Montmorillonite

Cleavelandite — See Plagioclase — Albite

Clinochlore — See Chlorite

CLINOHUMITE $(Mg, Fe)_9 (Si O_4)_4 (F, OH)_2$ Monoclinic   Humite group

Putnam Co. Reported as rare but highly modified crystals (Dana, J.D.-1892; Trainer-1938).

CLINOZOISITE Ca_2 Al_3 Si_3 O_{12} (OH) calcium aluminum silicate hydroxide   Monoclinic   Epidote group

Essex Co. Clinozoisite and grossular were reported in wollastonite at Willsboro (De Rudder and Beck-1963).

CLINTONITE $Ca(Mg, Al)_3(Al_3, Si)O_{10}(OH)_2$ Monoclinic   Mica group

Orange Co. Seybertite (Clintonite) is reported at Amity (Dana, J.D.-1892).

COALINGITE $Mg_{10}Fe_2'''(CO_3)(OH)_{24} \cdot 2H_2O$ Trigonal

Richmond Co. Present in serpentinized harzburgite-dunite on Staten Island (Okulewicz-1977).

COBALTITE   Co As S cobalt arsenic sulfide   Cubic

Essex Co. Small grains reported at Lake Sanford but identification was not exact (Wheeler-1950).

Collophane — See Apatite

Colophonite — See Garnet (Andradite)

COLUMBITE $(Fe, Mn)(Nb, Ta)_2O_6$ Orthorhombic

Saratoga Co. Reported with chrysoberyl at Greenfield (Palache-Berman-Frondel-1944).

Westchester Co. Columbite was abundant at Baylis quarry as masses and crystals, some 3 inches long; also at Kinkel quarry, Bedford (Black-1948; Manchester-1931; Agar-1933; Tan-1966).

COPIAPITE $Fe''Fe'''_4(SO_4)_6 \cdot (OH)_2 \cdot 20H_2O$ Triclinic

Putnam & Westchester Co. Unconfirmed report at Anthony's Nose, pyrrhotite mine (Zodac-1933).

CORDIERITE (Iolite) $Mg_2Al_4Si_5O_{18}$ magnesium aluminum silicate,   Orthorhombic

Lewis Co. Inclusions in Grenville gneiss (Smyth and Buddington-1926).

Westchester Co. Cordierite was reported in schist and in emery at Peekskill (Friedman-1956).

CORUNDUM Al_2O_3 aluminum oxide   Trigonal

Emery is a grayish black to black granular aggregate of corundum that is admixed with magnetite or hematite and spinel.

Orange Co. Small bluish and pink corundum crystals are reported with spinel and rutile in crystalline limestone at Warwick (Palache, et. al.-1944).

Westchester Co. There are four major emery localities in the Cortlandt complex of basic and ultrabasic intrusive igneous rocks. Minerals that have been reported in the rocks adjacent to the emery deposits include allanite, andalusite, cordierite, högbomite, hypersthene, olivine, sapphirine, sillimanite and staurolite (Friedman-1956).

Coulsonite — See Magnetite

COVELLITE   Cu S copper sulfide   Hexagonal

St. Lawrence Co. Microscopic traces occur in sulfides of magnetite deposits from Parish, and from Benson Mines (Leonard-1951).

Ulster Co. Covellite was reported as an alteration of chalcopyrite at Ellenville (Ingham-1940).

Crocidolite — See Amphibole

Cummingtonite — See Amphibole

CUPRITE Cu_2O copper oxide   Cubic

Rockland Co. Reported with malachite in trap rock 2 miles from Ladentown (Dana, J.D.-1892).

Cyanite — See Kyanite

Cyrtolite — See Zircon

DANBURITE   Ca B_2 Si_2 O_8 calcium borosilicate   Orthorhombic

St. Lawrence Co. Crystalline masses and occasional partly translucent light brown danburite crystals occur in veins in a green pyroxene rock about 5 miles south of Russell (Brush and Dana-1880; Agar-1921). Glassy residual grains in large altered gray danburite crystals occur in the McLear pegmatite (Shaub-P.O.: Yedlin-1940).

DATOLITE   Ca B Si O_4 (OH) calcium borosilicate hydroxide Monoclinic

Putnam Co. Found in vein in syenite at the Tilly Foster Mine, near Brewster (Trainer-1941).

Warren Co. Microscopic crystals in cavities with chabazite, etc. near Schroon Lake (Rowley-1957).

Diamond   C carbon   Cubic

There are several peridotite dikes in and around Syracuse, Onondaga County and in and around Ithaca,Tompkins County. Although periodically tested, no diamonds have ever been reported (Gill-1928; Sinkankas-1959). An unconfirmed find was made in Grass River near Massena, St. Lawrence Co., in 1909 (Sinkankas-1959).

Diopside — See Pyroxene

Dipyr — See Scapolite

DOLOMITE   Ca Mg (CO$_3$)$_2$ calcium magnesium carbonate   Trigonal

The mineral dolomite is the major constituent of several important sedimentary and metamorphic rock formations in the state. The term "dolostone" is often used for the sedimentary rock dolomite to avoid confusion with the mineral of the same name. The Grenville crystalline limestones of St. Lawrence Co. are a series of metasediments which are estimated to be 2,000 feet thick. They are differentiated into 15 units most of which are silicated dolomites (dolostones) (Brown & Engel-1956).

The principal rock of the Inwood formation of New York and Westchester Counties is a crystalline dolomitic marble (Schuberth-1968).

The Little Falls dolomite formation is a siliceous dolomite (dolostone) and is noted for the occurrence of exquisite quartz crystals that are known as "Herkimer diamonds". This formation occurs extensively in Herkimer, Montgomery and Saratoga Counties with small outcrops at Lake George in Warren County. Small dolomite crystals sometimes occur with the quartz crystals (Cushing-1905a; Newland & Vaughn-1942).

Lockport Dolomite (Dolostone)   Penfield, Monroe Co.

The Lockport formation of western New York contains thick beds of magnesian limestone (Lockport dolomite, a dolostone). Numerous cavities contain fine crystals of dolomite, calcite, celestite, and other minerals.

Monroe & Wayne Co. Fine white rhombohedral dolomite crystals up to 5 mm. on an edge occur in or frequently line cavities in the Lockport dolomite (dolostone) (Giles-1920; Jensen-1942) (See also p. 35).

Montgomery & Herkimer Co's. Gray, white to buff dolomite crystals occur in cavities in Little Falls dolomite (dolostone) west of Fonda, also at Middleville, etc.

Niagara Co. Gray, white to pinkish crystals often line cavities in the Lockport formation. Excavation for the Erie Canal west of Lockport produced fine examples. (Awald-1958). There is one operating quarry nearby.

Oneida Co. Crystals line cavities in the Lockport. (Monahan-1928).

Putnam Co. Dolomite is plentiful as white to gray cleavable masses with clinochlore, etc. and occasional crystals that are pseudomorphs of dolomite after chondrodite are reported at the Tilly Foster Mine, Brewster. (Trainer-1938, 1940).

St. Lawrence Co. Dolomite sometimes occurs with tourmaline at Pierrepont, etc. Fine pink saddle-shaped crystals occur in vugs in the Ogdensburg dolomite (dolostone) at the Barrett quarry near Norfolk (Robinson and Alverson-1971; VanDiver-1977).

Saratoga Co. Small rhombs of dolomite are associated with quartz crystals in cavities in the dolomite (dolostone) at the Gailor quarry (Rowley-1951).

Westchester Co. Dolomite is an abundant constituent of the Inwood marble (Schuberth-1968).

Dravite — See Tourmaline

DUMORTIERITE Al_7 $(B\,O_3)(Si\,O_4)_3$ O_3 aluminum borosilicate Orthorhombic

New York Co. Acicular crystals of dumortierite were reported as tufts in granite, also in pegmatite with orthoclase and muscovite at excavations 171st St. and Fort Washington Ave., etc. (Schaller-1905).

Westchester Co. Slender bluish fibrous masses of dumortierite were seen in pegmatite at Valhalla (Waite-1940).

Edenite — See Amphibole

Elbaite — See Tourmaline

Emery — See Corundum

Enstatite — See Pyroxene

EPIDOTE Ca_2 $(Al, Fe)_3$ Si_3 O_{12} (OH) calcium aluminum iron silicate hydroxide Monoclinic

Clinton Co. Tiny crystals and stringers of epidote occur in feldspar at Chateaugay mines, Lyon Mountain (Whitlock-1907).

Franklin Co. It is present in miarolitic cavities in granite gneiss on Owl's Head Mountain (Robinson and Alverson-1971).

Orange Co. Epidote crystals occur at many contact zones at Twin Lakes and near Monroe (Ayres-1945).

Putnam Co. Fine grained epidote and striated crystals up to a few cm. long occur at Mahopac iron mine (Martens-1927). Masses and dark green crystals of epidote up to 1 inch long were observed at Tilly Foster Mine, near Brewster (Trainer-1938).

Rensselaer Co. Epidote was reported to be widely distributed in quartz veins in graywacke east of Troy (Balk-1953).

Dolomite   Tuckahoe, Westchester Co.

Warren Co. Fine grained to coarse crystalline to massive veins of epidote occur in gabbro; crystals and groups were reported in vugs near Schroon Lake (Rowley-1957).

Westchester Co. Baylis quarry, Bedford (Tan-1966).

EPISTILBITE   Ca (Al$_2$ Si$_6$) O$_{16}$•5 H$_2$O calcium aluminosilicate hydrate   Monoclinic   Zeolite group

Westchester Co. Bundles of yellowish to white crystals of epistilbite 3 to 4 mm. long were associated with bertrandite on beryl (Pough-1936).

EPSOMITE   Mg SO$_4$•7 H$_2$O magnesium sulfate hydrate   Orthorhombic

Tompkins Co. White powdery coatings and aggregates of extremely small epsomite crystals were observed on Moscow and Genesee shales near Portland Point (Martens-1925).

ERYTHRITE   Co$_3$ (As O$_4$)$_2$•8 H$_2$O cobalt arsenate hydrate   Monoclinic

Putnam Co. Tiny erythrite crustations on serpentine and magnetite at the Tilly Foster Mine, near Brewster (Januzzi-1959).

Eupyrchroite — See Apatite

FAYALITE   Fe$_2$ Si O$_4$ iron silicate   Orthorhombic   Olivine group

St. Lawrence Co. A green fayalite-ferrohedenbergite granite forms a belt 0.5 to 1 mile wide near Inlet on northeast side of Cranberry Lake (Buddington and Leonard-1962).

FELDSPAR — See anorthoclase, microcline, orthoclase, perthite, plagioclase (albite, oligoclase, andesine, labradorite, and bytownite; anorthite has not been reported in the state).

FERGUSONITE   Y Nb O$_4$ yttrium niobium oxide   Tetragonal

Essex Co. Fergusonite as massive in allanite and as crystals was found in a syenitic pegmatite 4 miles northwest of Crown Point Center (Rowley-1962; Tan-1966).

Flint — See Quartz (Chalcedony)

FLUOCERITE   (Ce, La) F$_3$ Hexagonal

Essex Co. Yellow-brown to orange alteration of allanite may be fluocerite in a syenitic pegmatite 4 miles northwest of Crown Point Center (Rowley-1966; Tan-1966).

New York Co. Reported at Fourth Ave. and 90th St. (Chamberlain-1885).

Fergusonite   near Crown Point, Essex Co.

Fluorapatite — See Apatite

FLUORITE   Ca F$_2$ calcium fluoride   Cubic

Fluorite is a common mineral that is found in sedimentary rocks such as limestones and dolomites (dolostones); it is also found in some granites and with some lead and zinc ores.

Clinton Co. A fluorite-bearing granite occurs at the Palmer Hill group of iron mines (Newland and Kemp-1908; Kemp and Alling-1925).

Essex Co. White, yellow, pink and green fluorite occurs in the Barton Hill iron ore bed (Kemp and Ruedemann-1910).

Jefferson Co. Pale green crystals up to 5 inches on an edge were found about 1862 in a fluorite vein that ran under Muscalonge Lake from the northeastern shore (Buddington-1934).

Monroe Co. Excellent quality cubic fluorite crystals up to 3 inches on an edge and some modified crystals occur in cavities in the Lockport dolomite (dolostone). Colors range from clear to light yellow and light blue to greenish. The crystals often show zoning and are sometimes enclosed in clear selenite (Giles-1920; Hawkins-1925; Jensen-1942).

Niagara Co. Light to dark blue fluorite crystals occur in the Lockport formation near Lockport, etc. (Awald-1958).

Orange Co. White to purple fluorite occured at the Atlas limestone quarry (Cosminsky-1947). (Yttrian fluorite) is reported as altered crystals on hornblende (Shephard-1852; Palache-Berman-Frondel-1951).

Putnam Co. Small colorless, yellow and orange crystals and purple masses of fluorite were reported at the Tilly Foster Mine at Brewster. Hexoctahedral and tetrahexahedral forms were reported (Trainer-1938-1939-1940-1941-1942).

St. Lawrence Co. An immense cavity lined with large cubic crystals of light green fluorite was discovered at Macomb in the autumn of 1888. This furnished groups nearly two feet across and single crystals up to a foot across. Fifteen tons of fine crystals were reported (Kunz-1892; Newland-1919; Cushing and Newland-1925).

Sharp bright green elongated cubes up to 2 inches on an edge were reported at Benson Mines (Alverson-1975).

Small pink and green fluorite veinlets and masses occur along a road cut south of route 58 at Fine (Jensen-P.O.; Tan-1966).

Rossie. Transparent light green hexoctahedral crystals averaging 15 mm. diameter were on calcite rhomb (Whitlock-1910a). Small veinlets of green fluorite occur in gneiss. The fluorite fluoresces blue under long wave ultra violet illumination (Jensen-P.O.).

Fluorite   Penfield, Monroe Co.

FORSTERITE Mg_2SO_4 magnesium silicate   Orthorhombic   Olivine group

Orange Co. The variety, boltonite, was listed at Warwick (Ries-1894).

Francolite — See Apatite

FOURMARIERITE $Pb\ U_4\ O_{13} \cdot 4\ H_2O$ Orthorhombic

Essex Co. Fourmarierite forms dense orange-red resinous material around periphery of altering uraninite crystals in syenitic pegmatite 4 miles northwest of Crown Point Center (Rowley-1962).

GALENA   Pb S lead sulfide   Cubic

Galena is the most important ore mineral of lead. While lead mines were worked spasmodically in the 19th century at Ancram in Columbia County, at Rossie in St. Lawrence County, and Ellenville in Ulster County, they were short lived. Today the St. Joe Minerals Corporation mines at Balmat and Edwards, produce lead as well as zinc ore. Elsewhere in the state, galena occurs at several localities too numerous to completely list here.

Columbia Co. Granular galena has been mined extensively near Ancram (Mather-1843).

Galena Crystals   Rossie, St. Lawrence Co.

Lewis Co. Brief attempts were made to mine lead ore near Martinsburg prior to 1850 (Miller-1910).

Monroe and Niagara Co's. Galena forms some fissure fillings in the Lockport dolomite (dolostone). Tiny cubo-octahedral crystals are sometimes seen (Awald-1958; Giles-1920; Jensen-1942).

During the excavation of the Erie Canal at Rochester, several hundred pounds of galena were found in a single cavity (Hall-1843).

Oneida Co. Reported in the Lockport dolomite (dolostone) near Clinton (La Buz-1968).

St. Lawrence Co. Galena was first noted in the roots of a fallen tree near Rossie. The first of several calcite-galena veins was opened in the winter of 1835–36 south of the village. Fine large cubic crystals of galena, some modified by octahedrons were encountered. The mines were worked intermittently and closed in 1868 shortly after the end of the Civil War (Beck-1842; Durant and Pierce-1878; Buddington-1934) (See also p. 45).

Galena is associated with sphalerite, pyrite, etc. at the St. Joe Minerals Corp. mines at Balmat and Edwards (Brown-1936b).

Sullivan Co. and Ulster Co. Galena is reported in Shawangunk Mountain zinc and lead deposits (Ingham-1940; Heusser-1977).

Westchester Co. Galena was reported at Old Sparta Copper Mine south

Galena   Balmat, St. Lawrence Co.

1. Amphibole, var. Tremolite (hexagonite)   Fowler, N.Y.

2. Ankerite with quartz on hematite   Antwerp, N.Y.

3. Ankerite with quartz and hematite   Antwerp, N.Y.

4. Apatite crystals   Pyrites, N.Y.

5. Apatite in calcite

Rossie, N.Y.

6. Artinite

Staten Island, N.Y.

7. Calcite crystal on dolomite crystals

Penfield, N.Y.

8. Celestite

Chittenango Falls, N.Y.

9. Chondrodite   Tilly Foster Mine, Brewster, N.Y.

10. Chrysoberyl-twin crystal   Saratoga County, N.Y.

11. Danburite crystal group   Russell, N.Y.

12. Dolomite crystal group   Penfield, N.Y.

13. Fluorite with dolomite crystals   Penfield, N.Y.

14. Garnet with hornblende   Gore Mt., N.Y.

15. Giesckite after nepheline　　　　　Natural Bridge, N.Y.

16. Hematite – botryoidal　　　　　Antwerp, N.Y.

17. Hematite-oolitic   Clinton, N.Y.

18. Labradorite   Saranac Lake, N.Y.

19. Labradorite – closeup Saranac Lake, N.Y.

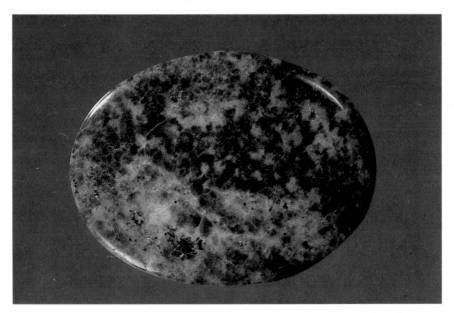

20. Lapis lazuli Edwards, N.Y.

21. Microcline–Amazonite   Valhalla, N.Y.

22. Millerite   Antwerp, N.Y.

23. Pyroxene – augite   Star Lake, N.Y.

24. Pyroxene – augite   Fine, N.Y.

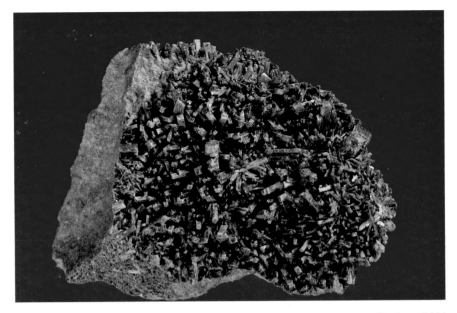

25. Pyroxene – augite   Pyrites, N.Y.

26. Pyroxene – diopside

De Kalb, N.Y.

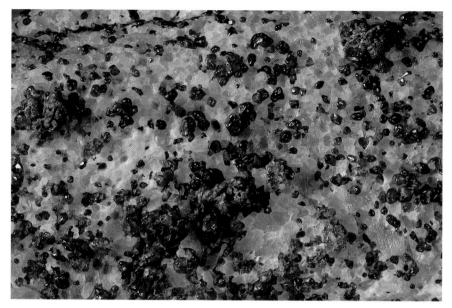

27. Pyroxene–diopside (coccolite)　　　　　　　　Cascadeville, N.Y.

28. Scapolite (wernerite)　　　　　　　　Olmstedville, N.Y.

29. Spinel and chondrodite   Amity, N.Y.

30. Sulfur on dolomite   Monroe Co., N.Y.

31. Zircon Rossie, N.Y.

32. Pyritized Nautiloid, Tornoceras sp. Alden, N.Y.

of Ossining (Manchester-1931). U-Galena is reported as a later mineral to form in fractures in cyrtolite (Kerr-1935; Hey-1963).

GARNET GROUP   Cubic

The garnets are a group of nesosilicates (orthosilicates). They form distinctive isometric crystals (rhombic dodecahedron, trapezohedron, etc.) that are often modified and may show combined forms. Garnets are common accessory minerals of metamorphic rocks (schists, gneisses, etc.) and some igneous rocks (granitic pegmatites, etc.).

Almandine (Almandite) $Fe_3 Al_2 (Si O_4)_3$ iron aluminum silicate

Almandine is the common red garnet in gneisses, schists and pegmatites, etc. It is found in sands off the shore of Lake Ontario and is present in many glacial erratics in the state.

Essex Co. Patches of red, fine granular almandite occur in anorthosite at many localities. It is also present in many gneissic rocks associated with the anorthosite (Buddington and Whitcomb-1941).

New York Co. Excavations in New York City along Broadway, etc. have been the source of many fine large garnet crystals in the past as well as gem quality garnets that have been cut (Manchester-1931; Manchester and Stanton-1917). A spessartitic almandine is reported at the Baylis Quarry, Bedford (Tan-1966).

Orange Co. A garnet pyroxene gneiss is reported at Bear Mountain (Lowe-1950; Dodd-1963).

Saratoga Co. Partly chloritized garnet crystals up to 1 inch have been noted at a pegmatite near Corinth (Tan-1966).

Warren Co. Garnet-rich deposits occur at several localities in the North Creek and Thirteenth Lake quadrangles (Miller-1914; Krieger-1937). The most famous and currently active mine is the Barton Mine on Gore Mountain near North Creek. Crude crystals up to a foot in diameter occur and garnets three feet in diameter have been reported. The garnet occurs in a dark gray metagabbro and each is surrounded by a rim or shell consisting of black hornblende, gray oligoclase and hypersthene. The garnet is approximately 85 to 65% pyralmandite and 15 to 35% lime garnet (Levin-1950; Shaub-1949; see p. 47).

Garnets as large as peas occur in a sillimanite garnet gneiss associated with graphite quartz schist at several localities near Hague.

Westchester Co. Crystals up to 3 inches have been found at the Kinkel and Baylis quarries, Bedford (Manchester-1931; Black-1948; Tan-1966).

Andradite $Ca_3 Fe'''_2 (Si O_4)_3$ calcium iron silicate

Essex Co. Several bands of garnet-pyroxene skarn occur near Willsboro.

It is often associated with wollastonite. The light brown to reddish-brown granular garnet is andradite (formerly called colophonite) (Dana, J.D.-1892; Buddington and Whitcomb-1941).

Putnam Co. Tilly Foster Mine, Brewster. Oil green dodecahedral crystals — rare (Dana, J.D.-1892; Trainer-1938).

St. Lawrence Co. Minute lemon-yellow andradite crystals occur at Balmat (Brown-1936a); also gray-green massive grossular.

Andradite occurs at Benson Mines (Palmer-1970). Brownish-black crystallized masses have been found at the Clifton Iron Mines near De Grasse (Jensen-P.O.).

Grossular (Grossularite) $Ca_3 Al_2 (Si O_4)_3$ calcium aluminum silicate

Essex Co. A grossular-clinozoisite sheet is injected into the wollastonite ore body (De Rudder and Beck-1963). Andraditic grossular reported at the Pokamoonshine Mine, Ausable quadrangle (Buddington-1950).

New York Co. Essonite has been reported (Manchester-1931).

Orange Co. Grossular is reported at the Bradley Mine near Monroe (Ayres-1945).

Spessartine (Spessartite) $Mn_3 Al_2 (Si O_4)_3$ manganese aluminum silicate

New York Co. Gem quality spessartite has been reported in granite (Manchester and Stanton-1917; Manchester-1931).

GEOCRONITE $Pb_5 Sb As S_8$ Monoclinic

St. Lawrence Co. Reported with galena (Steacy-1976).

GIBBSITE $Al (OH)_3$ aluminum hydroxide   Monoclinic

Dutchess Co. Reported at Clove Mine, Unionvale; also in Orange Co (Dana, J.E.-1892; Palache-Berman-Frondel-1944).

Glaucophane — See Amphibole

Goethite — See Limonite

GOLD   Au Cubic

Although several discoveries have been proclaimed, substantial results have never followed. Tiny flakes of gold in quartz have been reported. Assays of alluvial sands show gold ranging from a trace to perhaps $1.00 per ton (Newland-1933). Small flecks of amber mica from weathered Grenville marble have been erroneously mistaken for gold (Valiant-1899).

A pebble of milky quartz containing a small vein of gold was found in the glacial gravel that had been used to surface a driveway in the town of Greece, Monroe County in 1948 (Wishart).

Golden beryl — See Beryl

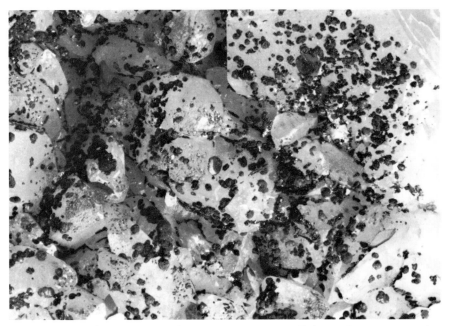

Goethite on Calcite   Balmat, St. Lawrence Co.

GRAPHITE   C carbon   Hexagonal

Graphite has been mined in the state from the early 19th century until the 1920's. A graphite deposit at Lead Hill (Chillson Hill) about 3 miles northwest of Ticonderoga was first mentioned. (Emmons-1842).

The graphite at Lead Hill is said to have been found on a mountain top farm when cows being driven to pasture across a rocky swamp slipped on a moss covered rocky ledge and dislodged the moss from the rock revealing a pure vein of graphite.

Graphite is chiefly present in metamorphosed limestones (marbles) (Ogilvie-1904), gneisses and schists or in contact deposits that are rich in pyroxenes. Graphite has been reported from Dutchess, Essex, Jefferson, Lewis, Orange, St. Lawrence, Saratoga, Warren and Westchester Counties (Alling-1919; Zodac-1940; Rowley-1955). Only a few localities are listed here.

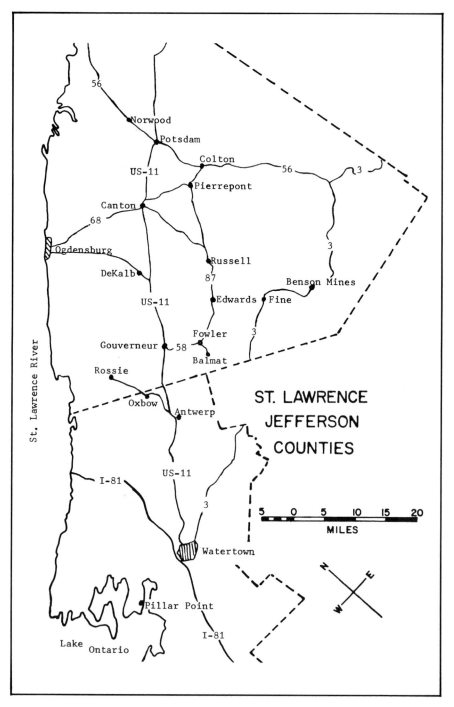

56

Norwood

Potsdam

Colton

US-11

56

3

Pierrepont

Canton

68

3

Ogdensburg

Russell

DeKalb

87

Benson Mines

US-11

Edwards Fine

Fowler

3

Gouverneur 58

Balmat

Rossie

Oxbow

Antwerp

ST. LAWRENCE
JEFFERSON
COUNTIES

US-11

I-81

3

5 0 5 10 15 20

MILES

Watertown

N

E

W

S

Pillar Point

I-81

Lake Ontario

St. Lawrence River

Essex Co. A vein of graphite several inches wide was reported as well as flakes with pyroxene and scapolite adjacent to pegmatite at Lead Hill, 3 miles northwest of Ticonderoga. A mine near Ticonderoga produced graphite as early as 1822 (Beck-1840). At a mine 7½ miles southwest of Crown Point Center and 10 miles from Ticonderoga, graphite flakes up to 3.0 mm. in length occurred in nearly pure crystalline limestone (marble) (Alling-1919).

Single graphite crystals up to 20 mm. diameter and rosettes of crystals 3.0 cm. in diameter were found near Bloomingdale (Alverson-1975).

Flakes of graphite up to 10 mm. diameter occur in a vein of rose quartz in gneiss a short distance north of Port Henry (Jensen-P.O.).

St. Lawrence Co. A graphite quartz schist was mined in the early 1900's southeast of Pope's Mills (Alling-1919).

Warren Co. A graphite quartz schist has been mined at several locations near Hague (Alling-1919).

Westchester Co. Reported at Bedford (Agar-1933).

Graphite in Quartz   Westport, Essex Co.

GREENOCKITE   Cd S cadmium sulfide   Hexagonal

St. Lawrence Co. Reported at Edwards and at Talcville (Cushing & Newland-1925).

GROUTITE   Mn O (OH) Orthorhombic

St. Lawrence Co. At Talcville, black acicular crystals form slender striated prisms 1 to 5 mm. long in cavities in talc (Segeler-1959).

Groutite with talc, etc.   Talcville, St. Lawrence Co.

Guitermanite — an impure jordanite

GUMMITE   A general term for secondary uranium oxides.

Westchester Co. Reported at Baylis and Kinkel quarries, Bedford (Agar-1933; Januzzi-1959; Tan-1966).

GYPSUM   Ca SO_4·2 H_2O calcium sulfate hydrate   Monoclinic

Gypsum is the commonest of the sulfate minerals in the state. Thick and extensive beds of rock gypsum of Silurian (Salinan) age occur in Erie County eastward to Onondaga County and beyond. The first discovery of gypsum in the state and possibly the first on record within the country is attributed to William Lindsay of Camillus, Onondaga County in 1792. Since that time and especially in this century, gypsum mines have been major contributors to the mineral industry of the state.

Pure gypsum is white to gray and often shows gradation to anhydrite. When clear and colorless, it is called selenite. Fibrous forms of gypsum are called satin spar.

Rock gypsum is an impure massive to granular gypsum containing carbonates, clay, etc. In New York State the rock gypsum is interbedded with limestone and shale. Individual localities for rock gypsum are not listed here but they occur in the following counties: Cayuga, Erie, Ge-

Gypsum, selenite – enclosing air bubble Penfield, Monroe Co.

nesee, Herkimer, Livingston, Madison, Monroe, Onondaga, Ontario and Wayne (Newland-1929).

The following are some localities for gypsum:

Clinton Co. At the Chateaugay iron mine at Lyon Mountain, selenite was found in one section of the mine between the 1513 and 2113 foot levels. One swallowtail twin 32 inches long was reported (Zimmer-1947).

Monroe Co. White, massive to crystalline gypsum and clear selenite occurs in cavities in the Lockport dolomite (dolostone). Some of the selenite is of optical grade (Jensen-1942).

Niagara Co. White to gray massive gypsum and transparent selenite occur in the Lockport dolomite (dolostone) (Awald-1958). Satin spar sold at some tourist shops in Niagara Falls in past years was imported from Derbyshire, England.

Onondaga Co. Fibrous gypsum was reported at Manlius (Eaton-1820).

Putnam Co. Tilly Foster Mine, Brewster. Small selenite crystals are reported on apophyllite (Trainer-1938).

St. Lawrence Co. Gypsum has been found at Balmat.

Gypsum, selenite   Penfield, Monroe Co.

HALITE   Na Cl sodium chloride   Cubic   Rock Salt

Salt has had a very prominent role in the mineral industry of New York State. The salt beds are widely distributed and underlie an area several thousand miles in extent. Missionaries from Canadian settlements along the St. Lawrence River visited well known natural salt "licks" in the neighborhood of Onondaga Lake in the mid 1600's but the occurrence of salt was not established until 1865 (Newland-1919; S. Smith-1929).

The Salina beds of Silurian age which carry the salt extend as a belt running east and west across the state. It is 12 miles wide at the Niagara River and extends eastward across the central group of counties south of Oneida Lake from which point it gradually tapers to an end not far from Schoharie. The Salina beds dip to the south, an average of 45 feet to a mile. As the salt is not exposed at the surface, it is reached only through wells and shafts. The crude salt as mined is coarse grained, grayish-white in color. Grains of anhydrite, carnallite, polyhalite and sylvite have been reported (Alling-1928). The occurrence of Silurian salt

Halite   Himrod, Yates Co.

in New York State is most recently documented (Kreidler-1957). The Salina beds extend westward through Ontario into Michigan where they also contain extensive salt deposits (Dorr and Eschman-1970; Heinrich-1976). Thin seams of halite have been found at Edwards in St. Lawrence Co. (Brown-1932; Gressens-1978).

HARMOTOME   (Ba, K) (Al, Si)$_2$ Si$_6$ O$_{16}$•6 H$_2$O barium potassium aluminosilicate hydrate   Monoclinic   zeolite group

Bronx Co. Reported as pale pink twinned crystals in narrow veins in gneiss at subway excavation in Southern Boulevard (Manchester-1931).

New York Co. Yellow, brown and cinnamon colored crystals over ½ inch were found during Harlem railroad improvements in 1871 at 43rd St. (Chamberlain-1888).

Westchester Co. Reported at Sing Sing (near Ossining) (Dana, J.D.-1892).

Hastingsite — See Amphibole

HAÜYNITE (Haüyne)   (Na, Ca)$_{4-8}$ (Al$_6$ Si$_6$) O$_{24}$ (SO$_4$, S, Cl)$_{1-2}$ sodium calcium aluminosilicate sulfate sulfide chloride   Cubic & Triclinic   Sodalite group

Harmotome   near Sing Sing, Westchester Co.

St. Lawrence Co. At the Edwards mine of St. Joe Minerals Corp. a mass
of bright blue haüynite bearing rock (lapis lazuli) about 3 ft. by 8 ft.
was found within the ore zone on the first mining sublevel, D3 stope,
at 2700 feet in 1969. This haüynite is non-cubic (Hogarth-1977). It was
later identified from several other parts of the mine. The lapis lazuli
was surrounded by a zone characterized by pyritic amphibole that has
a selvage rich in phlogopite (Lessing and Grout-1971)

Lapis Lazuli. This is a complex aggregate of several minerals including haüynite or lazurite which provides the blue color, calcite and silicates. Specks of bright iron pyrite are invariably present. At Edwards,
non-cubic haüynite (Sapozhnikov and Ivanov-1976) is associated with
pargasite, diopside and calcite; locally, oligoclase, scapolite and anhydrite are common; pyrite is ubiquitous but uncommon (Hogarth, personal communications-1977). Lapis lazuli is, therefore, a rock name. It
is considered a gem material (Webster, R.-1972).

Hedenbergite — See Pyroxene

HEMATITE Fe_2O_3 iron oxide   Trigonal

Hematite occurs in igneous, sedimentary and metamorphic rocks, both
as primary constituent and as an alteration product. It is an ingredient

of the cementing materials of red sandstones and of the coloring materials of red clays, shales and slate.

Earthy hematite is brick red in color. The steel gray to iron-black hematite is often micaceous in part. Martite is hematite that is pseudomorphous after magnetite. It occurs with magnetite at several localities in the Adirondack region. The lack of its early recognition by mine companies and the fact that it is weakly magnetic often delayed the successful processing of the iron ore in many places. Turgite (Hydrohematite) is hematite with adsorbed water.

Hematite, ground and probably mixed with oil or grease, was used as a mineral pigment for personal ornamentation by the Seneca Indians (Ritchie-1954).

There were two principal districts in the state where hematite was mined for iron ore but mining operations ceased many years ago: There were hematite mines in Jefferson and St. Lawrence Counties (See p. 43) and the Clinton hematites (See p. 44).

Clinton Co. The presence of martite in the magnetite at Arnold Hill and Palmer Hill caused difficulty in milling and was partly instrumental to closing the mine (Kemp and Alling-1925).

Hematite, fossiliferous   Ontario, Wayne Co.

Dutchess Co. Lustrous black botryoidal crusts of turgite occur on limonite at the old Amenia mine and at old Clove mine at Unionvale (Zodac-1951a).

Essex Co. "Halos" of hematite surround hornblende and biotite at Rose Rock Quarry (Tan-1966).

Fulton Co. "Red paint" ore was mined locally many years ago (Thompson-P.O.).

Herkimer Co. Fossiliferous hematite is exposed along Ohisa and Otsquaga Creeks near Edicks (Rickard and Zenger-1964).

Jefferson Co. The hematite deposits are in a narrow belt from between Keene and Antwerp northwest to the Shirtliff Mine, 3½ miles north northwest of Philadelphia.

The Sterling Mine, 2¾ miles north of Antwerp was opened in 1836. The last operations were in the period 1904–1912. The hematite included red ochre, massive and botryoidal red, steel gray compact and micaceous types. Occasionally tiny black crystals up to a millimeter in size occurred in vugs. The Sterling Mine and the mine dumps were the source of fine specimens of millerite, ankerite, stilpnomelane, quartz crystals, etc. (Buddington-1934) (See p. 44).

Monroe Co. A 12 inch thick bed of fossiliferous hematite occurs in the Genesee gorge north of Rochester in prominent view on the east side of the gorge north of Driving Park Bridge. Martite is present (Alling-1946).

Oneida Co. The iron industry in the area began in 1797. In addition to oolitic and fossiliferous hematite beds, thin beds of specular hematite are reported. Use of the hematite as an iron ore ceased during World War I, but the hematite was used until recent years as a paint pigment and as a coloring agent for cements (Newland and Hartnagel-1908; Dale-1953) (See also p. 44).

Putnam Co. Hematite is reported as stains on serpentine at the Tilly Foster Mine, Brewster (Trainer-1938).

St. Lawrence Co. Lustrous black hematite and occasional groups of small "iron rose" crystals were found in cavities in a dense gray quartzite about 3 miles south of Pierrepont (Robinson and Alverson-1971). Hematite is abundant and martite is associated with magnetite at Benson Mines (Leonard and Vlisidis-1961; Palmer-1970). Earthy red hematite and small specular crystals occur at the Balmat zinc mine (Pough-1940); hematite is present in the Balmat-Edwards district (Lea and Dill-1968).

Wayne Co. Hematite was mined in open cuts north of Ontario Center, 15 miles east of Rochester. The ore trenches are now filled with water. This is the "Furnaceville" iron ore of the Clinton Group (Silurian Age) (Cooper-1957) (See also p. 44).

HEULANDITE   (Na, Ca)$_{4-6}$ Al$_6$ (Al, Si)$_4$ Si$_{26}$ O$_{72}$•24H$_2$O sodium calcium aluminosilicate hydrate   Monoclinic   Zeolite group

New York Co. Found as narrow veins on faces of gneiss at excavations (Manchester-1931).

Putnam Co. Small crystals were noted in pyroxene at Tilly Foster Mine, Brewster (Trainer-1939).

Warren Co. near Schroon Lake, tiny crystals were found associated with apophyllite, datolite, etc. (Rowley-1957).

Hexagonite — See Amphibole (Tremolite).

HISINGERITE   Fe$'''_2$ Si$_2$ O$_5$ (OH)$_4$•2 H$_2$O   Monoclinic

Putnam Co. Occurrence reported at Tilly Foster Mine, Brewster (Trainer-1938).

HOEGBOMITE (Högbomite)   (Mg, Fe)$_2$ (Al, Ti)$_5$ O$_{10}$ Hexagonal

Westchester Co. Cortlandt Twp., south southeast of Peekskill. Small hoegbomite crystals up to 0.04 mm. are reported along margins of spinel grains (Friedman-1952).

Hornblende — See Amphibole

HORTONOLITE   (Fe$''$, Mg, Mn)$_2$ SiO$_4$ Magnesian fayalite. Orthorhombic

Orange Co. Intimately associated with magnetite and in calcite in an iron mine at Monroe (Dana, J.D.-1892).

HUMITE   (Mg, Fe)$_7$ (Si O$_4$)$_3$ (F, OH)$_2$ magnesium iron silicate fluoride hydroxide   Orthorhombic

Putnam Co. Large partly altered humite crystals as well as fine red modified crystals occurred with magnetite at the Tilly Foster Mine, Brewster (Trainer-1938).

Hyalite — See Opal

HYDROMAGNESITE   Mg$_5$ (CO$_3$)$_4$ (OH)$_2$•4 H$_2$O   Monoclinic
   Hydromagnesite often occurs as an alteration of serpentine rocks.

Putnam Co. Tilly Foster Mine, Brewster. White to chalky coatings on serpentine (Trainer-1938).

Richmond Co. Staten Island. Small clusters of white radiating hydromagnesite crystals with artinite (Reasenberg-1968). Reported in serpentinized dunite on Staten Island (Okulewicz-1977).

Westchester Co. on serpentine (Shepard-1852).

HYDROTALCITE $Mg_6 Al_2 (CO_3) (OH)_{16} \cdot 4 H_2O$ Trigonal

Jefferson Co. Reported at Antwerp and Oxbow (Palache, Berman, Frondel-1944).

Putnam Co. White fibrous and grayish-white foliated to lamellar at the Tilly Foster Mine, Brewster (Trainer-1938, 1943).

St. Lawrence Co. Optical data reported (Larsen-1921). "Houghite" (pseudomorph after spinel) is reported at Rossie and Summerville (Palache, Berman, Frondel-1944).

HYDROZINCITE $Zn_5 (CO_3)_2 (OH)_6$ zinc carbonate hydroxide Monoclinic

St. Lawrence Co. Gray masses reported with sphalerite, etc. fluoresce pale blue-white (Dill-1976; Van Diver-1977).

Hypersthene — See Pyroxene

ICE H_2O Hexagonal
Water exists in three forms:
a) Solid — snow, ice, sleet, hail, frost. Tiny hexagonal crystals are incomparably exquisite and varied. The snow crystals that grow slowly assume the most solid forms. Crystals that grow rapidly will assume

Ice   Niagara Falls (American Falls) 1963

Ice–Frost pattern

branching forms (e.g. frost crystal patterns on windowpanes) (Bentley and Humphreys-1931). Snow usually covers the ground in most areas of the state from December through March.

The ice bridge at Niagara Falls and ice cascades on waterfalls throughout the state are scenic wonders of the winter season.

b) Liquid — water. The scenic beauty of the state is enhanced in many areas by the water of brooks, streams, rivers, lakes and ponds.

c) Aqueous vapor — which is present in the atmosphere. When this vapor condenses, it forms dewdrops on blades of grass and leaves of plants. While dewdrops have no crystal form, they create unique art patterns.

Iddingsite — See Olivine

Idocrase — See Vesuvianite

ILLITE   This is a group of mica-clay minerals with a complex formula. Illite is invariably present in sediments (clays, shales, etc.) of marine origin (Grim-1953).

Monroe Co. Illite constitutes 85% of the Maplewood shale (Grim-p.c.).

Tompkins Co. The clay fraction of the Enfield shale is predominently illite (Martin-1954).

ILMENITE Fe Ti O$_3$ iron titanium oxide   Trigonal
Ilmenite is an important ore of titanium. In many of its occurrences it is associated with magnetite.

Essex Co. The titaniferous magnetite deposits of the Lake Sanford area were discovered in 1826 by prospectors who were hunting for silver but active mining did not begin until 1941. Ilmenite is usually intergrown with magnetite. Ilmenite crystals up to 10 cm. long are reported partially altered to gray-tan leucoxene in which the ilmenite parting is preserved. (Stephenson-1945; Wheeler-1950; Kays-1965). Leucoxene is composed chiefly of anatase, etc.

Orange Co. Crystals are reported in serpentine and white limestone at Warwick, Amity and Monroe (Palache, Berman, Frondel-1944).

Putnam Co. Tabular crystals were reported in gneiss, etc. at Tilly Foster Mine, Brewster (Trainer-1938).

Westchester Co. Found at the Kinkel Quarry, Bedford (Manchester-1931; Black-1948).

ILVAITE Ca Fe''$_2$ Fe''' (SiO$_4$)$_2$ (OH) calcium iron silicate hydroxide   Orthorhombic

St. Lawrence Co. Distinct crystals several millimeters long have been noted, some associated with willemite (Brown-1936; Pough-1940).

Iolite — See Cordierite

IRON Nickel-Iron   Fe, Ni   Cubic   Meteoritic Nickel-Iron
Nickel-iron is an alloy of nickel and iron that is an almost ubiquitous constituent of meteorites.

Meteorites are more likely to be found on arid plains than in heavily vegetated areas. Hence only 9 meteorite occurrences are reported for New York State while Kansas and Texas have a combined total of over 180.

There are three classes of meteorites of which two have been reported in New York State. Many are reported or are brought into museums for identification but almost all turn out to be pieces of slag, concretions, etc.

Siderites, or iron meteorites, consist almost entirely of nickel-iron. Most siderites will exhibit an octahedral or hexahedral structure. Ataxites do not.

Aerolites, or stones, consist chiefly of silicate minerals with a variable nickel-iron content that averages about 13%. Chondrites are aerolites that contain small spheroidal aggregates of enstatite, bronzite or hypersthene, sometimes with olivine. Achondrites are aerolites which do not have chondrules.

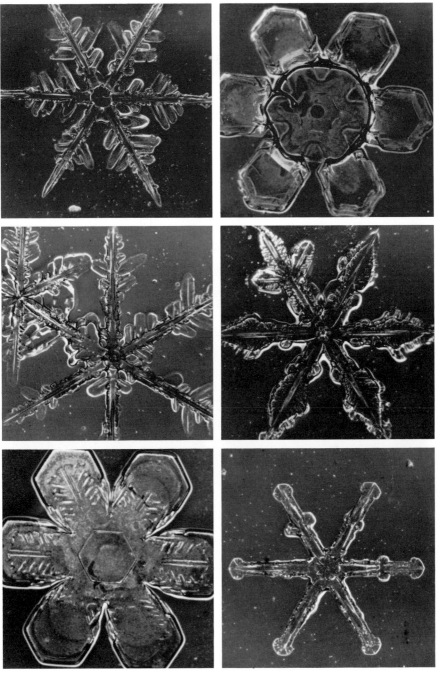

Snow crystals (Photo by Dr. Lothar Engelmann)

Ref: Nininger-1933; Farrington-1915; Palache, Berman, Frondel-1944; Mason-1962; Hey-1966.

METEORITES THAT HAVE BEEN REPORTED IN NEW YORK STATE

BETHLEHEM, Albany County. Syn. Albany Co.; Troy.
Stone. Crystalline spherical olivine-bronzite chondrite. Seen to fall 7:30 a.m., August 11, 1859. Known weight about 11 grams (0.4 ounce). (Wells-1859; Shepard-1860; Ward-1904; Farrington-1915; Mason-1962; Hey-1966).

BURLINGTON, Otsego County. Syn. Cooperstown; Otsego County.
Iron. Medium octahedrite. Found before 1819. A mass weighing about 150 pounds was ploughed up but only about 12 pounds has been preserved. (Silliman-1844; Farrington-1915; Nininger-1952; Mason-1962; Hey-1966; Buchwald-1976)

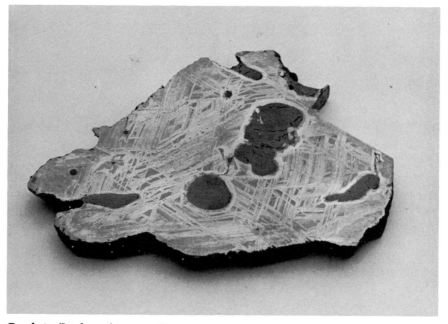

Cambria (Lockport) meteorite
Siderite – polished
Troilite nodules are gray
(Courtesy, Center for Meteorite Studies, Tempe, Arizona)

CAMBRIA, near Lockport, Niagara County. Syn. Lockport.
Iron. Fine octahedrite. This iron meteorite was found in 1818 while cultivating field. It was irregular elongated in shape, 46 cm. (18

inches) long and 14 cm. (5.5 inches) wide. Troilite nodules occurred in the interior of the iron. Some depressions on the surface contained remains of troilite that had weathered. (Silliman-1845; Ward-1904; Cohen-1905; Farrington-1915; Nininger-1952; Mason-1962; Hey-1966; Buchwald-1976)

MOUNT MORRIS, Livingston County.
Stone. Olivine-bronzite chondrite. A mass of about 12½ grams was found in 1897 on the Landers farm 1½ miles south of Mount Morris. (Whitlock-1913; Mason-1962; Hey-1966)

SCHENECTADY, Schenectady County.
Stone. H-4 chondrite (Van Schmus and Wood-1967). Fell at 8:30 p.m. Friday 12, April 1968. A 283.3 gram stone meteorite was found two days later. (Fleischer, R.L., et. Al.-1970)

Schenectady meteorite, Aerolite–Chondrite
(Courtesy, Schenectady Museum, Schenectady, N.Y.)

SENECA FALLS, Seneca County. Syn. Seneca River.
Iron. Medium octahedrite. This iron meteorite, weighing about 9 pounds, was found in 1850 while digging a ditch on a farm on the Cayuga side of the Seneca River. It was about 10 cm. (4 inches) in diameter and 17¾ cm. (7 inches) long. (Root-1851; Shepard-1853; Ward-1904; Farrington-1915; Mason-1962; Hey-1966; Buchwald-1976).

SOUTH BYRON, Genesee County.
Iron. Nickel-rich ataxite. A mass weighing nearly 6 kg (13.28 lbs) was picked up in 1915 by a farmer while excavating a ditch about ½ mile west of South Byron. (Ward-1904; Mason-1962; Hey-1966; Buchwald-1976).

TOMHANNOCK CREEK. Rensselaer County. Syn. Ironhannock Creek, Rensselaer Co.
Stone. Brecciated olivine-bronzite chondrite. A stone weighing about 1½ kg (3.3 lbs) was discovered about 1863 near the base of a large tree on the bank of Tomhannock Creek. (Bailey-1887; Ward-1904; Farrington-1915; Mason-1962; Hey-1966)

YORKTOWN, Westchester County.
Stone. Olivine hypersthene chondrite. Fell Sept. 1869. A stone weighing about ½ kg (1.1 lbs) was found. (Mason & Wiik-1960; Mason-1962; Hey-1966)

JAROSITE $K Fe_3 (SO_4)_2 (OH)_6$ Trigonal   A secondary mineral

St. Lawrence Co. Reported as a brown earthy alteration product on pyritic schist near Fowler-Balmat (Kinsland-1976).

Jasper — See Quartz

Jenkinsite — See Serpentine

JORDANITE $Pb_{14} As_6 S_{23}$ lead arsenic sulfide   Monoclinic

St. Lawrence Co. Jordanite is associated with galena, calcite, diopside, etc. in the St. Joe Minerals Corp. Mine at Balmat (Brown-1959; Ramdohr-1969; Lessing-1969). Guitermanite is an impure jordanite.

KAOLINITE $Al_2 Si_2 O_5 (OH)_4$ Monoclinic

Lewis Co. Greenish-gray masses reported as essentially kaolin occur in quartz cavities in Lyonsdale Twp. (Dale-1924).

New York Co. A white clay forming patches in a deeply weathered granodiorite was noted in subway excavation east of the Harlem River (Kerr-1930)

Richmond Co. Kaolinite is reported in a clay outcrop in a transported glacial till along the west bank of a small creek near Princess Bay station (Kerr-1932).

St. Lawrence Co. Occurs at Rock Island road cut (Van Diver-1977).

Westchester Co. Occurs in Bedford pegmatites (Agar-1933).

KASOLITE   Pb (UO_2) Si $O_4 \cdot H_2O$ lead uranyl silicate hydrate   Monoclinic

Essex Co. Sharp pale yellow cubical pseudomorphs after uraninite up to ⅜ inch in syenitic pegmatite near Crown Point Center (Rowley-1962; Tan-1966).

KYANITE Al_2 Si O_5 aluminum silicate   Triclinic

Dutchess Co. Present in phyllite schist on the east slope of Clove Valley 1½ miles north of Clove Valley Station (Barth and Balk-1934).

Westchester Co. Present in sillimanite-staurolite schist near Golden's Bridge (Chase and Brock-1976).

Labradorite — see Plagioclase

LANGITE Cu_4 (SO_4) $(OH)_6 \cdot 2$ H_2O Orthorhombic

Westchester Co. There is an unconformed report of bluish-green prisms of langite having been found on the dumps of an old pyrrhotite mine at Anthony's Nose (Zodac-1933).

LANTHANITE   (La, Ce)$_2$ $(CO_3)_3 \cdot 8$ H_2O Orthorhombic

Essex Co. In syenitic pegmatite northwest of Crown Point Center, radiated and tufted groups of crystals and crusts of matted crystals occur on allanite (Kemp and Ruedemann-1910; Rowley-1962; Tan-1966). Also at Sanford Mine, Moriah, on allanite (Blake-1858; Palache, Berman, Frondel-1951).

Lapis lazuli — See Haüynite

LAUMONTITE   Ca $(Al_2$ $Si_4)$ $O_{12} \cdot 4$ H_2O calcium aluminosilicate hydrate   Monoclinic   Zeolite group

New York Co. Noted as narrow veins in gneiss (Manchester-1931)

Putnam Co. Tilly Foster Mine, at Brewster. Small veins containing groups of white crystals found in gneiss (Trainer-1938).

Leuchtenbergite — See Chlorite

Leucoxene — See Ilmenite

LIMONITE   a general term for hydrous iron oxides, mostly goethite. Limonite is an abundant material always occurring as a secondary product of other iron minerals including sulfides (especially pyrite, marcasite and pyrrhotite), oxides and iron-bearing silicates. It is present in the "rusty" gneisses and the pyrite deposits of St. Lawrence and Jefferson Counties (Prucha-1957). It is a common alteration of pyrite and marcasite crystals and inclusions in the Devonian and other shales in the state (Trainer-1932; Fisher-1951).

Small deposits of "bog ore" have been found in marshes and boggy places in Livingston, St. Lawrence, and Wayne Counties and elsewhere. All the occurrences of limonite are too numerous to mention.

Dutchess and Columbia Co's. The Maltby limonite mine near Millerton is reported to have opened in 1750. Many small mines were in operation off and on during the 1800's. The limonite ore varied from earthy and pulverulent (ocherous) to brown compact material. Mammillary, botryoidal and stalactitic forms were reported (Mather-1843; Smock-1889; Newland-1919)

Livingston Co. Limonite (bog ore) that was found in small quantities in marshy spots near Avon produced a yellowish to brownish pigment that was used by the Seneca Indians as paint stones (Ritchie-1957).

Orange Co. Atlas quarry at Pine Island. Yellowish brown stains in and on small pseudomorphs after pyrite in limestone (Zodac-1940).

Putnam Co. Tilly Foster Mine, Brewster. Common as stains and coatings; also pseudomorphous after biotite (Trainer-1938, 1940).

Richmond Co. Limonite ore, some of which was oolitic, was mined on Staten Island (Newland-1901; Manchester-1931). Mammillary, botryoidal and stalactitic forms and yellow ochre reported on the island (Chamberlain-1887).

St. Lawrence Co. Limonite occurred in the gossan of the zinc mines at Balmat.

LINNAEITE $Co_3 S_4$ Cubic

Putnam Co. Tilly Foster Mine, Brewster. Tiny steel-gray octahedral crystals on magnetite were reported (Januzzi-1959).

Lizardite — See Serpentine

LOELLINGITE (Löllingite. Obs. Leucopyrite) $FeAs_2$ iron arsenide   Orthorhombic

Orange Co. Present in diorite rock at Edenville (Beck-1842; Whitlock-1903; Newland-1919).

Reported at Monroe and Edenville (Palache, Berman, Frondel-1944).

St. Lawrence Co. Cobaltian loellingite was reported from the Clifton Mine near De Grasse (Leonard-1951; Leonard and Vlisidis-1960).

MAGHEMITE Gamma $Fe_2 O_3$ iron oxide   Cubic
Maghemite is formed by the slow weathering of magnetite.

Northern Adirondacks. About 1 mile south of Skerry, the ilmenomagnetite in a diabase dike is partly altered to maghemite (Buddington, Fahey and Vlisidis-1969).

MAGNESITE   Mg CO_3 magnesium carbonate   Trigonal
Magnesite occurs mainly as an alteration of magnesium rocks.

Orange Co. Small veins in serpentine near Greenwood Furnace (Beck-1842).

Putnam Co. Small groups of white crystals and cleavages with talc and mica were reported at the Tilly Foster Mine, Brewster (Trainer-1938).

Richmond Co. Noted in serpentine and magnesian marble (Beck-1842). Reported with artinite on serpentine (Okulewicz-1977).

Rockland Co. Small veins were noted in serpentine at several places (Beck-1842; Newland-1901).

MAGNETITE   Fe'' Fe'''$_2$ O_4 Cubic
Magnetite is a common accessory mineral in igneous and metamorphic rocks and also occurs as segregated masses of considerable size. It has been an important ore mineral of iron of the Adirondacks and the Hudson Highlands. Some of the earliest discoveries in the state were made by surveyors when their magnetized compass needles were affected by masses of magnetite. Magnetite localities were indicated on the early maps made during the French occupation of the Champlain Valley. Magnetite deposits began to be first worked in this area about 1800 (Wessels-1961) (See p. 39). Titaniferous magnetite may contain as much as 7.5% TiO_2. Ilmeno-magnetite is magnetite with micro-intergrowths of ilmenite.

The principal Adirondack magnetite deposits that are low in titanium occur in the borders of the Adirondack highlands in Clinton, Essex, Franklin, Washington and Warren Counties (Newland-1919; Broughton et. al. 1966; Newland and Kemp-1908) (See also p. 39).

Clinton Co. At Lyon Mt. the magnetite occurs as irregular grains in a gneissic granite (Gallagher-1937).

Essex Co. Magnetite is a common constituent of many of the igneous and metamorphic rocks of the county. In several regions great sheets, lenses and pods of magnetite occur. Mining operations have been an important activity in the county for nearly 200 years. The largest area of titaniferous magnetite occurs in both anorthosite and gabbro near Lake Sanford. Ilmenite is intimately intergrown with the magnetite. The presence of vanadium may be due to the presence of coulsonite. Leucoxene is present as an alteration of ilmenite (Newland-1919; Balsey-1943; Stephenson-1945).

Magnetite, octahedral crystal   Mineville, Essex Co.

Several magnetite ore bodies occur in the Mineville area where the first mine was opened in 1846. A granular ore at the Lovers Pit produced excellent modified octahedral crystals up to an inch on an edge in the 1890's (Kemp and Ruedemann-1910). Excellent examples of magnetite showing octahedral parting were found. Apatite in the magnetite ore contained rare earths (McKeown and Klemic-1956) (See p. 125).

Mining operations at Mineville ceased October 27, 1934.

Herkimer Co. Magnetite ore was discovered five miles north of Dolgeville about 1840 in an area of syenite and granite gneisses. Magnetite ore was mined intermittently from 1839 to 1913 (Beck-1842; Cushing-1905a; Newland and Kemp-1908; Tuttle-1977).

Lewis Co. Briefly mined near Port Leyden (Miller-1910).

New York Co. Oriented inclusions of magnetite and hematite in muscovite were studied from 26 localities on Manhattan Island (Frondel and Ashby-1937).

Onondaga Co. Small crystals and irregular grains were noted in a peridotite dike (Maynard and Ploger-1946).

Orange Co. A species once reported as "diamagnetite" from Monroe appears to be a pseudomorph of magnetite after ilvaite (Palache, Berman, Frondel-1944).

The Stirling mine in southeastern Orange County was discovered in 1750. The Forest of Dean Mine just outside of Monroe Township is one of the oldest mines in the Highlands of the Hudson, having begun operation in 1756. The granular magnetite is associated with granite. Other magnetite mines were operated near Sterling Forest, Monroe and Warwick in the 1800's (Newland-1919). (See p. 41.) Lodestone was reported at an abandoned iron mine on the top of Bull Hill, near Monroe (Zodac-1939b).

Magnetite   Monroe, Orange Co.

Putnam Co. The Tilly Foster Mine at Brewster (see p. 41), was named after the man, Tilly Foster, who was born in Carmel in 1793. Magnetite was first mined on the Foster property in 1810. The ore deposit was a thick lens over 500 feet long occurring in gneiss. The mine has now been closed for many years and is filled with water. The Tilly Foster Mine was a very prolific source for minerals and over 60 different minerals have been listed. In addition to the massive magnetite, fine dodecahedral magnetite crystals, some up to an inch in size, rarely twinned were found, often associated with chondrodite, clinochlore, dolomite, etc. (Manchester-1931; Trainer-1938, 1940, 1941, 1942, 1943; Nuwar-1971).

Magnetite, dodecahedral crystals   Tilly Foster Mine, Putnam Co.

There were several famous magnetite mines in Putnam County that ceased operations many years ago near Carmel north of Mahopac Falls, near Peekskill, etc. (Newland-1919; Colony-1921).

St. Lawrence Co. The magnetite ore at Benson Mines area near Star Lake was mentioned as early as 1847 and has been worked intermittently since about 1899. The most recent mining activity started in July 1941. The magnetite ore occurs in bands of gneiss is very extensive (Newland and Kemp-1908; Dale-1935; Hartnagel and Broughton-1951; Palmer-1970).

The Clifton Mines near De Grasse about 10 miles north of the Benson Mines were first operated about 1858. The mines lay idle for many years around the turn of the century until 1941 when the mines were reopened. They are now closed (Hartnagel & Broughton-1951). Magnetite is in the Balmat-Edwards District (Lea and Dill-1968).

Many other magnetite occurrences at other localities in the state have been listed (Whitlock-1903).

MALACHITE $Cu_2 (CO_3) (OH)_2$ copper carbonate hydroxide
Monoclinic
While malachite is uncommon in the state, several occurrences are listed where it has been observed.

Essex Co. Microscopic crusts and acicular crystals have been noted in a syenitic pegmatite northwest of Crown Point Center (Rowley-1962; Tan-1966).

Jefferson Co. Reported at Muscalonge Lake (Hough-1854).

Lewis Co. Malachite occurs as an alteration of chalcopyrite in Grenville calcite of a vein filling in Lyonsdale Twp. (Dale-1924).

Niagara Co. Spots of malachite occur with azurite and chrysocolla on gray sandstone near Lewiston (Awald-1958).

Orleans Co. Malachite was noted as occurring in cavities of Pentamerus in the Reynales formation near Medina (Hall-1843).

Putnam Co. Tilly Foster Mine, Brewster. Malachite was noted with chalcopyrite (Trainer-1938).

St. Lawrence Co. Reported at Benson Mines (Robinson and Alverson-1971; Van Diver-1977).

Warren Co. Green films of malachite and microscopic crystals occur with chalcopyrite at Schroon Lake (Rowley-1957).

Westchester Co. Malachite and azurite occur as stains on gneiss at White Plains (Fluhr-1931). Reported at old copper and lead mines near Ossining (Torrey-1888; Manchester-1931).

MANASSEITE $Mg_6 Al_2 (CO_3) (OH)_{16} \cdot 4 H_2O$ Hexagonal

Orange Co. Listed with hydrotalcite, dolomite, serpentine at Amity (Palache, Berman, Frondel-1944).

MARCASITE $Fe S_2$ iron sulfide   Orthorhombic   Dimorphous with pyrite.
Marcasite concretions and pyrite concretions can form under very similar conditions. Sometimes both minerals are present in the same specimen.

Erie Co. The "marcasite" concretions that are found in the Ledyard shale (Devonian) near the town of Alden, have been shown by X-ray to be pyrite. Pyrite has also been identified in many other shales in Erie County (Izard and Clemancy-1967). For additional references, see under Pyrite.

Monroe Co. and Niagara Co. Tiny thin bladed striated blackish bronze colored marcasite crystals up to ¼ inch long often occur on calcite and dolomite crystals that occur in the Lockport dolomite (dolostone) (Giles-1920; Jensen-1942; Awald-1958). These crystals were once misidentified as "achmite" (acmite) and rutile (Beck-1842).

Nassau Co. Brassy yellow crystallized nodules of marcasite are reported in lignite beds near Glen Cove; also near Oyster Bay (Rocks and Minerals, Vol. 30, 26, no's. 11-12, 1954; no. 247, p. 372, 1955).

St. Lawrence Co. Marcasite was reported at Balmat-Edwards (Lea and Dill-1968). Marcasite occurred with crystallized dolomite in cavities in the Ogdensburg dolomite (dolostone) at Norwood.

Ulster Co. Small crystals on and in calcite are reported (Whitlock-1905).

Marialite — See Scapolite

Marmatite — See Sphalerite

Martite — See Hematite

Meionite — See Scapolite

MELANTERITE Fe $SO_4 \cdot 7$ H_2O Monoclinic

Putnam Co. Whitish efflorescence on pyrrhotite on dumps of old pyrrhotite mine at Anthony's Nose is reported (Zodac-1933).

Tompkins Co. Associated with epsomite, gypsum, etc. on shales near Ithaca (Martens-1925).

Westchester Co. An incrustation of melanterite was reported on wall of abandoned emery mine northeast of Croton (Zodac-1939a).

MELILITE A mineral group of general formula (Na, Ca)$_2$ (Mg, Al) (Si,Al)$_2$ O$_7$ Tetragonal

Herkimer Co. Reported in alnoite dike near Manhein (Smyth-1893).

Onondaga Co. Reported in peridotite dike at Green Street, Syracuse (Smyth-1902).

Tompkins Co. Reported in peridotite dikes in vicinity of Ithaca (Martens-1924).

Meta-autunite — See Autunite

Meta-bentonite — See Montmorillonite

Mica — see Biotite, Illite, Muscovite, Phlogopite

MICROCLINE   K Al Si$_3$ O$_8$ potassium aluminosilicate   Triclinic
Feldspar group
Potash feldspar — dimorphous with orthoclase.

Microcline is a common constituent of many acidic igneous rocks. It may occur together with orthoclase in granite, but is more common in granite pegmatites where it is invariably intergrown with albite to form perthite. Color is gray, buff, salmon, and shades of pink to red. Green microcline is amazonite (amazonstone).

Clinton Co. Lyon Mountain. Large microperthite crystals with well developed crystal faces are found in miarolitic cavities in the magnetite mine (Gallagher-1937).

Essex Co. Large crystals near Crown Point Center about 4 feet to 5 feet long are exposed in old quarry wall (Rowley-1962). At Olmsteadville, a blue adularescent microcline occurred with scapolite, idocrase, etc. (Shaub-1953; Sinkankas-1957).

Orange Co. Granite quarry, Mt. Adam (Cosminsky-1947).

Putnam Co. Tilly Foster Mine, Brewster (Trainer-1938).

St. Lawrence Co. Perthite and anorthoclase were reported in a pegmatite occurring at a roadcut south of rte. 58, near rte. 3, near Fine (Tan-1966).
   The feldspar at the McLear pegmatite consists of granular microcline-perthite and albite (Shaub-1929).

Saratoga Co. near Overlook. Large microcline crystals reported (Rowley-1942a; Tan-1966).

Warren Co. Crystals of microcline more than 1.5 ft. in length were reported at the Chestertown pegmatite prospect (Tan-1966).

Westchester Co. Giant microcline crystals up to 5 feet long are reported as well as some perthite at the Bedford quarries (Manchester-1931; Agar-1933; Tan-1966). Material obtained from a pegmatite east of Valhalla was used for construction of Kensico Dam contained well developed green to bluish green crystals of amazonite up to 8 inches long streaked with albite; microcline perthite in graphic granite (Newland-1916; Alling-1926; Manchester-1931).

MICROLITE   (Na, Ca)$_2$ Ta$_2$ O$_6$ (O, OH, F) sodium calcium tantalum oxide hydroxide fluoride   Cubic

New York Co. Found in oligoclase at excavation at 39th St. and 6th — 7th Ave's (Chamberlain-1888).

Microcline   Bedford, Westchester Co.

MILLERITE   Ni S nickel sulfide   Trigonal

Jefferson Co. Some of the finest millerites in the world were found in the Old Sterling Mine, 2¾ miles north of Antwerp. The millerite occurred as radiating groups of capillary crystals in vugs in hematite with ankerite, etc. (Shepard-1852; Valiant-1899; Buddington-1934).

Mizzonite — See Scapolite

MOLYBDENITE   Mo S_2 molybdenum sulfide   Hexagonal
Although molybdenite is reported in several areas, it only occurs in small amounts.

Clinton Co. Reported as closely associated with titanite at the Chateaugay Mine, Lyon Mountain (Whitlock-1907).

Essex Co. Observed as streaks and scales in pegmatite (Kemp and Ruedemann-1910).

Lewis Co. Occurrences of molybdenite disseminated in pegmatite veins in granite, etc. Near Lowville have been described (Newland-1919; Buddington-1934).

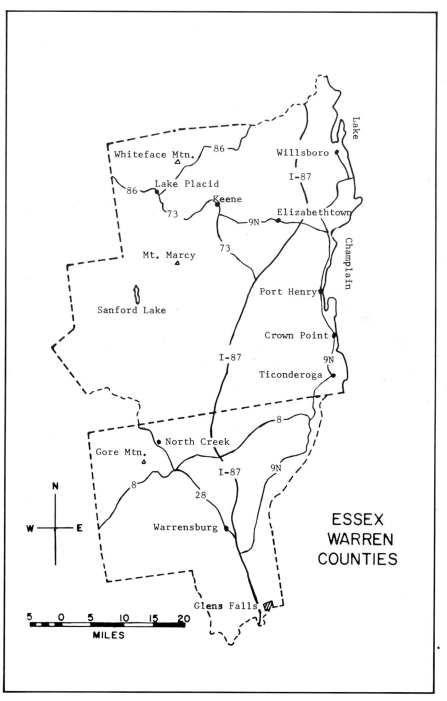

ESSEX
WARREN
COUNTIES

Millerite   Antwerp, St. Lawrence Co.

New York Co. Molybdenite was quite plentiful in excavations for the Columbia College campus at Fourth Ave. and 49th St. (Chamberlain-1888).

Orange Co. Flakes and foliated masses of molybdenite were noted in crystalline white limestone (marble) in the Atlas limestone quarry at Pine Island (Zodac-1940).

St. Lawrence Co. Flakes of molybdenite were observed with pyroxene near Fine (Jensen-P.O.). Reported at the McLear pegmatite and elsewhere (Buddington-1934; Dale-1935; Engel-1962; Tan-1966).

Westchester Co. Reported at the Baylis and Kinkel quarries, Bedford (Tan-1966). Several other molybdenite localities in the state have been reported (Whitlock-1903; Newland-1919).

MONAZITE   (Ce, La, Nd, Th) PO$_4$ Monoclinic
Monazite is a phosphate of the rare earths, mainly cerium.

Essex Co. Small percentages occur in rare earth-bearing apatite at Mineville (Mc Keown and Klemic-1956). Small monazite crystals up to ⅞ inch long were found in a syenitic pegmatite northwest of Crown Point Center (Rowley-1962; Tan-1966).

New York Co. Several minor occurrences of monazite are reported in schist at the northern part of Manhattan Island (Palache, Berman, Frondel-1951). Many crystals of monazite and xenotime were found in an excavation for a new Speedway at 181st St. and the Harlem River (Chamberlain-1895).

Numerous crystals were also found at an excavation at 171st St. and Fort Washington Ave. (Hovey-1896).

Saratoga Co. Microscopic crystals and a few masses of monazite were found in the Overlook pegmatite, Town of Day (Rowley-1960; Tan-1966).

Westchester Co. Monazite crystals about ⅛ inch in size are reported with sillimanite at Yorktown Heights (Palache, Berman Frondel-1951).

MONTICELLITE Ca Mg Si O$_4$ Orthorhombic

Essex Co. A monticellite-bearing marble is reported in Mt. Marcy quadrangle (Jaffe & Jaffe-1975).

Lewis Co. Reported in the Lake Bonaparte quadrangle (Valley and Essene-1977).

MONTMORILLONITE (Na Ca) $_{0.33}$ (Al, Mg)$_2$ Si$_4$ O$_{10}$ (OH)$_2$•nH$_2$O sodium calcium aluminum magnesium silicate hydroxide hydrate Monoclinic

Essex Co. Pale pink earthy coatings of montmorillonite occur on microcline in syenitic pegmatite (Rowley-1962; Tan-1966). Montmorillonite is reported as an alteration product of wollastonite at Willsboro (De Rudder & Beck-1963).

Oneida Co. Metabentonite, a mineral of the montmorillonite group (Kerr & Hamilton-1949; Glossary of Geology-1973) is reported in thin beds of yellowish to gray clay (Kay-1953).

St. Lawrence Co. Pink earthy coatings lined some cavities of the McLear pegmatite.

Mountain Leather — See Amphibole

MUSCOVITE K Al$_2$ (Al Si$_3$) O$_{10}$ (OH)$_2$ potassium aluminosilicate hydroxide Monoclinic Mica group
Muscovite is a common rock forming mineral of granites and granite

pegmatites. It also occurs in schists and gneisses. The occurrences are too numerous to list here.

New York Co. Muscovite is a predominent constituent of the Manhattan schist (Schuberth-1968). Inclusions of tourmaline and other minerals in muscovite from New York City have been studied (Frondel-1936, 1940); magnetite inclusions in muscovite have been described (Frondel and Ashby-1937).

Putnam Co. Crystal groups were reported at the Tilly Foster Mine, Brewster (Trainer-1941).

St. Lawrence Co. Sericite is a fine grained member of the mica group usually muscovite. It occurs as alteration of various aluminosilicates. It is best recognized in thin section. Reported in the Russell area (Buddington and Leonard-1962) and also occurs in many other counties in the state.

Saratoga Co. Large crystals of muscovite were reported at Batchellerville (Tan-1966).

Warren Co. Pale green muscovite crystal plates were reported at Horicon (Rowley-1955).

Muscovite enclosing iron oxides   Batchellerville, Saratoga Co.

Westchester Co. Small muscovite crystals were present in all quarries at Bedford (Black-1948). Book mica up to 6 inches in diameter was reported at the Baylis quarry (Tan-1966).

NATROLITE Na_2 $(Al_2$ $Si_3)$ O_{10}•2 H_2O sodium aluminosilicate hydrate   Orthorhombic   Zeolite group

Putnam Co. Tilly Foster Mine, Brewster. Slender crystals about 1 inch long were noted on the surface of a granite gneiss (Trainer-1942).

NEPHELINE (Na, K) Al Si O_4 sodium potassium aluminosilicate   Hexagonal

Lewis Co. Crystals of nepheline pseudomorphed to Gieseckite (an aggregate of micaceous character) were noted at Diana and Natural Bridge (Dana, J.D.-1892; Agar-1923; Buddington-1939; Moyd-1976).

Norbergite — See Under Chondrodite

Oligoclase — See Plagioclase

OLIVINE The name olivine refers to a group of minerals consisting of the series Forsterite — Fayalite (Mg_2 Si O_4 — Fe''_2 Si O_4), Orthorhombic   Iddingsite is a mixture of silicates formed by alteration of olivine, fayalite, etc.

Essex Co. Olivine is a common constituent of gabbros (Kemp and Ruedemann-1910). It is present in layers of cumberlandite at the Split Rock Mine near Westport (Sack-1977).

Herkimer Co. Abundant in alnoite dike near Manheim (Smyth-1893).

Onondaga Co. Pale yellow glassy grains of olivine occur in peridotite dike (Maynard and Ploger-1946); in peridotite at Clintonville (Smith-1931).

Putnam Co. Light green olivine is abundant at the Mahopac iron mines near Brewster (Gillson-1926). It is reported at the Tilly Foster mine, Brewster (Colony-1921; Trainer-1938). Olivine (dunite) is reported at Tompkins Hill (Berkey and Rice-1919).

Richmond Co. Both unaltered and partially altered olivine is reported in a serpentinized harzburgite-dunite on Staten Island (Okulewicz-1977).

Rockland Co. An olivine-rich zone occurs in the Palisades diabase (Colony-1933; Schuberth-1968).

St. Lawrence Co. Bright red iddingsite is reported as an alteration of fayalite in a fayalite granite near Inlet (Buddington & Leonard-1962).

Warren Co. Olivine is an essential mineral in primary gabbro (Levin-1950).

Westchester Co. Olivine is present in the peridotite and the olivine pyroxenite of the Cortlandt Complex southwest of Peekskill. (J.D. Dana-1881; Berkey and Rice-1919; Shand-1942; Dolgoff-1958)

OPAL Si $O_2 \cdot nH_2O$ silicon oxide hydrate   amorphous

Diatomaceous earth is a light colored siliceous earth composed principally of opaline fragments of diatoms (microscopic plants) that grow in fresh water and secrete siliceous skeletons.

Hyalite is a colorless variety of opal that most often occurs as globular glassy crusts on pegmatite minerals. Hyalite frequently fluoresces green.

Essex Co. Microscopic botryoidal fluorescent crusts of hyalite occur on feldspar in a syenitic pegmatite northwest of Crown Point Center (Rowley-1962; Tan-1966).

Herkimer Co. Thick deposits of Post Pleistocene diatomaceous earth are reported at Beaver Meadow, Big Crooked Lake, Chub Pond, Roilly Pond and White Lead Lake, etc. (Cox-1893; Newland-1919).

Putnam Co. Noted as a gray-white hyalite coating of hisingerite at the Tilly Foster Mine, near Brewster (Trainer-1938).

Westchester Co. Highly fluorescent crusts of hyalite occur on smoky quartz at the Kinkel quarry, Bedford (Black-1948; Tan-1966).

ORPIMENT $As_2 S_3$ arsenic sulfide   Monoclinic

Orange Co. Slight traces of orpiment were reported 1 mile north of Edenville (Whitlock-1903; Newland-1919).

St. Lawrence Co. Associated with realgar at Balmat.

ORTHOCLASE $KAlSi_3O_8$ potassium aluminosilicate Monoclinic   Feldspar group   Potash feldspar   dimorphous with microcline

See also: Microcline

Orthoclase is a common constituent of many igneous rocks. It may occur together with microcline in granite, but microcline is the more common in granite pegmatites.

Clinton Co. Orthoclase crystals coat vugs in granite (Whitlock-1907).

Essex Co. Adularia reported at Olmsteadville (Rowley-1948; Tan-1966). Moonstone is reported at Leib's farm near Bloomingdale (Sinkankas-1976).

New York Co. Terminated crystals of orthoclase were reported (Manchester-1914).

Warren Co. Orthoclase was intergrown with scapolite at the serendibite locality, Johnsburg (Larsen and Schaller-1932).

Westchester Co. It is intergrown with microcline at the Kinkel and Baylis quarries, Bedford (Tan-1966).

Pargasite — See amphibole

PECTOLITE $NaCa_2Si_3O_8(OH)$ sodium calcium silicate hydroxide   Triclinic

Rockland Co. Reported as radiating crusts on diabase (Zodac-1951).

PERICLASE   Mg O Cubic

Putnam Co. Tilly Foster Mine, Brewster. Cubic parting in serpentine is possibly due to replaced periclase (Palache, Berman, Frondel-1944).

PEROVSKITE   Ca Ti O_3 Orthorhombic, pseudocubic
Perovskite occurs as an accessory mineral in ultrabasic igneous rocks.

Herkimer Co. Present in alnoite dike near Manheim (Smyth-1893).

Onondaga Co. Small honey-yellow crystals of perovskite with square cross sections are abundant inclusions of the serpentine in peridotite dike at Syracuse (Maynard and Ploger-1946).

Tompkins Co. Present in the freshest peridotite of dikes in and near Ithaca (Cole-1959).

Perthite — See Microcline

Pharmacolite   Ca H (As O_4)•2 H_2O calcium arsenate hydrate   Monoclinic

Orange Co. An unconfirmed report of occurrences with magnetite in the town of Monroe (Beck-1842).

PHLOGOPITE   K Mg_3 (Al Si_3) O_{10} (F, OH)$_2$ potassium magnesium aluminosilicate hydroxide   Monoclinic   Mica group
Phlogopite is the yellowish-brown to dark brown "amber" mica common to metamorphosed limestones (marbles), etc. It is sometimes green in color. Phlogopite is widespread in the crystalline limestones (marbles) especially near igneous contact zones of Essex, Jefferson, Lewis and St. Lawrence Counties.

Essex Co. Phlogopite that occured in the crystalline limestones of many graphite mines was difficult to separate from graphite during milling operations.

Phlogopite, crystal   Oxbow, Jefferson Co.

Lewis Co. Golden amber colored mica was given an early popular name of "cat gold" (Valiant-1899, p. 86).

Onondaga Co. Phlogopite is present in peridotite dikes at Syracuse (Maynard and Ploger-1946).

Orange Co. Dark brown phlogopite crystals were found at the Rich Mine (Ayres-1945). Fine large crystals were reported at Atlas limestone quarry, near Pine Island (Cosminsky-1947).

Putnam Co. Greenish mica at the Mahopac iron mines was considered phlogopite (Colony-1921); later reported as muscovite (Gillson-1926).

St. Lawrence Co. Large phlogopite crystals up to 12 cm. in diameter occur in salmon calcite at an old mica mine near Pyrites (Agar-1921; Jensen-P.O.). Phlogopite was adjacent to haüynite at Edwards Mine (Lessing and Grout-1971). Crystals up to 3 inches in diameter occurred with salmon calcite and pyroxene at the contact zone at a road cut near Fine (Jensen-P.O.; Tan-1966).

Green phlogopite from Talcville has been described (Ming-1971). Large dark brown crystals occur in dolomite at the Pierrepont black tourmaline locality (Whitlock-1903; Agar-1921; Jensen-P.O.). Analyses of phlogopite from Edwards were given (Craw-1850).

Phlogopite crystal in dolomite Pierrepont, St. Lawrence Co.

Phlogopite, cleavage of a multiple crystal Pierrepont, St. Lawrence Co.

PHOSPHURANYLITE $Ca (UO_2)_4 (PO_4)_2 (OH)_4 \cdot 7 H_2O$ Orthorhombic
Unconfirmed report at Bedford (Black-1948).

PICKERINGITE $Mg Al_2 (SO_4)_4 \cdot 22 H_2O$ mon.

Essex Co. White efflorescent incrustations on pyrrhotite were noted in
syenitic pegmatite northwest of Crown Point Center (Rowley-1962;
Tan-1966).

Polycrase   Overlook, Saratoga Co.

PLAGIOCLASE   A series of triclinic feldspars of general formula (Na,
Ca) Al (Al, Si) $Si_2 O_8$. The end members are albite (Ab) Na Al $Si_3 O_8$
and anorthite (An) Ca $Al_2 Si_2 O_8$. The series is:

	Ab	*An*
Albite	(100-90%)	(0-10%)
Oligoclase	(90-70%)	(10-30%)
Andesine	(70-50%)	(30-50%)
Labradorite	(50-30%)	(50-70%)
Bytownite	(30-10%)	(70-90%)
Anorthite	(10-0%)	(90-100%)

(Anorthite has not been reported in the state).

ALBITE   sodium aluminosilicate
Albite is not common in New York State. It occurs in some pegmatites,

gneisses, etc. Colors are white, gray and creamy-white. It occurs in perthite where it is intergrown with microcline.

Cleavelandite is a lamellar or platy variety.

Peristerite is a moonstone with bluish reflections.

Clinton Co. Lyon Mountain. Small colorless crystals were reported in miarolitic cavities in granite (Whitlock-1907).

Essex Co. Near Crown Point Center. Small crystals occurred in cavities in pegmatite. Some cleavelandite was present (Rowley-1962; Tan-1966).

Adularescent albite colored deep red by hematite inclusions was reported at Mineville. (Sinkankas-1959).

Peristerite, massive and in crystals is reported at Newcomb (Sinkankas-1959).

Franklin Co. Dark brown sunstone has been reported at Owl's Head Mountain, 10 miles south of Malone (Robinson and Alverson-1971; (Sinkankas-1976).

Putnam Co. A component of gneiss (Trainer-1938).

St. Lawrence Co. Macomb. Peristerite was found in a pegmatite vein and was occasionally crystallized. Individual crystals up to an inch or more in size are reported (Alverson-1975; Whitlock-1903).

Warren Co. Small crystals were reported to occur in vugs in gabbro and bladed aggregates were noted (Rowley-1957). A large 1½" crystal coated with chlorite was reported near Warrensburg.

Westchester Co. Albite is present in pegmatites at Bedford (Tan-1966).

Peristerite of good quality found in a quarry near Valhalla was cut into gems (Manchester-1931).

OLIGOCLASE sodium calcium aluminosilicate

Essex Co. Near Crown Point Center. Large white oligoclase crystals occurred in pegmatite and was also intergrown with microcline (Rowley-1962; Tan-1966).

Herkimer Co. and Hamilton Co. Present in gneiss (Nelson-1968).

New York Co. Oligoclase was reported at an excavation (Manchester-1931). It is the common feldspar in Manhattan schist (Schuberth-1968).

Orange Co. Oligoclase was noted at an old granite quarry on Mt. Adam (Cosminsky-1947).

Putnam Co. Tilly Foster Mine (Trainer-1938).

St. Lawrence Co. Oligoclase is present in gneiss (Engel and Engel-1953).

Warren Co. It is present in diorite, some crystals were observed (Rowley-1957).

Westchester Co. Oligoclase was reported at the Baylis and Kinkel quarries (Tan-1966).

ANDESINE

Essex Co. Andesine occurs in pegmatites near Crown Point Center and Ticonderoga (Tan-1966).

Saratoga Co. Overlook quarry (Tan-1966).

Warren Co. At the Gore Mt. Garnet Mine, grains to masses of andesine that ranged in size up to several inches across the cleavage occurred with hornblende as segments of the "envelopes" next to the garnets (Miller-1914; Shaub-1949). Andesine also occurs in a pegmatite near Chestertown (Tan-1966).

ANDESINE-LABRADORITE

Essex Co. The high peaks of the Adirondacks are underlain solely by anorthosite which is generally coarse grained and consists principally of plagioclase feldspar that varies in composition between calcic andesine and sodic labradorite. Calcic andesine is common. Almost all of the rocks in the Adirondack region have been subjected to varying degrees of metamorphism. The anorthosite is sometimes referred to as a meta-anorthosite.

The plagioclase of the Marcy type anorthosite is blue-gray and crystals up to 70 mm. in length have been reported. The plagioclase of the Whiteface type anorthosite is granulated and whiter. Augite, magnetite and garnet are also present. Excellent outcrops of anorthosite occur in the Mt. Marcy, Mount Whiteface and Lake Sanford areas.

Near Upper Jay and elsewhere, the plagioclase sometimes exhibits a dark blue to golden bronze chatoyance (Kemp and Alling-1925; Alling-1930; Barth-1930; Buddington-1939, 1953, 1969; Stephenson-1945; Broughton, et al.-1966; Van Diver-1969; Boone, Romey and Thompson-1969; Isachsen and Moxham-1969). This plagioclase is usually labradorite.

St. Lawrence Co. Sunstone is reported at Benson Mines (Robinson and Alverson-1971; Sinkankas-1976).

BYTOWNITE   calcium sodium aluminosilicate

St. Lawrence Co. Bytownite was reported as an accessory mineral in skarn (Leonard-1951).

PLATINUM   Pt Cubic

Clinton Co. A mass that weighed 104 grams was found in the glacial drift near Plattsburgh. It contained 46% platinum and 54% chromite (Dana, J.D.-1892).

Pleonaste — See Spinel

POLYCRASE (Y, Ca, Ce, U, Th) (Ti, Nb, Ta)$_2$ O$_6$ Orthorhombic
Polycrase — Euxenite group

Saratoga Co. Crystals of polycrase up to 1 cm. long were noted in coarse granite pegmatite in the southeast corner of the town of Day (Smith and Kruesi-1947). It was intergrown with monazite at the Overlook quarry (Rowley-1960; Tan-1966), but had previously been erroneously reported as aeschynite-samarskite (Rowley-1976).

POLYHALITE K$_2$ Ca$_2$ Mg (SO$_4$)$_2$•2 H$_2$O Triclinic
Grains of polyhalite are present in Silurian salt beds (Alling-1928).

PREHNITE Ca$_2$ Al$_2$ Si$_3$ O$_{10}$ (OH)$_2$ calcium aluminosilicate hydroxide   Orthorhombic

Putnam Co. Prehnite is reported as coatings on gneiss and microcline at the Tilly Foster Mine, near Brewster (Whitlock-1903; Trainer-1941).

Rockland Co. It is reported with pectolite on diabase near Nyack (Zodac-1951).

Warren Co. Colorless to white terminated crystals and groups of prehnite occur in veins in the wall of a road cut near Schroon Lake (Rowley-1957).

PROUSTITE Ag$_3$ As S$_3$ silver arsenic sulfide   Trigonal

St. Lawrence Co. See pyrargyrite

PUMPELLYITE Ca$_2$ Mg Al$_2$ (Si O$_4$) (Si$_2$O$_7$) (OH)$_2$•H$_2$O calcium magnesium aluminum silicate hydroxide hydrate   Monoclinic

St. Lawrence Co. A ferrian variety of pumpellyite occurs as minute to extensive replacements, veinlets and vug linings in a variety of wall rocks and ore types in the magnetite district (Leonard-1951).

PYRARGYRITE Ag$_3$ Sb S$_3$ silver antimony sulfide   Trigonal

St. Lawrence Co. Small ruby red grains and hair-like crystals under 0.02 mm. in length were found in a vug with small calcite and barite crystals and iron oxides at Balmat. The grains were microprobed and were estimated to have a composition pyrargyrite (60%) — proustite (40%)

PYRITE Fe S$_2$ iron sulfide   Cubic   Dimorphous with marcasite
Pyrite is the most common and widespread of all sulfide minerals. In New York State, pyrite is occasionally found as small cubic or dodecahedral crystals, sometimes modified by other crystal forms. It occurs as small nodules in shales and as granular masses in beds of "rusty" gneiss. Pyrite commonly alters to limonite.

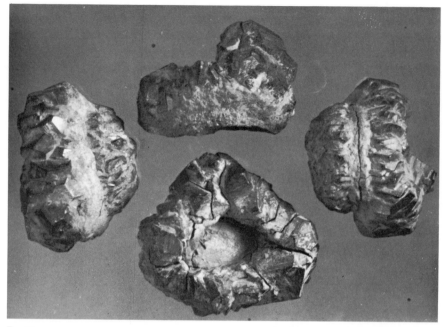

Pyrite   Schoharie Creek, Schoharie Co.

Pyrite concretions and marcasite concretions can form under very similar conditions. Sometimes both minerals are present in the same specimen. Pyrite occurrences are too numerous to list here. Many have been listed elsewhere (Whitlock-1903; Beck-1842).

Many of the western New York occurrences described in the literature as marcasite have been shown to be pyrite (Izard and Clemancy-1967).

In St. Lawrence and Jefferson Counties, there are numerous occurrences of "rusty" gneiss that are generally less than 20 feet thick though a lens 80 feet in thickness has been reported at Pyrites. Mining of the pyrite ore for its sulfur content began in 1883–84 and ceased in 1920–1921 (Buddington-1917; Newland-1919; Buddington and Ruedemann-1934; Prucha-1957).

Clinton Co. Small brilliant crystals were reported at the Chateaugay iron mines, Lyon Mountain (Whitlock-1907).

Columbia Co. Large cubes were found in graywacke in the Parish of New Concord (Eaten-1820).

Erie and Niagara Counties Nodular concretions occur in the Devonian shales and limestones at many localities. Near Alden, the pyrite concretions often contain beautifully preserved fossils. Previously called marcasite, these concretions have been reported to be pyrite (Izard and

Clemancy-1967). Minute pyrite crystals occur in the Lockport dolomite (Awald-1958).

Jefferson Co. See p. 143.

Livingston Co. A pyrite layer representing the Tully limestone horizon occurs at Leicester (Trainer-1932).

Monroe Co. Minute dodecahedral crystals modified by the octahedron occur in cavities in the Lockport dolomite (Hawkins-1926; Jensen-P.O.).

New York Co. Crystals in calcite were reported in excavation at Broadway and 207th St. (Manchester-1931).

Orange Co. A large slab of limestone coated with pyrite was found at the Atlas limestone quarry near Pine Island (Cosminsky-1947).

Pyrolusite in Talc   near Fowler, St. Lawrence Co.

Oneida Co. Pyritized fossils occur in the Frankfort shale at Holland Patent (Palache, Berman, Frondel-1944).

Ontario Co. Lenticular pyrite occurs in the horizon of the Tully limestone (between the Genesee shales and the Hamilton beds) in a discontinuous layer from Canandaigua Lake westward to Lake Erie. The pyrite layers are from 10 to 50 feet on an edge and from one to four inches thick (Clarke and Luther-1904). Fossils that were found in the pyrite layer represent a dwarf fauna (Loomis-1903).

Putnam Co. Small crystals up to ¼ inch, also massive veins and coatings occurred at the Tilly Foster Mine, Brewster (Trainer-1938).

Schoharie Co. Small groups of partly altered pyritohedral crystals occur in shale at Schoharie Creek (Shepard-1852; Jensen-P.O.).

St. Lawrence Co. Pyrite is commonly associated with sphalerite, etc. at the St. Joe Minerals Corp. mines at Balmat and Edwards (Brown-1936). The pyrite has been analysed for minor elements (Doe-1962). (See also p. 74.)

Ulster Co. Pyrite crystals were found at the Neward Cement Mine at Rondout (Whitlock-1905).

Westchester Co. Pyrite is reported at the Kinkel quarry, Bedford, etc. (Black-1948).

Yates Co. Small nodules of pyrite up to 6 mm. occur in shale in Willow Grove Gulley, 3 miles south of Penn Yan (Jensen-P.O.).

PYROLUSITE   Mn O_2 manganese oxide   Tetragonal
Pyrolusite is a secondary mineral that is usually found as inclusions or dendritic coatings.

Essex Co. Dendrites on feldspar at pegmatite quarry northwest of Crown Point Center (Rowley-1962; Tan-1966).

Lewis Co. Dendrites on calcite crystals at Sterlingbush (Whitlock-1910).
   Dendrites occurred on quartz in veins of Grenville calcite in Lyonsdale Twp. (Dale-1924).

Putnam Co. Tilly Foster Mine near Brewster. Dendrites were reported on feldspar (Trainer-1939)

Rensselaer Co. Pyrolusite dendrites occurred on quartz crystals near Chatham (Hallenbeck-1959).

St. Lawrence Co. Dendrites occur in schist near Fowler.

Washington Co. Dendrites were reported on slate (Whitlock-1902).

Westchester Co. Pyrolusite dendrites were found on feldspar, beryl, etc. at the Baylis and Kinkel quarries (Manchester-1931; Black-1948; Tan-1966)

PYROMORPHITE Pb_5 $(PO_4)_3$ Cl lead phosphate chloride   Hexagonal

Westchester Co. Pyromorphite was reported at the old Sparta copper mine, south of Ossining (Whitlock-1903; Manchester-1931).

Pyrope — See Garnet

PYROXENE A mineral group of general formula AB Si_2 O_6. In the orthorhombic series A and B are Mg, Fe^{+2} and Mn with minor Al, Fe^{+3}; in the monoclinic series, A = Na, Ca; B = Mg, Fe, Al, Cr.

Pyroxenes are common rock forming silicate minerals closely related in crystal form and composition.

The following pyroxenes have been reported in New York State: (Beck-1842; Ries-1895; Buddington-1939).

Orthorhombic
Enstatite	Mg_2 Si_2 O_6 magnesium silicate
Bronzite	Ferroan enstatite
Hypersthene	(Mg, Fe)$_2$ Si_2 O_6 magnesium iron silicate

Monoclinic
Diopside	Ca Mg Si_2 O_6 calcium magnesium silicate
Hedenbergite	Ca Fe Si_2 O_6 calcium iron magnesium silicate
Augite	(Ca, Na) (Mg, Fe, Al, Ti) (Si, Al)$_2$ O_6 calcium sodium magnesium iron aluminum silicate
Aegirine	Na Fe Si_2 O_6 sodium iron silicate

The pyroxenes found in New York State include:

Acmite is a synonym of aegirine.

Aegirine which occurs in certain igneous rocks.

Augite is an essential constituent of many basic igneous rocks and in certain metamorphic rocks.

Bronzite is a ferroan enstatite often having a bronze-like or pearly metallic luster.

Coccolite is a granular diopside that usually occurs in metamorphic limestones

Diallage is a dark green to brown variety of usually augite or diopside that occurs in lamellar or foliated masses. It has a conspicuous parting parallel to the front pinacoid.

Diopside is a white to light green pyroxene that occurs in some metamorphic rocks, especially as a contact metamorphic mineral in crystalline limestone.

Enstatite is grayish-white to green or brown pyroxene found in pyroxenites, peridotites, gabbros, etc.

Hedenbergite occurs occasionally in contact zones of granites and limestone.

Pyroxene–Augite   Russell, St. Lawrence Co.

Hypersthene is a grayish to greenish-black or dark brown pyroxene occurring in many gabbros, metagabbros, etc.

Malacolite is a synonym for a gray to greenish variety of diopside.

Pigeonite is near diopside in composition.

Salite is a grayish-green to black variety of diopside.

Uralite is a green or grayish-green fibrous variety of amphibole that is pseudomorphous after pyroxene (usually augite).

Alterations: Pyroxenes commonly alter to serpentine, talc, etc.

Bronx Co. Pyroxenes are occasionally found (Manchester-1931).

Clinton Co. Dark green to black, prismatic augite crystals were reported at the Chateaugay mines, Lyon Mountain (Whitlock-1907).

Essex Co. Augite is a common constituent of the gabbros, etc. (Kemp and Ruedemann-1910; Buddington-1939). Medium sized stout augite crystals were found near Olmsteadville (Rowley-1948); very large augite crystals were recorded at Chillson Hill, Ticonderoga (Nason-1888). The clinopyroxene associated with wollastonite at Willsboro is salite (De Rudder and Beck-1963).

Diopside. Bright green granules of diopside (coccolite occur in blue calcite with granules of scapolite (Rocks and Minerals, vol. 27, no's. 11-12, 1952); diopside crystals were associated with vesuvianite at Olmsteadville (Shaub-1953).

Hedenbergite. A green pyroxene in a quartz nordmarkite is hedenbergite (Buddington-1939).

Hypersthene is a common constituent of gabbro and is also in anorthosite (Kemp and Ruedemann-1910). A dike of hypersthene rock occurs in anorthosite at Roaring Brook (De Waard-1970; Van Diver-1977).

Salite. Analyses of salites from several locations are given (Buddington-1950).

Franklin Co. Analyses of augite and hypersthene are given (Buddington-1950).

Herkimer Co. Hypersthene occurs in syenite in the Ohio quadrangle (Nelson-1968).

Jefferson and Lewis Co's. Augite is present in gabbro southeast of Gates Corners and in quartz syenite gneiss southwest of Harrisville (Buddington-1950, etc.).

New York Co. Pyroxenes were occasionally found (Manchester-1931).

Orange Co. Well formed diopside crystals were reported at the Atlas limestone quarry near Pine Island (Cosminsky-1947). Augite and coccolite occur near Amity and Warwick (Whitlock-1903; Manchester-1931).

Pyroxene–Diopside (Malacolite)　　　　Sing Sing, Westchester Co.

Putnam Co. At the Tilly Foster Mine near Brewster, augite is associated with pyrrhotite, etc. It was formerly mistaken for diopside (Trainer-1938-1943). Stout dark green diopside crystals with dolomite and green laminated masses of diallage are described (Trainer-1938). Enstatite is reported as coarse crystalline, lamellar, gray and olive-green masses (Trainer-1938, 1943). Dark green enstatite has a bronze-like surface (bronzite).(Trainer-1938).

St. Lawrence Co. Augite is a constituent of syenite gneisses and pyroxenites (Buddington-1939). Small crystals up to 2 cm. occur at old mica pits near Pyrites (Agar-1921; Jensen-P.O.). Terminated augite crystals up to 2 inches long, somewhat corroded, occur in vugs in road cuts southeast of Fine and near Russell (Jensen-P.O.). Crystals 4 to 5 inches in diameter were observed in pegmatite near Star Lake (Dale-1935). Dark green square augite prisms were noted south of Edwards (Alverson-1975). Good pyroxene crystals altered to uralite occur with dolomite at the black tourmaline locality at Pierrepont (Jensen-P.O.; Van Diver-1977).

Some of the finest diopside crystals in the world have been found in a wooded rock knob of silicated marble in a cow pasture (historically known as the Calvin Mitchell farm) 3 miles northeast of Richville). The first crystal was found in the 1880's. The diopside crystals are glassy, translucent to transparent and have a single excellent termination. Crystals up to 1 inch wide and 3 inches long have been reported (Cushing and Newland-1925; Sinkankas-1959; Robinson-1973); Gemstones over 14 carats in weight have been cut from this diopside.

The zinc ore body at Balmat is enclosed in a silicated limestone predominently of diopside or its alteration minerals. By alteration, the diopside has supplied a large part of the abundant serpentine and talc found in the ore deposits (Brown-1936a, 1947; Brown and Engel-1956).

Good gray diopside crystals up to 1 inch long occur in salmon calcite at an old mica mine near Pyrites (Agar-1921). A good locality for diopside is near Edwards (Carl and Van Diver-1971; Robinson and Alverson-1971; Van Diver-1977). Diopside crystals occur at the Mc Lear pegmatite (Shaub-1921).

A ferrohedenbergite is described near Inlet (Buddington and Leonard-1962). Scattered narrow dikes or sheets of hypersthene occur throughout the several rock types from Carthage, in Jefferson Co., northeasterly to South Edwards (Buddington-1939).

Tompkins Co. Chromian diopside is reported in peridotite dikes near Ithaca (Martens-1924).

Warren Co. Augite occurs in both the anorthosite and the gabbro at Gore Mt. Garnet mine (Levin-1950). Diopside that is partly altered to serpentine, occurs with serendibite at Johnsburg (Larsen and Schaller-1932). Diopside crystals up to 3 inches long, partially replaced by muscovite occur near Horicon (Rowley-1955). Hypersthene is a constituent of both anorthosite and gabbro at Gore Mt. Garnet Mine. It is often abundant in the hornblende envelopes surrounding the garnets. Good crystals over 4 inches long have been found (Shaub-1949).

Westchester Co. Pyroxene is reported at the old Bedford quarries (Tan-1966). Grayish-white crystals of malacolite were found in an old quarry at Sing Sing (near Ossining) (Manchester-1931). Hypersthene is a chief constituent of all norites in the Cortlandt Complex south and east of Peekskill (Berkey and Rice-1919; Shand-1942).

PYRRHOTITE $Fe_{1-x}S$ iron sulfide   Hexagonal

Essex Co. Several pyrrhotite dikes up to 15 inches wide were noted in the wall of a quarry in syenitic pegmatite northwest of Crown Point Center (Rowley-1962; Tan-1966); also veins of pyrrhotite containing apatite crystals were seen near Lincoln Pond (Rowley-1967).

Jefferson Co. Pyrrhotite often occurs with pyrite in "rusty" gneisses, some of which have been actively mined for sulfur (Buddington-1917; Newland-1919; Buddington and Ruedemann-1934; Prucha-1957).

New York Co. Tiny tabular pyrrhotite crystals were noted (Manchester-1931).

Orange Co. Pyrrhotite was reported at the Atlas limestone quarry, near Pine Island (Cominsky-1947) and near Monroe (Ayers-1945).

Putnam Co. Common in pure masses, occasional crystals Tilly Foster Mine, Brewster (Trainer-1948).

St. Lawrence Co. Pyrrhotite often occurs with pyrite in "rusty" gneisses (See ref. under Jefferson Co.). Masses of pyrrhotite occur in the zinc ore at Balmat (Doe-1966; Lea and Dill-1968).

Westchester Co. Present in the pyrrhotite mine at Anthony's Nose (Berkey and Rice-1919; Zodac-1933).

QUARTZ $Si O_2$ silicon oxide   Trigonal
Ref. Frondel-1962; Dake, Fleener, Wilson-1938; Goldring-1931, 1950; Broughton, Fisher, Isachsen, Richard-1966).
Many varieties of quartz occur in New York State. It is an essential constituent of igneous rocks such as granites and granite pegmatites. In metamorphic rocks, it occurs in gneisses and quartzites. In sedimentary rocks, it is an essential constituent of sandstone, quartz conglomerates and graywackes as well as being present in many shales.
Quartz is also present in the sands of many streams and lakes. It occurs in glacial gravels and cobbles often as milky quartz, chert, flint,

and as a rock constituent. Nodular masses and irregular layers of chert (flint) occur abundantly in the Onondaga limestone and some other sedimentary rocks in the state.

The common varieties of quartz found in the state are:

Agate is a translucent variety of quartz, a variegated chalcedony, with alternating bands of color or degrees of translucency, (rare).

Amethyst is a translucent to transparent crystalline quartz. The common colors of amethyst in the state are shades of purple to reddish-violet, (rare).

Basanite is a black jasper, (rare).

Chalcedony is a translucent to transparent microfibrous variety of quartz. The colors may be white, gray-green to black. The fracture is conchoidal, (common).

Chert is a rock consisting dominently of microfibrous quartz. The colors may be white, gray-green to black. The fracture is conchoidal. (common).

Citrine is a transparent yellow to yellow-brown crystalline quartz, (rare).

Drusy quartz refers to small projecting quartz crystals densely grouped and incrusting a surface, (rare).

Flint is a term that is properly applied to nodular concretions in chalk or limestone. Flint has been widely used as a synonym for chert especially for the dark gray or black variety of chert. There is no mineralogical difference between flint and chert. The term flint is used preferentially by archeologists for any cryptocrystalline varieties of quartz that have been used by primitive man. The fracture is conchoidal. The varieties and sources of flint found in New York State have been described (Wray-1948) (common).

"Herkimer diamonds" refer to the quartz crystals found in Herkimer County (common locally). (See pp. 33, 146.)

Jasper is massive, dense, cryptocrystalline and opaque. The colors may be shades of red, brown, yellow, dull green and blue to black. The colors are due to admixed materials such as iron oxides and are often variegated. The fracture of jasper is usually even, while chert and flint will have a conchoidal fracture.

Milky quartz is a milk-white nearly opaque variety of crystalline quartz, (common).

Rock crystal refers to transparent or nearly so and usually colorless quartz. It may or may not be in distinct crystals, (common).

Rose quartz is a pink to rose-red massive crystalline variety. The color is due to the presence of titanium, (once common locally in pegmatites). Asterism which is often observed in rose quartz is best seen in polished spheres of the material under strong illumination. It is due to reflected light from microscopic oriented inclusions of rutile, (rare).

Smoky quartz is a crystalline variety that is often transparent. The color is in shades of smoky brown from nearly colorless to nearly black (common).

Quartz and its varieties are too abundant to list all occurrences (see Whitlock-1903).

Albany Co. Quartz crystals were reported at Glenmont, New Scotland and Watervliet (Whitlock-1903).

Bronx Co. Pale colored amethyst was found in an excavation at Dodgewood Rd. and Independence Ave. Small stones were cut (Rocks and Minerals, No. 243, p. 616-1954).

Clinton Co. Quartz is abundant at the Chateaugay mines, Lyon Mountain (Whitlock-1907). Jasper was reported at Ausable (Whitlock-1903).

Essex Co. Rose quartz was found near Port Henry (Kemp & Ruedemann-1910).

Greene Co. The site of aboriginal flint quarries was at "Flint Mine Hill" near Coxsackie. Colors of the flint in the shale beds are green, blue, red and black. The great piles and chips of broken flint are evidence of extensive quarry work and fashioning of flint objects for many centuries. It is believed that the first Indians found the hill and began to work it over 5,000 years ago (Parker-1924; Wray-1948) (see p. 11).

Quartz enclosing air bubble   Herkimer Co.

Quartz, "Herkimer diamonds"   Herkimer Co.

Herkimer Co. "Herkimer diamonds" were first noticed to any extent in large quantities when digging a canal before 1797 in the area of Little Falls. The superbly beautiful, perfectly transparent crystals of rock crystals are found in various parts of Herkimer County, especially at Middleville, Fairfield, Little Falls and Salisbury. They are commonly found in cavities or vugs in the siliceous dolomite rock, Little Falls dolomite (dolostone). Loose crystals are often found in the soil. Crystals up to 6 inches long and more have been found. Black anthraxolite is common as inclusions in the quartz crystals or associated with them in cavities. The larger crystals often contain inclusions of water that may also contain small bubbles of air. When these crystals are near the surface of the ground, the winter cold often causes the liquid to freeze, thus shattering the crystals, leaving only fragments. Sometimes these crystals will break along incipient cleavage planes (La Buz-1969; Tuttle-1973) (see p. 33).

Jefferson Co. Large quartz crystals without prisms occur at an old iron mine near Antwerp. (Beck-1842). Medium sized crystals occur in vugs with hematite, ankerite, etc. at the old Sterling iron mine near Antwerp.

Lewis Co. Tabular quartz in a boxwork structure and drusy quartz occurred at an old mine east and north of Port Leyden (Dale-1924; Slo-

Quartz conglomerate   Olean, Cattaraugus Co.

cum-1948). A large geode of pale amethyst crystals up to ¾ inch diameter was found at the Carbola talc mine near Natural Bridge (Jensen-P.O.). A two inch layer of jasper-pyrite-hematite-quartz was encountered when constructing a new shaft at Carbola in 1944.

Monroe Co. Drusy crystals and granular masses occur in the Lockport dolomite (dolostone) (Jensen-1942).

Montgomery Co. The siliceous dolomite (dolostone) north and west of Fonda contains an abundance of quartz crystals similar to the "Herkimer diamonds" of the Middleville area (Whitlock-1903).

New York Co. Clear and smoky crystals were reported (Manchester-1931).

Niagara Co. Small drusy crystals were noted in the Lockport dolomite (dolostone) (Awald-1958).

Oneida Co. "Herkimer diamonds" were reported near Newport (Kay and Grosman-1953).

Putnam Co. Milky and smoky quartz are common but crystals were rare at the Tilly Foster Mine, Brewster (Trainer-1938).

Rennselaer Co. Noted near Troy (Eaton-1820; Ruedemann-1930). Quartz crystals up to 3 inches long and enclosing chlorite were found in quartz vein west of Chatham (Hallenbeck-1959).

Quartz–Flint in various stages of being made into arrowheads
Coxsackie, Greene Co.

Quartz, Banded Jasper and Pyrite   Lewis Co.

Quartz-Chalcedony   Rochester, Monroe Co.

Quartz crystals   Saratoga Co.

Quartz-crystals   Antwerp, St. Lawrence Co.

Quartz-crystallized   Ellenville, Ulster Co.

St. Lawrence Co. Vugs in the massive milky quartz of the Mc Lear pegmatite contain pale smoky quartz crystals (Shaub-1929). The old iron mines in the town of Hermon and Fowler were the source of fine doubly terminated quartz crystals with a very short or no prism face. Crystals up to two inches in diameter were reported (Beck-1842; Durant & Pierce-1878). Rose quartz has been reported near Rossie (Agar-1921).

Milky quartz containing abundant black tourmaline crystals occurs at a limestone granite gneiss contact 1 mile northwest of Pierrepont (Whitlock-1903).

Quartz, drusy on calcite   Anthony's Nose, Westchester Co.

Saratoga Co. Fine prismatic quartz crystals, some pale smoky, some doubly terminated and some naturally recemented crystals occurred in dolomite (dolostone) at Gailor quarry at north edge of Saratoga Springs (Rowley-1951). Rose Quartz, some asteriated and of gem quality, occurred at the Overlook quarry near Linwood (Rowley-1942; Tan-1966).

Ulster Co. Large doubly terminated quartz crystals with numerous inclusions were found in the old cement mines near Rondout (Whitlock-1903, 1905). Clear prismatic quartz crystals often densely coating surfaces in vugs were found at the former lead mines at Ellenville (Beck-1842; Whitlock-1903).

Warren Co. Clear crystals similar to "Herkimer diamonds" were abundant on Diamond Island in Lake George (Whitlock-1903).

Westchester Co. Milky, smoky, and rose quartz were abundant in the Baylis and Kinkel quarries at Bedford. (See p. 31.) Crystals of smoky quartz up to 8 inches long with roughened surface were found (Newland-1906; Manchester-1931; Agar-1933; Black-1948; Sinkankas-1959; Tan-1966).

REALGAR   As S arsenic sulfide   Monoclinic

St. Lawrence Co. Realgar is associated with jordanite etc. at Balmat (Lessing-1969; Van Diver-1977).

RHODONITE   Mn SiO_3 manganese silicate   triclinic

St. Lawrence Co. Crystalline pink rhodonite reported at Balmat (Dill-1976).

Riebeckite — See Amphibole

Ripidolite — See Chlorite

RUTILE   Ti O_2 titanium oxide   Tetragonal

Essex Co. Needles of rutile up to 15 mm. were reported near Newcomb (Nason-1888).

New York Co. Noted at a Broadway and 218th St. excavation (Manchester-1914, 1931).

Orange Co. Rutile is reported in the crystalline limestone near Amity, etc. (Palache, Berman, Frondel-1944).

St. Lawrence Co. Small rutile crystals up to 3 mm. long were found in marble at a quarry southwest of Gouverneur (Jensen-P.O.).

Warren Co. Noted at the serendibite locality (Larsen and Schaller-1932; also at Brant Lake (Rowley-1955). Small dull geniculated twins of rutile were reported near Athol (Rowley-1976).

Westchester Co. Microscopic crystals of rutile are responsible for asterism in rose quartz at Kinkel quarry, Bedford (Manchester-1931; Jensen-P.O.).

SAMARSKITE   (Y, Ce, U, Ca, Pb) (Nb, Ta, Ti, Sn)$_2$ O$_6$ Monoclinic

Saratoga Co. The mineral reported as samarskite-aeschynite at Overlook quarry (Rowley-1942) has been identified as polycrase (Rowley-1976).

Lewis Co. Black massive samarskite was reported near Lyons Falls (Ardelio-1957).

SAPPHIRINE $(Mg, Al)_8 (Al, Si)_6 O_{20}$ Triclinic

Westchester Co. Small grains of sapphirine up to 1.3 mm. long were noted in hornfels as well as emery and cordierite sillimanite schist in Cortlandt township southeast of Peekskill (Friedman-1952).

Satin Spar — See Gypsum

SCAPOLITE   (Syn. Wernerite)   A group name   Tetragonal
Scapolite is a metamorphic mineral occurring in metamorphic limestones and calcareous rocks adjacent to intrusive igneous rocks (granites, etc.) or their metamorphic equivalents (gneisses). Scapolite is tetragonal and forms excellent prismatic crystals. Notable specimens have been found in Lewis, St. Lawrence and Essex Counties.

Scapolites have a variable composition with marialite and meionite as end members.

Marialite $3 Na (Al, Si_3) O_8 \cdot Na Cl$ sodium aluminosilicate chloride
Meionite $3 Ca (Al_2 Si_2) O_8 \cdot Ca CO_3$ calcium aluminosilicate carbonate

Scapolite   Newcomb, Essex Co.

Mizzonite and Dipyre are intermediate members. Wernerite is an old term for scapolite (Goldsmith-1976).

Essex Co. Crystals of dipyre up to 10 cm. long were found near Newcomb (Nason-1888). Excellent scapolite crystals were reported at Mineville (Kemp and Ruedemann-1910). Scapolite crystals were found with pyroxene at Lead Hill graphite mine northwest of Ticonderoga (Alling-1917). Grains, irregular masses and large well developed crystals of scapolite occur near Olmsteadville (Rowley-1948; Shaub-1953).

Jefferson & Lewis Co's. Both meionite and mizzonite are found near Natural Bridge (Smyth and Buddington-1926; Buddington-1939) Large crystals up to 3 inches long and fine groups have been found near Diana (Smithsonian Museum collection).

Scapolite   near Pyrites, St. Lawrence Co.

Orange Co. Scapolite was reported at the Tuxedo Park quarry and crystals up to 10 inches long near Monroe (Ayres-1945). Dark green scapolite was found southwest of Mt. Adam and gray-green crystals occurred at the Atlas limestone quarry (Cominsky-1947) and at Edenville (Buerger-1927), Mizzonite was reported in gneiss (Pegau and Bates-1941).

Putnam Co. Grayish-white scapolite with some crystals of dipyre occurred at the Tilly Foster Mine near Brewster (Trainer-1940).

St. Lawrence Co. Meionite was reported near Hailesboro (Carl and Van Diver-1971). Scapolite was associated with pyroxene near Oxbow (Agar-1921). Sharp crystals up to 3 inches were found at old phlogopite prospects near Pyrites (Agar-1921; Jensen-P.O.; Alverson-P.O.).

Warren Co. Scapolite was associated with serendibite at Johnsburg (Larsen & Schaller-1932).

Shorl — See Tourmaline

Schroeckingerite   Na Ca$_3$ (UO$_2$) (CO$_3$)$_3$ (SO$_4$) F•10 H$_2$O

Westchester Co. Schroeckingerite was reported at the Kinkel quarry, Bedford (Armstrong-1935). Re-examination of this material showed it to be Beta-Uranotile (Steinocher and Novacek-1939) which is considered a synonym of Beta-Uranophane (Frondel-1958).

SCORODITE   Fe^{+3} As O$_4$•2 H$_2$O Orthorhombic

Orange Co. Reported with arsenopyrite (Shepard-1852).

Putnam Co. Scorodite was reported at the arsenopyrite mine 3 miles north northwest of Carmel. It was found in abundance in 1918 and 1919 in veins up to 8 inches wide and as stalactites in the mine (Martens-1924).

Selenite — See Gypsum

SERENDIBITE   Ca$_4$ (Mg, Fe, Al)$_6$ (Al, Fe)$_9$ (Si, Al)$_6$ B$_3$ O$_{40}$ Triclinic

Grayish-blue serendibite occurred with diopside, phlogopite, etc. in metamorphosed limestone near Johnsburg (Larsen & Schaller-1932).

Sericite — See Muscovite

SERPENTINE

Faust & Fahey-1962; Fleischer-1975). A group of rock-forming minerals of general formula A$_3$ Si$_2$ O$_5$ (OH)$_4$. A=Mg, Fe″, Ni. Individual members of the serpentine group, excepting chrysotile, are best identified by X-ray diffraction. Serpentines are always secondary minerals that have been formed by the alteration of magnesium-rich silicate minerals (e.g.

Serpentine, with Chrysotile veins   Thurman, Warren Co.

diopside, olivine, etc.) present in igneous rocks (e.g. peridotites, dunites) or metamorphism of magnesian limestones and dolomites. The colors are usually green, greenish-yellow, greenish-gray, and sometimes brown, black, white or variegated. The following three members of the serpentine group are found in New York State:

Antigorite $(Mg, Fe)_3 Si_2 O_5 (OH)_4$. It is platy or lamellar, color is brownish-green. Jenkinsite = Ferroan antigorite.

Chrysotile (Syn. Serpentine asbestos) $Mg_3 Si_2 O_5 (OH)_4$ magnesium silicate hydroxide   Color gray-white or greenish-yellow. Fibrous or silky.
 Deweylite is a mixture of chrysotile or lizardite plus stevensite.

Lizardite $Mg_3 Si_2 O_5 (OH)_4$ magnesium silicate hydroxide   Platy. Color is variable.

The following names that have been given to serpentines are now obsolete:

Bowenite — hard compact greenish-white to yellow-green (Antigorite).

Marmolite — pale green (chiefly lizardite).

Serpentine pseudomorph after Chondrodite   Tilly Foster Mine, Putnam Co.

Picrolite — columnar — fibers not separable or elastic; (generally anti-gorite or chrysotile).

Retinalite — honey yellow (chrysotile).

Williamsite — massive light green, usually containing specks of chromite; sometimes considered an admixture of the serpentine group minerals with stevensite.

Other useful definitions:

Ophicalcite — a recrystallized limestone composed of serpentine and calcite.

Pseudomorph — in alteration to serpentine, the form of the crystal or form of the original mineral has not changed.

Serpentinite — a rock consisting almost entirely of serpentine.

Essex Co. Green serpentine up to ½ inch in diameter in calcite (ophicalcite) occurs at Moriah near Port Henry (Kemp and Ruedemann-1910).

Lewis Co. Serpentine occurs with talc at talc mines 2 miles east of Natural Bridge.

Onondaga Co. Serpentine pseudomorph after olivine occurs in peridotite dikes in and near Syracuse (Maynard and Ploger-1946).

Orange Co. Chondrodite altered to serpentine is reported at Edenville (Buerger-1927). Jenkinsite was found with magnetite at the Clove mine, Monroe (Shepard-1852; Dana, J.D.-1892; Manchester-1931; Faust and Fahey-1962).

Putnam Co. Serpentine was found in many forms and colors at the Tilly Foster Mine, Brewster (Trainer-1938, 1939, 1940, 1942). Bowenite, chrysotile, marmolite, picrolite, retinalite, and williamsite were reported. Serpentine was also recorded as pseudomorphs after brucite, clinochlore, chondrodite, enstatite, etc. (Trainer-1938) and after periclase (Palache, Berman, Frondel-1944).

Richmond Co. A serpentine from Staten Island was identified as lizardite (Faust and Fahey-1962). Deweylite was reported on Staten Island (Newland-1901). Chrysotile and lizardite are reported (Okulewicz-1977).

St. Lawrence Co. At Balmat, serpentine occurs as replacements of diopside in the silicated limestone adjacent to the ore body (Brown-1947; Brown and Engel-1956). Nodules of light green serpentine occur in the crystalline limestone (Grenville marble) near Oxbow and Somerville (Agar-1921) clinochrysotile and lizardite are reported at talc mine near Talcville (Faust and Fahey-1962).

Tompkins Co. Alteration of olivine to serpentine is reported in peridotite dikes in and near Ithaca, New York (Cole-1959).

Warren Co. Chrysotile asbestos occurs in veinlets with average fiber length of ¼ inch in yellow-green serpentine that occurs in rounded and irregular patches in crystalline limestone at Thurman (Newland-1919).

Westchester Co. Good quality dark red serpentine was obtained at an excavation near Port Chester.

Seybertite — See Chlorite

SIDERITE $Fe\ CO_3$ iron carbonate   Trigonal

Columbia Co. A gray compact siderite was mined near Livingstone between 1875 and 1901 (Newland-1942).

Jefferson Co. Siderite is reported at the Sterling Iron mine near Antwerp (Buddington-1934).

Putnam Co. Small botryoidal masses were reported on schist at the Tilly Foster Mine, Brewster (Trainer-1939).

St. Lawrence Co. Siderite occurred as crystals, massive and in botryoidal forms at old iron mines near Rossie (Durant and Pierce-1878).

Ulster Co. Siderite occurs in talcose slate near Napanoch (Palache, Berman, Frondel-1951).

Sillimanite with Magnetite in Gneiss   Benson Mines, St. Lawrence Co.

SILLIMANITE $Al_2 Si O_5$ aluminum silicate   Orthorhombic

Bronx Co. A sillimanite schist is reported at Pelham Bay Park (Seyfert and Leveson-1968).

Oneida Co. Sillimanite gneiss occurs near Remsen (Hawley and Potter-1960).

Putnam Co. Sillimanite is present in the Manhattan schist at Yorktown Heights (Bodelsen-1948).

Saratoga Co. Pink xenoliths of sillimanite are reported in pegmatite at Batchellerville (Tan-1966).

St. Lawrence Co. In Russell and Hammond quadrangles, sillimanite-quartz nodules occur in gneiss, schist and feldspathic quartzite (Buddington and Leonard-1962). Sillimanite gneiss occurs at Benson Mines (Dale-1935; Palmer-1970; Jensen-P.O.). Sillimanite is present in magnetite schist, etc. in the Balmat-Edwards District (Brown and Engel-1956).

Warren Co. A sillimanite schist and a sillimanite garnet gneiss occur in the township of Hague (Alling-1917).

Westchester Co. Sillimanite occurs in schists near Golden's Bridge (Chase and Brock-1976).

SILVER   Ag Cubic

There have been many unconfirmed reports of silver having been found in the state. Early references mention "hearsay" rumors (Hough-1860; Mather-1843). Native silver was reported in 1825 at a lead mine that was operated during the Revolutionary War south of Sing Sing in Westchester Co. (Torrey-1888).

Lewis Co. No evidence is reported of an "old silver mine" in Lyonsdale Twp., near Port Leyden (Dale-1924; Slocum-1948).

St. Lawrence Co. A small occurrence of native silver was once reported at Balmat (Dill-1975).

Ulster Co. At Ellenville, 7.5 ounces of silver per ton of lead ore was reported (Newland-1919).

SINHALITE   Mg Al BO$_4$ Orthorhombic

Warren Co. Sinhalite occurs with serendibite, etc. near Johnsburg (Schaller and Hillebrand-1955).

SKLODOWSKITE   Mg (UO$_2$)$_2$ Si$_2$ O$_7$•6 H$_2$O Monoclinic

Essex Co. Occurs as yellow acicular crystals with uraninite, etc. (Rowley-1962; Tan-1966).

SMITHSONITE   Zn CO$_3$ zinc carbonate   Trigonal

Lewis Co. Reported as incrusting calcite crystals in calcite-quartz vein, near Port Leyden (Dale-1924).

Smoky Quartz — See Quartz

Spessartine — See Garnet

SPHALERITE   Zn S zinc sulfide   Cubic

Sphalerite is an important ore of zinc that is often associated with galena and other sulfides. It is also a common sulfide mineral that occurs in many limestones.

Lewis Co. Reported in quartz-calcite vein near Port Leyden (Dale-1924).

Monroe Co. Clear to translucent brilliant red-brown crystals up to ¾ inch, also opaque crystals up to an inch or more and masses occur in cavities and seams in the Lockport dolomite (dolostone) (Jensen-1942).

Niagara Co. Lustrous resinous fissure fillings and crystals up to 2 inches with color, brown to yellow, in the Lockport dolomite (dolostone) near Lockport (Awald-1958).

Oneida Co. Grains and cleavable red-brown masses occur in Lockport dolomite (dolostone) (Monahan-1928).

Orleans Co. Zinc in peat soils at Manning is believed derived from sphalerite in underlying Lockport dolomite (dolostone) (Cannon-1955).

St. Lawrence Co. Balmat-Edwards District (Cushing and Newland-1925; Smyth-1917) (See p. 46).

The occurrence of sphalerite was noted over a century ago (Emmons-1838). The primary sphalerite is dark chocolate brown, contains iron, and is associated with pyrite. Secondary sphalerite is light yellow (Brown-1936); clear yellow crystals in vugs are reported (Robinson-1971; Alverson-1975) small amounts of manganese and cadmium etc. are present (Doe-1960, 1962). The mine at Edwards has been operating since 1915 (Brown-1936). The light yellow sphalerite at Balmat is fluorescent. Small amounts of sphalerite occur with galena veins at Rossie (Buddington-1934).

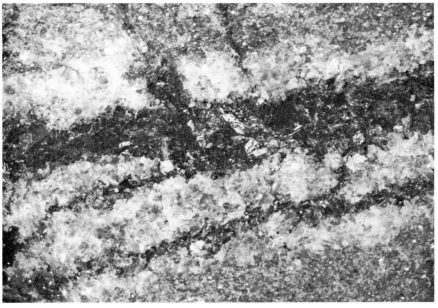

Sphalerite veins in Marble   Balmat, St. Lawrence Co.

Saratoga Co. Sphalerite is present in the Gailor quarry at Saratoga Springs (Rowley-1951).

Sullivan Co. and Ulster Co. Sphalerite was abundant at Ellenville and near Summitville (Newland-1919).

Sphene — See Titanite

SPINEL Mg Al$_2$ O$_4$ magnesium aluminum oxide   Cubic

Ceylonite and pleonaste are ferroan spinel. Picotite is a chromian spinel. Spinel is generally abundant in certain areas of the crystalline limestones (Grenville marble) near contacts with igneous intrusives (granites, etc.) or their metamorphic equivalents. Chondrodite and phlogopite are commonly associated with the spinels. Crystals are octahedral, and generally under 6 mm. in size except near Monroe in Orange County where black crystals 16 inches around the base and weighing 59 pounds were reported (Frondel-1935).

Jefferson Co. Light blue to purple spinel crystals up to ½ inch were reported near Oxbow (Beck-1842) Also little lilac colored spinel crystals were associated with chondrodite (Agar-1921; Buddington-1934).

Lewis Co. near Natural Bridge, grains and octahedra of purple spinel up to 6 mm. occur in calcite (Agar-1921; Smyth and Buddington-1926).

Orange Co. A belt of crystalline limestone (marble) from Amity southward to Andover and Sparta, New Jersey contains abundant spinel with phlogopite, chondrodite, etc. (Beck-1842; Palache, Berman, Frondel-1944). Found near Greenwood (Cominsky-1947; Ayres-1945); also at O'Neil mine south of Monroe (McElroy-1939); Pleonaste was reported in sand of stream bed near Bear Mt. (Pegau and Bates-1941).

Spinel crystal   Amity, Orange Co.

Putnam Co. Tilly Foster Mine, Brewster. Tiny crystals were reported with chondrodite (Trainer-1938). Black (pleonaste) to dark green spinel were noticed in microscopic study (Gillson-1926).

Richmond Co. Picotite is reported in serpentine on Staten Island (Okulewicz-1977).

Tompkins Co. Picotite is reported in peridotite dikes near Ithaca (Martens-1924).

Westchester Co. A green ferroan spinel (pleonaste) is associated with magnetite, etc. in the Cortlandt complex (Shand-1942; Friedman-1956).

SPODUMENE   Li Al Si$_2$ O$_8$ lithium aluminosilicate   Monoclinic

Spodumene is a lithium bearing pyroxene-like mineral. It is very rare in the state.

Essex Co. Spodumene has been reported in a pegmatite northwest of Crown Point Center (Rowley-1962; Tan-1966).

STAUROLITE   (Fe, Mg)$_2$ Al$_9$ Si$_4$ O$_{23}$ (OH) iron magnesium aluminum silicate hydroxide   Orthorhombic

Dutchess Co. Present in phyllitic schist (Barth and Balk-1934).

New York Co. Reported in schists at Golden's Bridge (Chase and Brock-1976); in Manhattan schist (Whitlock-1903).

STEVENSITE   Mg$_3$ Si$_4$ O$_{10}$ (OH)$_2$ Monoclinic

Essex Co. Stevensite occurs as a wall rock alteration of the wollastonite deposit at Willsboro (De Rudder and Beck-1963).

STILBITE   Na Ca$_2$ (Al$_5$ Si$_{13}$) O$_{36}$·14 H$_2$O sodium calcium aluminosilicate hydrate   Monoclinic   Zeolite group

Bronx and New York Co's. Narrow veins in and radiated on gneiss at subway excavations along Southern Boulevard (Manchester-1931).

Clinton Co. Stilbite occurred as drusy crusts of colorless crystals and yellow to brown sheafs at the Chateaugay mines, Lyon Mountain (Whitlock-1907).

Franklin Co. Stilbite occurs in miarolitic cavities in granite gneiss at Owl's Head Mountain (Robinson and Alverson-1971).

Putnam Co. At the Tilly Foster Mine, Brewster, stilbite is reported to occur in gneiss (Trainer-1938, 1942; Whitlock-1903).

Rockland Co. Stilbite was found in vugs in diabase near Nyack (Zodac-1951).

STILPNOMELANE   K (Fe'', Fe''', Al)$_{10}$ Si$_{12}$ O$_{30}$ (OH)$_{12}$ Triclinic

Jefferson Co. Stilpnomelane is abundant as golden-bronze to brown velvety coatings with hematite, ankerite, etc. in vugs in quartz at the Old Sterling Mine near Antwerp. The name "chalcodite" was proposed in 1851; analysis by Brush showed it to be stilpnomelane (Brush-1858).

STRONTIANITE   Sr CO$_3$ strontium carbonate   Orthorhombic

Jefferson Co. Strontianite was reported at Muscalonge Lake, Chaumont Bay and Theresa (Shepard-1852).

Niagara Co., etc. Strontianite was reported in Lockport dolomite (dolostone) of western New York (Giles-1920).

Schoharie Co. Discovery of a large vein of strontianite in a cliff near Schoharie was announced in 1835 (Emmons-1838). White to bluish-gray, fibrous, massive and acicular crystals were reported (Grabau-1906; Newland-1919).

SULFUR   S Orthorhombic

Sulfur occurs sparingly in some sedimentary rocks where it forms by action of ground water on metallic sulfides or by the reduction of gypsum.

Monroe, Ontario and Niagara Co's. Crude crystals and masses of sulfur occurred occasionally in gypsum mines (Newland-1929); also in vugs and seams in the Lockport dolomite (dolostone) (Giles-1920; Jensen-1942; Awald-1958).

St. Lawrence Co. Sulfur was reported to have formed by decomposition of pyrite at old iron mines in Rossie (Durant and Pierce-1878).

SYLVITE   K Cl potassium chloride   Cubic

Present in small amounts in halite beds of the state (Alling-1928).

Livingston Co. Found associated with halite at Retsof in 1977.

TALC   Mg$_3$ Si$_4$ O$_{10}$ (OH)$_2$ Monoclinic

Dutchess Co. Massive talc is reported near Fishkill (Beck-1842).

Essex Co. Talc occurs as an alteration of the wall rock at the Willsboro wollastonite deposit (De Rudder and Beck-1963).

Lewis Co. Talc occurs with serpentine at the Carbola Talc Co. Mine at Natural Bridge (Newland and Hartnagel-1936).

Orange Co. Several locations for talc are reported near Amity and Monroe (Beck-1842).

Putnam Co. Talc has been reported at the Tilly Foster Mine, Brewster (Trainer-1941).

Richmond Co. Present in serpentine on Staten Island (Beck-1842).

St. Lawrence Co. For nearly a century talc has been one of the major economic minerals of the state. The first commercial mine opened in 1878 (Elberty and Lessing-1971). Mines are currently active near Fowler and Balmat. The talc is derived by alteration of tremolite which is also present in varying amounts (Cushing & Newland-1925; Brown-1936).

TENNANTITE $(Cu, Fe)_{12} As_4 S_{13}$ copper iron arsenic sulfide   Cubic

St. Lawrence Co. The presence of tennantite at the Balmat zinc mine was first reported by Brown (1959). Massive tennantite with quartz and chalcopyrite was reported in 1976.

TETRAHEDRITE $(Cu, Fe)_{12} Sb_4 S_{13}$ copper iron antimony sulfide   Cubic

St. Lawrence Co. Small lustrous, crystals of tetrahedrite associated with pyrite were reported to coat calcite (Robinson-1971).

THOMSONITE $Na Ca_2 (Al_5 Si_5) O_{20} \cdot 6 H_2O$ sodium calcium aluminosilicate hydrate   Orthorhombic   Zeolite group

New York Co. Reported in gneiss (Manchester-1931).

Putnam Co. Reported at the Tilly Foster Mine, near Brewster (Trainer-1942).

Westchester Co. Radiated masses of thomsonite up to 4 inches in size in cracks were reported to occur in syenite (Philips-1924); reported at Piermont (Dana-1892).

THORITE $Th Si O_4$ thorium silicate   Tetragonal

Uranothorite, a highly uranoan thorite, was described by Collier in 1880 from an unspecified location in the Lake Champlain region of New York (Frondel-1958).

Essex Co. Black to orange-yellow crystals of thorite (uranothorite) occurred in a syenitic pegmatite near Crown Point Center (Rowley-1962; Tan-1966).

Saratoga Co. Yellow massive thorite (uranothorite) is reported with polycrase, monazite, etc. in a pegmatite at Day; also a crystal $3/8 \times 1\frac{1}{2}''$ (Rowley-1976).

Thucholite — See Uraninite

Tirodite — See Amphibole

TITANITE Ca Ti Si O₅ calcium titanium silicate Monoclinic Syn.
Sphene

Titanite, or sphene, is widely distributed as an accessory mineral in acidic igneous rocks (granites, granite pegmatites, syenites, diorites, etc.) and in many metamorphic rocks (gneisses, crystalline limestones) as well as some beds of magnetite ore.

Clinton Co. Dark brown to black crystals up to 15 mm. were found in vugs in granite gneiss at Chateaugay mines, at Lyon Mountain (Whitlock-1907).

Essex Co. Near Olmsteadville, pinkish colored titanite crystals were associated with vesuvianite (Shaub-1953). Small yellow to brown titanite crystals were reported on the south shore of Harris Lake. Some large ones were altering to rutile (Nason-1888). Microscopic titanite crystals are reported to occur in a syenitic pegmatite near Crown Point Center (Rowley-1962; Tan-1966).

Jefferson and Lewis Co's. Good crystals of titanite occur at the contact between crystalline limestone and granite near Oxbow and near Natural Bridge (Agar-1921; Robinson and Laverson-1971; Van Diver-1977).

Titanite (Sphene) Tilly Foster Mine, Putnam Co.

Orange Co. Titanite as tiny crystals to crystals 3 inches on edge were found at the contact of crystalline limestone and granite at the Atlas limestone quarry and elsewhere (Ayres-1945; Cosminsky-1947).

Putnam Co. At the Tilly Foster Mine, Brewster, transparent to translucent yellow to orange and greenish titanite crystals up to 2 inches long were reported. In 1891, several hundred crystals were found and a few gems were cut (Trainer-1938; 1942; Sinkankas-1959).

St. Lawrence Co. Titanite crystals up to 5 cm. long are abundant with actinolite in quartz at McLear pegmatite near DeKalb Junction (Shaub-1929; Tan-1966). Crystals up to 2 cm. occur in pegmatite east of Fine and south of the Oswegatchie River (Jensen-P.O., 1955; Tan-1966). Large crystals were reported in contact zones at the Jayville iron mine (Dale-1935). Reported at talc mines (Engel-1949).

Warren Co. Titanite was present in metamorphosed limestone near Johnsburg (Larsen & Schaller-1932).

Westchester Co. Small crystals were reported at the Bedford feldspar quarries (Agar-1933; Black-1948; Tan-1966).

Titanite (Sphene)   Putnam Co.

TORBERNITE   Cu $(UO_2)_2$ $(PO_4)_2 \cdot 8-12$ H_2O copper uranyl phosphate hydrate   Tetragonal

Westchester Co. Reported on feldspar at Bedford quarries (Agar-1933; Tan-1966).

TOURMALINE   a group name for a group of boron silicates of general formula A X_3 Y_6 B_3 Si_6 (O, OH)$_{27}$ (OH)$_3$ (OH, F) A=Na, Ca; X=Li, Mg, Fe″, Fe‴, Al, Cr, Mn: Y=Al, Fe, Cr   Trigonal

Thorough studies and chemical analyses have been made of many tourmalines including several from New York State localities (Dunn et. al.-1977). Color, crystal habit or other physical and chemical properties cannot be used for the easy identification of members of the tourmaline group.

Achroite is a name that was given to a colorless to grayish-white transparent to translucent variety of elbaite from Elba, Italy. The color-less tourmaline from DeKalb is uvite.

Buergerite is ferric iron tourmaline. It has not been reported in the state.

Dravite, a sodium magnesium tourmaline, is usually brown or light green in color. Most of the brown tourmalines of St. Lawrence County and Essex County that have been called dravite are now identified as uvite (Dunn et. al.-1977).

Elbaite, a lithium-aluminum tourmaline, occurs in shades of pink and red or various shades of green.

Schorl is ferrous iron tourmaline. Most black tourmalines from gran-ite pegmatites are schorl. Most of the black tourmaline from Pierrepont in St. Lawrence Co. is uvite (Dunn et al-1977).

Uvite is calcium magnesium tourmaline. Most uvites are brown in color. The brown tourmalines from the DeKalb, Gouverneur and Rich-ville localities are uvite (Dunn el al-1977).

The common occurrence of tourmaline in New York State is in granite pegmatites where it is usually black. Tourmaline also occurs in meta-morphic limestones (e.g. Grenville marble) where it is usually brown. It is an accessory mineral in many granites, some gneisses, and also occurs in some river and lake sands.

Essex Co. Large crystals were reported along the shore of Harris Lake, near Newcomb (one crystal was 8 inches long and 4 inches wide); also numerous brown, green and greenish-black crystals with some cut into small gems (Nason-1888). On the south shore of Goodenow River, large crystals were found in Grenville marble (Balk-1932). Large crystals of tourmaline were found in pegmatite near Crown Point Center. Some crystals had a core of microcline surrounded by a shell of tourmaline (Rowley-1962; Tan-1966).

Jefferson Co. Brown tourmaline occurs in marble at several localities near Oxbow (Agar-1921).

New York Co. A study of brown muscovite from pegmatite on Fort Washington Ave. in New York City revealed over 100 tourmaline inclusions ranging in color from brownish-black to yellow-brown (Frondel-1936). A 9½ inch long, 10 pound crystal of black tourmaline was found in quartz at Fort Washington Ave. and 171st St. Gem quality tourmalines were found at Broadway and 218th St. and at 225th St. (Manchester-1931; Schuberth-1965).

Orange Co. Small brown crystals occurred in marble at the Atlas limestone quarry near Pine Island (Zodac-1940). Variously colored crystals were reported near Warwick and Edenville, etc. (Beck-1842).

Putnam Co. Black tourmaline crystals were reported in gneiss at the Tilly Foster Mine, Brewster, as well as brown crystals in calcite (Trainer-1938).

St. Lawrence Co. Brown tourmaline is common in the crystalline limestone (Grenville marble) at many localities (Whitlock-1903). The most famous is on the Dale Bush (Gomer Jones) farm 4½ miles north of Gouverneur where fine crystals and crystal groups have been found associated with tremolite (Dana, J.D.-1892; Cushing and Newland-

Tourmaline, Uvite   Richville, St. Lawrence Co.

Tourmaline, Uvite   Pierrepont, St. Lawrence Co.

1925; Agar-1921). The brown tourmaline that occurs at localities near Gouverneur has sometimes been called dravite but has recently been recognized as uvite, a calcium magnesium variety of tourmaline (Dunn et al.-1977). A white or colorless tourmaline was found near DeKalb (Dana-1892). Although it has been called acroite, it is uvite (Dunn et al.-1977).

Black tourmaline is a common constituent of many pegmatites and granites in the county (Agar-1921, 1923). The best known black tourmaline locality is on Grannis Brook at the Bower Powers farm about 3 miles west of the town of Pierrepont. Fine crystals and groups of black tourmaline occur with quartz, dolomite, mica, and uralite (Whitlock-1903; Martin-1916; Agar-1921; Dunn-1977). Most of this black tourmaline is uvite (Dunn et al.-1977). Reddish brown tourmalines from Balmat and the talc mines near Fowler are also uvites.

Saratoga Co. Large black terminated tourmaline crystals up to 9 inches or more in length and complex crystal masses were found at the Overlook quarry (Rowley-1942; Tan-1966). During World War II, about 500 pounds of large crystal sections from this quarry were sold in the United Kingdom (Frondel-1948).

Warren Co. Crystals of brown tourmaline that were reported as dravite and up to 7 inches in length were found with graphite, etc. in the town of Horicon (Rowley-1955). The tourmaline at Horicon is uvite (Dunn et al.-1977). Microscopic blue-green acicular crystals were enclosed in quartz near Schroon Lake (Rowley-1957).

Westchester Co. Black tourmaline was abundant at the Bedford quarries especially at the Kinkel quarry. In 1928, a magnificent group was reconstructed by Weishaas and Manchester. Thirty-two crystals, each averaging 2 inches in diameter and from 8 inches to 18 inches in length were mounted in a radiating group (Manchester-1931; Weidhaas-1959).

Tourmaline, Schorl   Bedford, Westchester Co.

Travertine — See Calcite

Tremolite — See Amphibole

TROILITE   Fe S Hexagonal

Niagara Co. The Cambria iron meteorite was found in 1818 while cultivating a field near Lockport. Troilite nodules occurred in the meteorite and remains of troilite were found in surface depressions where the mineral had weathered (Farrington-1915).

Turgite — See Hematite

U-Galena — See Galena

Uralite — See Amphibole

URANINITE   U O₂ uranium oxide   Cubic

Essex Co. Cubic crystals up to 3 mm. on an edge occur in feldspar in a pegmatite northwest of Crown Point Center (Rowley-1962).

New York Co. Reported (Manchester-1914).

Orange Co. Associated with pyrite in low grade magnetite ore at the Miles Standish mine near Warwick (Heinrich-1958).

Putnam Co. Associated with magnetite and hornblende in pegmatite at the Phillips pyrite mine (Heinrich-1958).

St. Lawrence Co. McLear pegmatite, near DeKalb. Small cubes of uraninite and thucholite up to 5 mm. along an edge occur in milky quartz. Age is 1,094 million years. Twin crystals are rare (Shaub-1940; Heinrich-1958; Tan-1966). Thucholite is a mixture of uraninite and hydrocarbons (See p. 32).

Saratoga Co. Was found at Batchellerville (Tan-1966) and in the Overlook area (Rowley-1976 pc.).

Westchester Co. Reported at Bedford quarries (Kerr-1935).

Uraninite and Thucholite in Quartz   DeKalb, St. Lawrence Co.

URANOPHANE Ca $(UO_2)_2$ Si_2 O_7•6 H_2O calcium uranyl silicate hydrate   Monoclinic

Uranophane is common in small quantities in pegmatites of New York state (Tan-1966).

Essex Co. Canary-yellow to orange-yellow crusts on feldspar cleavages occur in pegmatite northwest of Crown Point Center (Rowley-1962; Tan-1966).

Saratoga Co. Was found at the Corinth feldspar pegmatite (Tan-1966).

Westchester Co. Reported on feldspar and beryl (Agar-1933; Black-1948; Tan-1966).

Uvite — See tourmaline

VANADINITE Pb_5 $(VO_4)_3$ Cl lead vanadate chloride   Hexagonal

Westchester Co. Reported at the old copper mine at Sparta, south of Ossining (Manchester-1931).

VAUQUELINITE Pb_2 Cu (Cr O_4) (PO_4) (OH) Monoclinic

Westchester Co. Green to brownish-green in small mammillary concretions at old lead mine, 1 mile south of Sing Sing (Torrey-1848; Manchester-1931).

VERMICULITE A mineral group of general formula (Mg, Fe, Al)$_3$ (Al, Si)$_4$ O_{10} (OH)$_2$•4 H_2O magnesium iron aluminum silicate hydroxide hydrate   Monoclinic

Lewis Co. Confirmed report in calcite-quartz vein near Port Leyden (Dale-1924).

New York and Queens Co's. A greenish mica prominent in weathered zone of granodiorite, in subway tunnel excavations (Kerr-1930).

Onondaga Co. Found in peridotite dike in Syracuse (Maynard & Ploger-1946).

VESUVIANITE Ca_{10} Mg_2 Al_4 (Si O_4)$_5$ (Si_2 O_7)$_2$ (OH)$_4$ calcium magnesium aluminosilicate hydroxide   Tetragonal   Syn. — Idocrase. Vesuvianite occurs typically in contact metamorphosed limestones.

Essex Co. Light brown to golden brown to chocolate brown crystals and groups were found in pockets of Grenville marble west of Olmsteadville (Rowley-1948).

St. Lawrence Co. Small crystals were found near Rossie and at Vrooman's Lake (Hough-1853; Durant and Pierce-1878).

Vesuvianite   Olmsteadville, Essex Co.

VONSENITE   Fe''$_2$ Fe''' BO$_5$ Orthorhombic

St. Lawrence Co. Dark gray to black granular masses occur in skarn of Jayville and Clifton magnetite deposits (Leonard & Vlisidis-1960).

Wad — a general term for soft manganese oxides not specifically identified.

WARWICKITE   (Mg, Ti, Fe''', Al)$_2$ (BO$_3$) O Orthorhombic

Orange Co. Brown to black slender crystals are associated with chondrodite, spinel, etc. in crystalline limestone at Warwick (Shepard-1838; Palache, Berman, Frondel-1951). This is the type locality for the mineral.

Water — See Ice

Wernerite — See Scapolite

WILLEMITE   Zn$_2$ Si O$_4$ zinc silicate   Trigonal

St. Lawrence Co. Small tabular crystals up to 2.5 mm. were found embedded in chlorite at Balmat (Brown-1936; Pough-1940, 1941).

WOLLASTONITE   Ca Si O$_3$ calcium silicate   Triclinic

Wollastonite is frequently found near contacts of metamorphosed lime-stone and igneous rocks (or their metamorphic equivalents) in the Adirondack area (Engel & Engel-1963).

Essex Co. Large bodies of white wollastonite occur with andradite in skarn south of Sugarloaf Mt. (Buddington & Whitcomb-1941).

Jefferson Co. Found near Natural Bridge (Agar-1921; Robinson & Alverson-1971). It is reported in the Lake Bonaparte quadrangle (Valley & Essene-1977).

Wollastonite and Andradite Garnet   Willsboro, Essex Co.

WULFENITE   Pb Mo O$_4$ lead molybdate   Trigonal

Westchester Co. Found sparingly in tabular crystals at old copper mine at Sparta, south of Ossining (Whitlock-1903).

WURTZITE   Zn S Hexagonal

St. Lawrence Co. Present at Balmat as aggregates and thin platelets with sphalerite and occasionally ilvaite (Ramdohr-1969).

XENOTIME   Y PO_4 yttrium phosphate   Tetragonal

New York Co. During excavations for a road bed along the Harlem River at 181st St., many small crystals were found embedded in oligoclase the largest 8 mm. (Hovey-1896; Chamberlain-1895).

Yttrofluorite — See Fluorite

ZEOLITES — a mineral group
See:

Chabazite	Laumontite
Epistilbite	Natrolite
Harmotome	Stilbite
Heulandite	Thomsonite

ZIRCON   Zr Si O_4 zirconium silicate   Tetragonal

Cyrtolite is an altered variety of zircon containing uranium and rare earths.

In the State, zircon is a common accessory mineral in igneous rocks (most commonly in granites and granite pegmatites); less commonly in metamorphic limestone (marble), and some sedimentary rocks (sandstones, etc.).

Broome & Delaware Co's. Zircon occurs as rounded grains to small crystals in Devonian shales, siltstone and sandstones in the Binghamton-Delhi area (Manley-1959).

Clinton Co. Lilac-brown crystals in pegmatite at Chateaugay iron mine, Lyon Mountain (Whitlock-1907).

Essex Co. Crystals up to 1 inch long were found near Mineville in 1897 (Kemp & Ruedemann-1910); crystals up to ½ inch in diameter were found in a syenitic pegmatite northwest of Crown Point Center (Rowley-1962; Tan-1966); small zircons were reported at the Rose Rock quarry south of Crown Point Center (Tan-1966).

The following ages were for zircons (Silver-1969).
1. in charnockite gneiss near Ticonderoga — 1130 ± 10 million years
2. in syenite pegmatite 2 miles south of Jay — 1100 ± 15 million years
3. in anorthosite 2 miles south of Jay — 1070 ± 20 million years
4. in pyroxene granulite at Lake Sanford — 1020 ± 10 million years

Franklin Co. Cyrtolite was reported at Owl's Head Mountain (Robinson & Alverson-1971).

Hamilton Co. Zircon is reported in a charnockite gneiss at Piseco Dome, etc. (Eckelmann-1977).

Jefferson Co. Zircon in marble near Natural Bridge is listed at 1025 to 1140 million years old (Eckelmann & Kulp-1957; Buddington & Leonard-1962).

Lewis Co. Zircon is reported in marble gneiss contact near Natural Bridge (Van Diver-1977).

Monroe Co. Zircon is a very common accessory mineral in detrital grains in crushed rocks of the Genesee Gorge (Alling-1946).

New York Co. Reported as inclusions in muscovite of Manhattan schist (Frondel-1940).

Orange Co. Zircon crystals were found in granite on Brooks Mt. and at Atlas quarry (Ayres-1945; Cosminsky-1947).

Putnam Co. Tilly Foster Mine, Brewster. A 1⅕ inch crystal was found in hornblende — clinochlore (Trainer-1938).

St. Lawrence Co. Crystals of zircon were reported in granite near Rossie (Emmons-1842; Van Diver-1977).

Saratoga Co. Small crystals of cyrtolite were reported at Overlook pegmatite (Rowley-1960; Tan-1966); also at Corinth Feldspar Company quarry (Tan-1966).

Washington Co. Reported in upper Fort Ann quarries (Tan-1966).

Westchester Co. Cyrtolite at Baylis and Kinkel quarries, Bedford, contain 5.5% hafnium (Lee-1928; Manchester-1931; Black-1948; Tan-1966). Age is about 350 million years (Eckelmann & Kulp-1957).

ZOISITE $Ca_2 Al_3 (Si_3 O_{12})$ (OH) calcium aluminum silicate hydroxide   Orthorhombic

Orange Co. Reported in magnetite ore at the Standish iron mine, Warwick (Colony-1921).

ORGANIC MATERIALS

AMBER is a fossil resin derived from coniferous trees.

Richmond Co. Clay pits near Kreischerville, Staten Island.

(Hollick-1905, 1905a, 1906, 1908).

Amber is found in deposits of Cretaceous sands and clays that represent part of the eastward extension of the Amboy clay series of the Raritan formation of New Jersey. The amber occurs in a lens-shaped stratum about 3 feet by 18 feet as irregular shaped fragments, some as large as a hickory nut and as occasional rounded drops. The amber is more or less transparent, yellow or reddish in color, opaque and grayish-white. Associated with the amber is closely packed vegetable debris, leaves, twigs, lignite and charred wood.

ANTHRAXOLITE is a hydrocarbon

Anthraxolite is a black carbonaceous material occurring in vugs and fractures in dolomites (dolostones) of Croixan and Canadian age throughout the Mohawk Valley. It is disseminated interstitially in the dolomites (dolostones) and is enclosed in quartz and calcite. Masses occur up to the size of a walnut (Dunn & Fisher–1954; Tuttle–1973).

Herkimer & Montgomery Co's. Very common in and with "Herkimer diamonds."

Saratoga Co. A black platey material embedded in calcite at the Gailor Quarry is graphite (Rowley–1951).

PEARLS

Fine small fresh water pearls of baroque shapes are yielded by various species of Unionidae in several streams and rivers of the state including the Grass River of St. Lawrence Co., the upper tributaries of the Hudson River, Pearl River in Rockland Co. and Flint Creek near the towns of Gorham and Potter in Ontario and Yates Counties (Kunz & Stevenson–1908; Kirchoff–1931; Sinkankas–1959).

Anthraxolite with quartz   Montgomery Co.

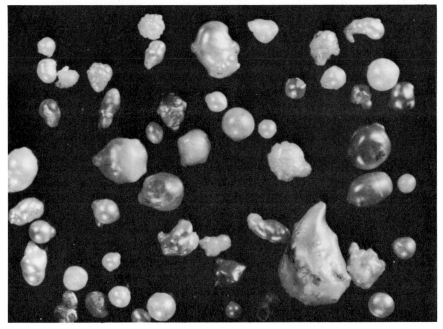

Fresh water pearls   Gorham, Yates Co.

Bibliography

Agar, William M. (1921) The Minerals of St. Lawrence, Jefferson and Lewis Counties, New York: Amer. Mineral., v. 6, no. 10, p. 148–153; v. 6, no. 11, p. 158–164.

(1923) Contact Metamorphism in the western Adirondacks: Amer. Philosophical Soc. Proc., v. 62, p. 95–174.

(1933) The pegmatites of Bedford, New York; 16th International Geological Congress, 9, p. 123–128.

Akerly, Samuel (1808) On the geology and mineralogy of the Island of New York; Amer. Mineral. Jour., no. IV, p. 191–196.

(1891) On the geology and mineralogy of the Island of New York; Amer. Mineral. Jour., 1, p. 191.

Alling, Harold L. (1917) The Adirondack graphite deposits; N.Y. State Mus. Bull. 199, 150 p.

(1918) Geology of the Lake Clear region; N.Y. State Mus. Bull. 207–208.

(1921) The Mineralography of the feldspars; Jour. Geol., v. XXIX, no. 3, p. 193–294.

(1926) The potash-soda feldspars; Jour. Geol. v. XXXIV, no. 7, part 1, p. 591–611.

(1928) The geology and origin of the Silurian salt of New York State; N.Y. State Mus. Bull. 275.

(1930) Feldspars in the Adirondack anorthosite; Amer. Mineral., v. 15, no. 7, p. 267–271.

(1946) Quantitative petrology of the Genesee Gorge sediments; Proc. Rochester Acad. Sci., v. 9, p. 5–63.

Alverson, Schuyler (1975) Personal communication.

Anderson, Keith Elliott (1947) Copper mineralization near Oxbow, Jefferson County, New York; unpublished M.S. thesis, University of Rochester, Rochester, New York.

Anderson, R. W. (1971) Gem Testing; Van Nostrand-Reinhold, New York, 384 p.

Ardelio, M. (1957) Personal observations

Arem, Joel (1973) Rocks and Minerals, Bantam, 145 p.

Armstrong, E. J. (1935) Schroeckingerite from Bedford, New York; Amer. Mineral., v. 20, p. 62–63.

Arnell, David R. (1809) A geological topographical history of Orange County; Medical Repository, 6, p. 313–318.

Awald, Clifford J. (1958) Minerals of the Niagara Frontier region; Science on the March, v. 38, no. 5, p. 98–107.

(1969) Minerals of the Niagara frontier; Rocks and Minerals, p. 323–331.

Ayres, V. L. (1945) Mineral localities of Monroe, New York and Bear Mountain Park; Rocks and Minerals, v. 20, no. 10, p. 468–470.

Bailey, S. C. H. (1865) On the minerals of New York Island; Lyceum Nat. Hist., N.Y. Ann. 8, p. 185–193.

(1887) On an aerolite from Rensselaer County, New York; Amer. Jour. Sci., 3rd Ser., v. 34, p. 60–62.

Baird, Gordon C. (1975) Pebbly phosphates in shale—a key to recognition of widespread submarine discontinuity of the Middle Devonian of New York; Unpublished PhD thesis, part III, Univ. of Rochester.

(1976) Personal communication.

Balk, Robert (1932) Geology of the Newcomb quadrangle; N.Y. State Mus. Bull. 290.

(1953) Structure of graywacke areas and Taconic Range, east of Troy, New York; Geol. Soc. Amer. Bull., v. 64, p. 811–864.

Balsey, J. R. (1943) Vanadium-bearing magnetite-ilmenite deposits near Lake Sanford, Essex County, New York; U.S. Geol. Surv. Bull. 940D.

Barth, Tom F. W. (1930) Mineralogy of the Adirondack feldspars; Amer. Mineral., v. 15, p. 129–143.

Barth, Tom F. W. and Balk, Robert (1934) Chloritoid from Dutchess County, New York; Amer. Mineral., v. 19, p. 345–350.

Bastin, Edson S. (1907) Feldspar and quartz deposits of southeastern New York; U.S. Geol. Surv., Bull. 315, p. 349–399.

(1910) Feldspar deposits of Westchester County, New York; U.S. Geol. Surv., Bull. 420, p. 60–63.

Bateman, Alan M. (1942) Economic Mineral Deposits; 898 p., Wiley, New York.

(1950) 2nd Ed., 916 p., Wiley, New York.

Bates, Barbara J. Mrs. (1973) Haüynite, alias Adirondack lapis lazuli; Lapidary Journal, v. 26, no. 12, p. 1777–1779.

Bauer, Max (1896) Edelsteinkunde; 2nd Ed., 766 pp., Tauchnitz, Leipzig.

(1932) 3rd Ed. by K. Schlossmacher, 871 pp., Tauchnitz, Leipzig.

Bauer, Max—Spencer, Leonard J. (1904) Precious Stones, Translated from the German with additions by L. J. Spencer; 627 pp., Griffin, London.

(1969) Ibid. published by Tuttle, Vermont, Japan.

Bayley, William S. (1908) Note on the occurrence of graphite-schist in Tuxedo Park; Econ. Geol. 3, p. 535–536.

Beck, Lewis Caleb, Report on the Mineralogical and Chemical Departments of the New York Geological Survey; N.Y. State Geological Survey Reports;

(1837) 1, p. 15–16.

(1838) 2, p. 7–73.

(1839) 3, p. 9–56.

(1840) 4, p. 45–111.

(1841) 5, p. 5–23.

(1842) Mineralogy of New York; Natural History of New York, Part III, 536 pp.

(1843) Analysis of hypersthene of New York; Amer. Jour. Sci., Ser. 1, 44, p. 35.

(1843) Analysis of allanite of Monroe, New York; Amer. Jour. Sci., Ser. 1, 44, p. 37.

(1844) Mineralogy of New York; Amer. Jour. Sci. 1, 46, p. 25–37.

(1850) Report on the mineralogy of New York; comprising additions which have been made since 1842; N.Y. State Cabinet, Annual Report 3, p. 109–153.

Behm, Juan J. (1954) The petrology of Richmond County (Staten Island); Staten Island Institute of Arts and Sciences Proceedings, v. 16, no. 1, p. 1–39.

Bentley, W. A. and Humphreys, W. J. (1931) Snow Crystals, 227 pp., McGraw-Hill.

Bergemann, C. (1852) Allanite from West Point; Amer. Jour. Sci., Ser. 2, p. 416–417.

Berkey, Charles P. (1911) Geology of the New York City (Catskill) Aqueduct; N.Y. State Mus. Bull. 146.

Berkey, Charles P. and Rice, Marion (1919) Geology of the West Point quadrangle; N.Y. State Mus. Bull. 225–226.

Berry, W. B. N. and Boucot, Arthur J. (1970) Correlation of the North American Silurian rocks; Geol. Soc. Amer. Special Paper 102.

Black, Daniel (1948) Some minerals of Bedford, New York; Rocks and Minerals, v. 23, no. 8, p. 710–712.

Blake, William P. (1858) Lanthanite and Allanite in Essex County, N.Y.; Amer. Jour. Sci., p. 245.

(1908) Tourmaline of Crown Point, N.Y.; Amer. Jour. Sci., v. 25, p. 123–124.

Blank, Horace R. (1978) Fossil laterite on bedrock in Brooklyn, New York: Geology, Vol. 6, No. 1, p. 21–24.

Bloss, F. Donald and Gibbs, Gerald V. (1963) Cleavage in quartz; Amer. Miner., v. 48, p. 821–838.

Bodelsen, O. W. (1948) Monazite occurrence at Yorktown Heights, N.Y.; Rocks and Minerals, v. 23, nos. 11–12, p. 908–909.

Bolton, Rev. Robert (1881) The History of the several towns, manors, and patents of the County of Westchester, 826 p. Vol. I, Roper, N.Y., Vol. II.

Boone, Gary M., Romey, William D. and Thompson, Dons (1969) Oscillatory zoning in calcic andesine-sodic labradorite relict phenocrysts in anorthosite of Oregon Dome and Giant Mountain, Adirondack Highlands; N.Y. State Museum and Science Service Memoir 18, p. 317–328.

Bradley, Walter M. (1909) On the analysis and chemical composition of the mineral warwickite; Amer. Jour. Sci., Ser. 4, 27, p. 179–184.

Braun, Fredrick (1896) On some new minerals from New York City; N.Y. Acad. Sci., 16, p. 44.

Breidenbaugh, E. S. (1873) On the minerals found at the Tilly Foster iron mines, N.Y.; Amer. Jour. Sci., Ser. 3, 6, p. 207–213.

Bristol, R. E., Leib, E. and Sawyer, V. (1967) Mineral locations in Adirondack Mountain area, New York State; 3rd Ed., Adirondack Gemstone Quarterly, Inc.

Broughton, John G. and Burnham, Robert D. (1944) Occurrence and uses of wollastonite from Willsboro, N.Y.; Amer. Inst. Min. and Met. Technical pub. 1737.

Broughton, John G., Fisher, Donald W., Isachsen, Ynvar W., and Rickard, Lawrence W. (1966) Geology of New York, a short account; Educational leaflet 20, The University of the State of New York, The State Education Department, New York State Museum and Science Service.

Brown, John S. (1932) Natural gas, Salt and Gypsum in Precambrian rocks at Edwards, New York; Amer. Assoc. Petroleum Geologists Bull., v. 16, p. 727–735.

(1936a) Structure and primary mineralization of the zinc mine at Balmat, New York; Econ. Geol., v. XXXI, no. 3, p. 233–258.

(1936b) Supergene sphalerite, galena and willemite at Balmat, New York; Econ. Geol., v. XXXI, no. 4, p. 331–354.

(1947) Porosity and ore deposition at Edwards and Balmat, New York; Geol. Soc. America, Bull., v. 58, p. 505–540.

(1959) Occurrence of Jordanite at Balmat, New York; Econ. Geol., v. 54, p. 136–139.

Brown, John S. and Engel, Albert, E. J. (1956) Revision of Grenville stratigraphy and structure in the Balmat-Edwards District, northwest Adirondacks, New York; Geol. Soc. America Bull. 67, p. 1500-1622.

Brown, John S. and Kulp, J. L. (1959) Lead isotopes from Balmat area, New York; Econ. Geol., v. 54, p. 137-139.

Brown, Samuel C. (1927) Notes on minerals from the Bedford, Westchester Co. Quarry; Amer. Mineral., v. 12, p. 354.

Bruce, Archibald (1814) White pyroxene from New York Island; Amer. Mineral. Journal, 1, p. 266.

Brush, George Jarvis (1854) On the chemical composition of Clintonite (New York); Amer. Jour. Sci., Ser. 2, p. 407-409.

(1858) On chalcodite; Amer. Jour. Sci., Ser. 2, 25, p. 198-201.

Brush, George Jarvis and Blake, John M. (1869) On hortonolite, a new member of the chrysolite group (from Monroe, N.Y.); Amer. Jour. Sci., Ser. 2, 48, p. 17-23.

Brush, George Jarvis and Dana, Edward Salisbury (1880) Crystallized danburite from Russell, St. Lawrence County, N.Y.; Amer. Jour. Sci., Ser. 3, 20:111.

Buchwald, V. F. (1976) Handbook of Iron Meteorites, 3 vol., 1418 pp; Center for Meteorite Studies, Arizona State University, Tempe, Arizona.

Buddington, Arthur F. (1917) Report on pyrite and pyrrhotite veins in Jefferson and St. Lawrence Counties, New York; N.Y. State Defense Council Bull., no. 1.

(1934) Geology and mineral resources of the Hammond, Antwerp and Lowville quadrangles; N.Y. State Mus. Bull. 296.

(1937) Geology of the Santa Clara quadrangle, New York; N.Y. State Mus. Bull. 309.

(1938) Memorial to Charles Henry Smyth, Jr.; Geol. Soc. Amer. Proceedings volume for 1937, p. 195-202.

(1939) Adirondack igneous rocks and their metamorphism; Geol. Soc. America Memoir 7.

(1948) Origin of granitic rocks of the northwest Adirondacks; Geol. Soc. America Memoir 28, p. 21-43.

(1950) Composition and genesis of pyroxene and garnet related to Adirondack anorthosite and anorthosite-marble contact zones; Amer. Mineral., v. 35, p. 659-670.

(1953) Geology of the Saranac quadrangle, New York; N.Y. State Mus. Bull. 346.

(1969) Adirondack Anorthositic Series: Origin of Granite and Related Rocks; N.Y. State Mus. and Sci. Service Memoir 18, p. 215-231.

Buddington, Arthur F., Fahey, Joseph and Vlisidis, Angelina (1955) Therometric and petrogenic significance of titaniferous magnetite; Amer. Jour. Sci., vol. 253, p. 497-532.

(1963) Degree of oxidation of Adirondack iron-oxide and iron-titanium oxide minerals in relation to petrogeny; Jour. Petr., 4, p. 138-169.

Buddington, Arthur F. and Leonard, Benjamin F. (1953) Chemical petrology and mineralogy of the hornblendes in northwest Adirondack granitic rocks; Amer. Mineral. v. 38, p. 891-902.

(1962) Regional geology of the St. Lawrence County magnetite district, northwest Adirondacks, New York; U.S. Geol. Surv., Prof. Paper 376.

Buddington, Arthur F. and Whitcomb, Lawrence (1941) Geology of the Willsboro quadrangle, New York; N.Y. State Mus. Bull. 325.

Buehler, Edward J. and Tesmer, Irving H. (1963) Geology of Erie Co.; Buffalo Soc. of Natural Science Bull., v. 21, no. 3.

Buerger, Martin J. (1927) Optical notes on some of the variable contact minerals from Edenville, New York; Amer. Mineral., v. 12, p. 374–378.

Burr, Freeman F. (1915) Occurrence of Amazonstone at North White Plains, New York; Sch. Mines Quarterly, 36, p. 186–188.

Buyce, M. Raymond (1969) Gems of New York State; Pub'l. by New York State Mus. and Science Service.

(1976) Personal communication.

Byrne, Peggy (1975) Mr. Anorthosite, A profile of Arthur F. Buddington; The Conservationist, vol. 30, no. 3, p. 10–13.

Cannon, Helen L. (1955) Geochemical relations of zinc-bearing peat to the Lockport dolomite, Orleans County, New York; U.S. Geol. Surv. Bull. 1000D.

Cannon, R. S., Jr. (1937) Geology of the Piseco Lake quadrangle; N.Y. State Mus. Bull. 312.

Carl, James D. and Van Diver, Bradford B. (1971) Some aspects of Grenville geology and the Precambrian/Paleozoic unconformity, northwest Adirondacks, New York; Geologic studies in the northwest Adirondack region; 43rd annual meeting, The New York State Geol. Ass'n.

Chamberlain, Arthur (1895) Xenotime crystals on Manhattan Island; The Mineral Collector, v. 11, no. 8, p. 123–124.

Chamberlain, Benjamin B. (1885) Field work in local mineralogy (Minerals of New York City; N.Y. Acad. Sci., Trans. 3, p. 48–50.

(1886a) Minerals of Harlem and Vicinity (New York City); N.Y. Acad. Sci., Trans. 5, p. 74–77.

(1886b) Minerals of Staten Island, New York; N.Y. Acad. Sci., Trans. 5, p. 227–230.

(1887) Minerals of Staten Island; N.Y. Acad. Sci. Trans. 5, p. 228–229.

(1888) The minerals of New York County, including a list complete to date; N.Y. Acad. Sci., Trans. 7, p. 211–235.

Chase, Pamela J. and Brock, Patrick W. G. (1976) Sillimanite and Sillimanite-Orthoclase Isograds in the Croton Falls quadrangle, Southeast New York; Geol. Soc. Amer. Northeast Section, Abstracts, 11th Annual Meeting, vol. 8, no. 2, Feb. 1976.

Chester, A. H. (1887) Mineralogical Notes; Amer. Jour. Sci., Ser. 3, 33, p. 283.

Clarke, John M. and Luther, D. Dana (1904) Stratigraphic and paleontologic map of Canandaigua and Naples quadrangles; N.Y. State Mus. Bull. 63.

Clarke, Noah T. (1920) The reconstruction of the Sterlingbush calcite cave; N.Y. State Mus. Bull. 219–220, p. 223–226.

Cleaveland, Parker (1816) An elementary treatise on mineralogy and geology, 1st Ed.

(1822) 2nd Ed, two volumes.

Coch, Nicholas Kyros (1961) Textural and mineralogical variations in some Lake Ontario beach sands; Unpublished M.S. Thesis, University of Rochester.

Cohen, E. (1905) Meteoritenkunde, Heft. 1, p. 312–315.

Cole, W. Storrs (1959) Geology of the Cayuga Lake basin; 31st annual meeting, New York State Geol. Ass'n.

Colony, Roy J. (1921) The magnetite iron deposits of southeastern New York; N.Y. State Mus. Bull. 249–250.

(1933) Structural Geology between New York and Schunemunk Mountain; 16th International Geological Congress, 9: p. 37.

Connally, G. Gordon (1960) Heavy minerals in the glacial drift of western New York; Proceedings, Rochester Acad. Sci., v. 10, 5, p. 241–278.

Cooper, Ruth (1957) The History of Iron Ore Mining in Ontario (N.Y.); History of the Town of Ontario (N.Y.), p. 56–61.

Cosminsky, P. R. (1947) A trip to Mt. Adam and Pine Island, Orange Co., New York Rocks and Minerals, v. 22, no. 3, p. 207–209.

Cox, Chas. F. (1893) Additional notes on recently discovered deposits of diatomaceous earth in the Adirondacks; Trans. N.Y. Acad. Sci., v. 13, p. 98–101.

Cozzens, Issachar, Jr. (1843) Geological history of Manhattan or New York Island, 114 p.; W. E. Dean, New York.

Craw, Wm J. (1850) Analysis of phlogopite from St. Lawrence County, N.Y.; Amer. Jour. Sci., Ser. 2, 10, p. 382.

Crawe, J. B. and Gray, Asa (1834) Sketch of the mineralogy of a portion of Jefferson and St. Lawrence Counties; Amer. Jour. Sci., Ser. 1, 25, p. 346–350.

Crosby, William Otis (1914) Physiographic relations of serpentine with special reference to the serpentine rock of Staten Island; Jour. Geol., v. 22, p. 582–593.

Crump, R. and Beutner, E. L. (1968) The Benson Mines iron deposit, St. Lawrence County, New York; Amer. Inst. Min. Eng., Graton-Sales volume, p. 49–71.

Cushing, H. P. (1905) Geology of the vicinity of Little Falls, Herkimer County, New York; N.Y. State Mus. Bull. 77.

(1905) Geology of the northern Adirondack region; N.Y. State Mus. Bull. 95.

Cushing, H. P., Fairchild, H. L., Ruedemann, Rudolf and Smyth, C. H., Jr. (1910) Geology of the Thousand Islands region; N.Y. State Mus. Bull. 145.

Cushing, H. P. and Newland, David H. (1925) Geology of the Gouverneur quadrangle; N.Y. State Mus. Bull. 259.

Cushing, H. P. and Ruedemann, Rudolf (1914) Geology of Saratoga Springs and vicinity; N.Y. State Mus. Bull. 169.

Cutbush, James (1824) Localities of minerals near West Point; Amer. Jour. Sci., Ser. 1, 7, p. 57–58.

Dahlberg, J. C. (1976) The Hudson River Chain and the Revolution; Lapidary Journal, vol. 30, no. 5, p. 1196–1201.

Dake, Henry C. (1943) Mineral Club History; Privately printed.

Dake, Henry C., Fleener, Frank L. and Wilson, Ben Hur (1938) Quartz Family Minerals.

Dale, Nelson C. (1924) The Box-vein of Lyonsdale, Lewis County, New York; New York State Mus. Bull. 251, p. 134–138.

(1934) Preliminary report on the geology of the Russell quadrangle; N.Y. State Mus. circular 15, 16 p.

(1935) Geology of the Oswegatchie quadrangle; N.Y. State Mus. Bull. 302.

(1953) Geology and mineral resources of the Oriskany quadrangle; N.Y. State Mus. Bull. 345.

Dana, Edward Salisbury (1875) Preliminary notice of chondrodite crystals from Tilly Foster mine, Brewster, New York; Amer. Jour. Sci., Ser. 3, 9, p. 63–64.

(1875b) On the chondrodite from the Tilly Foster mine, Brewster,

New York; Amer. Jour. Sci., Ser. 3, 10, p. 89–103.

(1876) On the optical character of chondrodite of the Tilly Foster mine; Amer. Jour. Sci., Ser. 3, 11, p. 139–140.

(1877) A Textbook of mineralogy, 1st Ed.

(1898) 2nd Ed.; Wiley, New York.

(1884) On a crystal of allanite from Port Henry, N.Y.; Amer. Jour. Sci., Ser. 3, 79, p. 479.

Dana, Edward Salisbury and Ford, W. E. (1932) A textbook of mineralogy. 4th Ed. revised, 851 p.; Wiley, New York.

Dana, James Dwight, A system of mineralogy; 1st Ed. (1837); 2nd Ed. (1844); 3rd Ed. (1850); 4th Ed. (1854); 5th Ed. (1868); 6th Ed. (1892) 1134 p. by Edward Salisbury Dana, Wiley, New York.

Appendix 1, (1899) 75 p.

Appendix 2, (1909) by E. S. Dana and W. E. Ford, 114 p.

Appendix 3, (1915) by W. E. Ford.

(1855) Note on hudsonite; Amer. Jour. Sci., Ser. 2, 19, p. 362.

(1873) Leucaugite from Amity, New York; Amer. Jour. Sci., Ser. 3, 6, p. 24.

(1874) On serpentine pseudomorphs and other kinds from the Tilly Foster iron mine, Putnam County, New York; Amer. Jour. Sci., Ser. 3, 8, p. 371–381, 447–459.

(1881) Origin of the rocks of the Cortlandt series; Amer. Jour. Sci., 3rd Ser., v. 20, p. 194–220.

(1884) Note on the Cortlandt and Stony Point (New York) hornblendic and augitic rock; Amer. Jour. Sci. Ser. 3, 28, p. 384–486.

Darton, Nelson Horatio (1882) Mineralogical localities in and around New York City and the minerals occurring in them; Sci. Amer. Supplement 14, p. 5492, 5566, 5796, 5797. (1883) Supplement 16, p. 6629.

Davis, Brian T. C. (1969) Anorthositic and quartz syenitic series of the St. Regis quadrangle, New York; N.Y. State Mus. and Sci. Service Memoir, p. 281–287.

Deer, W. A., Howie, R. A. and Zussman, J. (1962) Rock-forming Minerals, vol. 1, Ortho and Ring Silicates, 333 p., Wiley, New York.

(1963) Rock-forming Minerals, vol. 2, Chain silicates, 379 p., Wiley, New York.

(1962) Rock-forming Minerals, vol. 3, Sheet Silicates, 270 p., Wiley, New York.

(1962) Rock-forming Minerals, vol. 4, Framework Silicates, 435 p., Wiley, New York.

(1962) Rock-forming Minerals, vol. 5, Non-Silicates, 371 p., Wiley, New York.

DeRudder, Ronald D. (1964) Mineralogy, petrology, and genesis of the Willsboro wollastonite deposit, Willsboro quadrangle, New York; Unpublished Ph.D. thesis, University of Indiana, Bloomington, Indiana.

De Rudder, Ronald D. and Beck, Carl W. (1963) Clinozoisite from the Willsboro wollastonite deposit, New York; Geol. Soc. America, Special paper 76, p. 42–43.

(1963) Stevensite and talc-hydrothermal alteration products of wollastonite; Clays and Clay Minerals, Monograph No. 13, Earth science series.

Desautels, Paul E. (1968) The Mineral Kingdom, 251 p.; Grosset & Dunlap, New York.

(1971) The Gem Kingdom, 252 p.; Random House, New York.

(1974) Rocks and Minerals, 159 p.; Grosset & Dunlap, New York.

DeWaard, Dirk (1965) The occurrence of garnet in the granulite-facies terrane of the Adirondack highlands; J. Petrol. 6:165-191.

(1970) The anorthosite-charnockite series of rocks of Roaring Brook Valley in the eastern Adirondacks (Marcy massif); Amer. Mineral., v. 55, p. 2063-2075.

DeWaard, Dirk and Romey, William D. (1968) Petrogenetic Relationships in the Anorthosite-charnockite series of Snowy Mountain dome, south-central Adirondacks; New York State Museum and Science Service, Memoir 18.

Dill, David B. (1975, 1976) Personal communication.

Diller, J. S. and Whitfield, J. E. (1890) Dumortierite from Harlem, New York and from Arizona; Amer. Jour. Sci., Ser. 3, 37, p. 216.

Dodd, R. T. Jr. (1963) Garnet-pyroxene gneisses at Bear Mountain, New York: Amer. Miner., v. 48, p. 811-820.

Doe, Bruce R. (1960) The Distribution and Composition of Sulfide Minerals at Balmat, New York; 151 p., Unpublished PhD thesis, California Institute of Technology, Pasadena, Calif.

(1962) Distribution and composition of sulfide minerals at Balmat, New York; Geol. Soc. Amer. Bull., v. 73, p. 833-854.

Dolgoff, A. (1958) The Cortlandt complex; Field Guide Book, N.Y. State Geol. Ass'n, 30th Annual Meeting, p. 18-24.

Dollase, Wayne A. (1968) Refinement and comparison of the structures of zoisite and clinozoisite; Amer. Mineral., v. 53, p. 1882-1898.

Dorr, John A. Jr. and Eschman, Donald F. (1970) Geology of Michigan; The University of Michigan Press, 476 p.

Dunn, Pete J. (1977) Apatite, a guide to species nomenclature; The Mineralogical Record, v. 8, no. 2, p. 78-82.

Dunn, Pete J., Appleman, Daniel, Nelen, Joseph A. and Norberg, Julie (1977) Uvite, a new (old) common member of the tourmaline group and its implications for collectors: The Mineralogical Record, v. 8, no. 2, March-April 1977, p. 100-108.

Dunn, James R. and Fisher, Donald W. (1954) Occurrence, properties and paragenesis of anthraxolite in Mohawk Valley; Amer. Jour. Sci., v. 252, p. 489-501.

Durant, Samuel W. and Pierce, Henry B. (1878) History of St. Lawrence Co., New York, 1749-1878, 521 p.

Eager, Sam'l W. (1846-7) An Outline History of Orange County, 652 p. Callahan, New York.

Eaton, Amos (1820) An Index to the Geology of the Northern States.

(1824) A geological and agricultural survey of the district adjoining the Erie Canal in the State of New York; Part 1.

Eckel, Edwin Clarence (1901) The emery deposits of Westchester County, New York; Mineral Industry, 9, p. 15-17.

(1902) The quarry industry in southeastern New York; N.Y. State Mus. Report 54, 1, p. 141-176.

Eckelmann, F. Donald (1977) An investigation of zircon populations from charnockitic gneisses in southernmost Adirondacks: Geol. Soc. Amer. Abstracts Northeast Section 12th Annual Meeting, p. 258.

Eckelmann, Walter R. and Kulp, J. Lawrence (1957) Uranium-lead method of age determination: Part II, North American localities; Geol. Soc. Amer. Bull. 68, p. 1117-1140.

Edwards, Arthur M. (1896) Chondrodite on New York Island; Mineral Collector, vol. III, p. 48.

(1896) On the formation of hematite on Staten Island, New York; Mineral Collector, vol. III, p. 89.

Eggleston, Thos. (1891) Catalogue of Minerals and Synonyms; Wiley, New York.

Elberty, William T. and Lessing, Peter (1971) Geological studies of the northwest Adirondacks, New York; 43rd Annual Meeting, The New York State Geological Association.

Emmons, Ebenezer (1838) Geology of New York, report on Second District.

(1842) Geology of New York, Part II, Survey of the Second District counties; Clinton, Essex, Franklin, Jefferson, Hamilton, St. Lawrence, Warren.

Engel, Albert E. J. (1949) New York Talcs, their geological features; Mining Engineering, v. 1, no. 9, p. 345–348.

(1962) The Precambrian geology and talc deposits of the Balmat-Edwards district. Northwest Adirondack Mountains; U.S. Geol. Surv. open file report, 357 p.

Engel, Albert E. J. and Engel, Celeste G. (1953) Grenville series in the northwest Adirondack Mountains of New York, Part I, General features of the Grenville series; Geol. Soc. Am. Bull. 64, p. 1013.

(1958) Progressive metamorphism and granitization of the major paragneiss, northwest Adirondack Mountains, New York, Part I, Total Rock; Geol. Soc. Bull. 69, p. 1369–1414.

(1960) Part II, Mineralogy; Geol. Soc. Amer. Bull. 71, p. 1–58.

(1962a) Progressive metamorphism of amphibolite, northwest Adirondack Mountains, New York; Geol. Soc. Amer., Buddington volume, p. 37–82.

(1962b) Hornblendes formed during progressive metamorphism of amphibolites, northwest Adirondack Mountains, New York; Geol. Soc. Am. Bull., v. 73, p. 1499–1514.

English, George L. (1934) Getting Acquainted with Minerals, 324 p.; McGraw Hill, New York.

(1958) Revised edition by David E. Jensen, 362 p.; McGraw Hill, New York.

Fairbanks, Ernest E. (1923) A new occurrence of sapphirine; Amer. Mineral., v. 8, p. 165.

Fairchild, Herman LeRoy (1902) History and Work of the Rochester Academy of Science; Proceedings, Rochester (N.Y.) Acad. Sci., vol. III, p. 320–339.

(1919) Henry Augustus Ward; Rochester Acad. Sci. Proceeding, vol. 5, p. 241–251.

(1933) Building Stones of Rochester; Nature's Contributions to Local Edifices; The Rochester Historical Society of Rochester, Public Fund Series, vol. XII, p. 131–156.

Fairchild, Herman LeRoy and Warner, J. Foster Warner (1933) Building Stones of Rochester, Centennial History of Rochester; Rochester Historical Society, v. XII, p. 130–156.

Farrington, Oliver Cummings (1903) Gems and gem materials, 229 p.; Mumford, Chicago.

(1915) Catalogue of the meteorites of North America to January 1, 1909; Nat'l Acad. of Sci., vol. XIII, 513 p.

Faust, George T. and Fahey, Joseph J. (1962) The Serpentine group of Minerals; U.S. Geol. Surv. Prof. Paper 384A.

Fenn, H. N. (1824) Coal, gypsum and barites near Rochester; Amer. Jour. Sci., Ser. 1, 6, p. 56.

Fenton, Carroll Lane and Fenton, Mildred Adams (1945, 1952) Giants of Geology, 333 p.; Doubleday, Garden City, N.Y.

Fettke, Charles Reinhard (1912) Limonite deposits on Staten Island, New York; School of Mines Quarterly, 33, p. 382–391.

Finch, John (1829) Notice of the locality of bronzite at Amity, Orange County, New York; Amer. Jour. Sci., Ser. 1, 16, p. 185–186.

    (1831) Essay on the mineralogy and geology of St. Lawrence County; Amer. Jour. Sci., Ser. 1, 19, p. 220–228.

Fisher, Donald W. (1951) Marcasite fauna in the Ludlowville formation of western New York; Jour. Paleo., v. 25, no. 3, p. 365–371.

    (1959) Correlation of the Silurian rocks in New York State; N.Y. State Mus. and Sci. Service Geol. Surv., map and chart, Ser. 1.

    (1962) Correlation of the Cambrian Rocks in New York State; N.Y. State Mus. and Science Service, map and chart series, no. 2.

    (1965) Mohawk Valley strata and structure, Field trips in the Schenectady area; N.Y. State Geol. Ass'n, 37th Annual Meeting. p. A1 to A58.

Fisher, Donald W. (1976) James Hall; The Conservationist, p. 12–16, Nov.-Dec. 1976.

Fisher, Donald W. (1977) Personal Communication.

    (1978) Amos Eaton—Passionate Peddler of Science; Conservationist, Vol. 32, no. 4, Jan.-Feb. 1978.

Fleischer, Michael (1971, 1975) Glossary of Mineral Species. Mineralogical Record, Inc., Bowie, Maryland.

Fleischer, R. L., Lifshin, E., Price, P. B., Woods, R. T., Carter, R. W., and Fireman, E. L. (1970) Schenectady Meteorite; Icarus, 12, p. 402–406.

Flint, Richard Foster (1957) Glacial and Pleistocene Geology; Wiley, New York.

Fluhr, Thomas W. (1931) The Malchite of White Plains, N.Y.; Rocks and Minerals, v. 6, no. 2, p. 54–55.

Foot, Lyman (1822) Notices of the Geology and Mineralogy of Niagara Falls Region; Amer. Jour. Sci., Ser. 1, 4, p. 35–37.

Ford, William Ebenezer (1903) On the chemical composition of dumortierite (from New York City); Amer. Jour. Sci., Ser. 4, 14, p. 426–430.

Foster, Margaret D. (1962) Interpretation of the Composition and a classification of the Chlorites; U.S. Geol. Surv. Prof. Paper 414A.

Fowler, Samuel (1825) An account of some new and extraordinary minerals discovered in Warwick, Orange County, New York; Amer. Jour. Sci., Ser. 1, 9, p. 242–245.

Friederich, J. J. (1887) Minerals of New York; N.Y. Acad. Sci., trans. 6, p. 130.

Friedman, Gerald M. (1952) Sapphirine occurrence of Cortlandt, New York; Amer. Mineral., v. 37, p. 244–249.

    (1952) Study of hoegbomite; Amer. Mineral., v. 37, p. 600–608.

    (1956) The origin of spinel-emery deposits with particular reference to those of the Cortlandt Complex, New York; N.Y. State Mus. Bull. 351.

French, J. H. (1861) Gazetteer of the State of New York, 756 p.

Frondel, Clifford (1934) Selective incrustation of crystal forms; Amer. Mineral., v. 19, no. 7, p. 316–329.

    (1935) Catalogue of mineral pseudomorphs in the American Museum; Bull. American Museum of Natural History, vol. L XVII, Article IX.

(1935) The size of crystals; Amer. Mineral., v. 20, no. 6, p. 469–473.

(1936) Oriented inclusions of tourmaline in muscovite; Amer. Mineral., v. 21, no. 12, part 1, p. 777–799.

(1940) Oriented inclusions of staurolite, zircon and garnet in muscovite. Skating crystals and their significance; Amer. Mineral., v. 25, no. 1, p. 69–87.

(1941) Constitution and polymorphism of the Pyroaurite and Sjögrenite groups; Amer. Mineral., v. 26, no. 5, p. 295–315.

(1948) Tourmaline pressure gauges; Amer. Mineral., v. 33, p. 1–17.

(1952) Studies of uranium minerals (x); Uranopilite; Amer. Mineral., v. 37, p. 950–959.

(1958) Systematic Mineralogy of Uranium and Thorium; U.S. Geol. Surv. Bull. 1064.

(1962) The System of Mineralogy, Seventh edition, vol. III, Silica Minerals, 334 p., Wiley, New York.

Frondel, Clifford and Ashby, George F. (1937) Oriented inclusions of magnetite and hematite in muscovite; Amer. Mineral., v. 22, p. 104–121.

Frondel, Clifford and Montgomery, Arthur, co-editors (1951) Peter Zodac and Rocks and Minerals; Rocks and Minerals, v. 26, p. 451–453.

Frondel, Clifford, and Newhouse, W. H., and Jarrell, R. F. (1942) Spatial distribution of minor elements in single crystals; Amer. Mineral., v. 27, no. 11, p. 726–745.

Frondel, Judith W. (1964) Variation of some rare earths in allanite; Amer. Mineral., v. 49, nos. 9–10, p. 1159–1177.

Gallagher, David (1937) Origin of the Magnetite deposits at Lyon Mountain, New York; N.Y. State Mus. Bull. 311.

Gardner, H. F. (1920) The calcite cave in the New York State Museum; Amer. Mineral., v. 5, no. 1, p. 3–5.

Gebhard, John Jr. (1835) On the geology and mineralogy of Schoharie; Amer. Jour. Sci., Ser. 1, 28, p. 72.

Genth, F. A. (1853) Allanite from Orange County, New York; Amer. Jour. Sci., Ser. 2, 16, p. 86.

Giles, Albert W. (1920) Minerals of the Niagara limestone of western New York; Proc. Rochester Acad. Sci., v. 16, p. 57–72.

Gill, Adam Capen (1928) Personal Communication.

Gillette, Tracy (1940) Geology of the Clyde and Sodus Bay quadrangles; N.Y. State Mus. Bull. 320.

Gillson, Joseph L. (1926) Optical notes on some minerals from the Mahopac iron mine, Brewster, N.Y.; Amer. Mineral., v. 11, p. 281–286.

(1930) Genesis of Peekskill emery deposits; Abst. Amer. Mineral., 15, p. 121.

Gillson, Joseph L. and Kania, J. E. (1930) Emery deposits near Peekskill, New York; Econ. Geol., v. 25, p. 506–507.

Gilman, Daniel C. (1899) The life of James Dwight Dana, 409 p; Harper & Brothers, New York.

Glossary of Geology (1973); American Geological Institute.

Goldring, Winifred (1960) Handbook of Paleontology for Beginners and Amateurs, Part I: The Fossils; N.Y. State Mus. Handbook 9, third printing.

(1931) Part 2: The Formations; N.Y. State Mus. Handbook 10.

Goldschmidt, Victor (1913–1923) Atlas de Krystalformen, 9 vol., atlas and text.

Goldschmidt, V.M. (1937) The principles of distribution of chemical elements in minerals and rocks; Chem. Soc. London Jour., p. 656.

Goldsmith, Julian R. (1976) Scapolites, granulites and volatiles in the lower crust; Geol. Surv. Bull. 87, p. 161–168.

Gordon, C. E. (1911) Geology of the Poughkeepsie quadrangle; N.Y. State Mus. Bull. 148.

Gordon, Thomas F. (1836) Gazeteer of the State of New York, 801 p. Collins, Philadelphia.

Gosse, Ralph C. (1957) Strontianite at Schoharie, New York; Rocks and Minerals, v. 32, nos. 9–10, p. 462–463.

(1968) New York's banded gemstone; Rocks and Minerals, v. 43, no. 2, p. 83–84.

Grabau, Amadeus W. (1901) Guide to the Geology and Paleontology of Niagara Falls and vicinity; N.Y. State Mus. Bull. 45.

(1906) Guide to the geology and paleontology of the Schoharie valley in eastern New York; N.Y. State Mus. Bull. 92.

Gratacap, L. P. (1899) Notes on the Limonite beds on Ocean Terrace, Staten Island; Staten Island Nat. Sci. Ass'n., Proc., v. 7, no. 12, p. 2.

(1909) Geology of the City of New York, 232 p. Henry Holt, New York.

Greene, John C. (1968) The American Mineralogical Journal (1810–1814); reprint, p. VII–XVII.

Gresens, Randall L. (1978) Evaporates as precursors to massif anorthosite; Geology, Vol. 6, No. 1, p. 46–50.

Grim, Ralph E. (1953) Clay mineralogy, 384 p.; McGraw Hill, New York.

Groben, Mike (1976) The 1975 Annual Report of the Friends of Mineralogy, Ad hoc committee for mineral locality preservation; The Mineralogical Record, v. 7, no. 3, p. 101–104.

Hall, C. E. (1884) Laurentian magnetic iron ore deposits of northern New York; N.Y. State Geol. 4th Ann. Rep't., p. 23.

Hall, James (1843) Geology of New York, Part IV, Survey of the Fourth Geological District.

(1894) The Livonia salt shaft; its history and geological relations, etc.; N.Y. State Mus. 47th Annual report, p. 205–216.

Hall, James (1846–1894) Paleontology of New York, 13 Quarto Volumes, 4320 pages and 980 lithograph plates.

Hallenbeck, William H. (1959) Rock crystals with chlorite inclusions discovered in New York State; Rock and Minerals, v. 34, nos. 11–12, p. 483–486.

Hamlin, Chauncey J., et al (1938) Seventy-five years, a History of the Buffalo Society of Natural Sciences, 1861–1936; Buffalo Society of Natural Sciences Bull. XVIII.

Hardin, George A. (1893) History of Herkimer County.

Harrison, W. P. and Misiaszek, E. T. (1971) Some aspects of engineering geology in the St. Lawrence Valley and northwest Adirondack lowlands; Geological Studies of the Northwest Adirondack region; Fieldtrip guidebook, 43rd Annual meeting, the New York State Annual Meeting, Potsdam, New York, C–O to C–43.

Hartnagel, Chris A. (1907) Geologic map of the Rochester and Ontario Beach quadrangles; N.Y. State Mus. Bull. 114.

(1927) The mining and quarry industries in New York from 1919 to 1924; N.Y. State Mus. Bull. 273.

Hartnagel, Chris A. and Broughton, John G. (1951) The Mining and Quarry Industries of New York State, 1937 to 1948; N.Y. State Mus. Bull. 343.

Harnum, Eric G. (1968) A systematic study of the minerals of the Niagara Stone Division quarry; Rocks and Minerals, v. 43, no. 8, p. 563–568.

Hawes, G. W. (1878) Analysis of pyroxene from Edenville, N.Y.; Amer. Jour. Sci., Ser. 3, 16, p. 597.

Hawkins, Alfred C. (1925) Fluorite from Rochester, New York; Amer. Mineral., v. 10, p. 34–36.

(1926) Notes on pyrite and celestite from Rochester, New York; Amer. Mineral., v. 11, p. 165.

(1948) James Greenfield Manchester; Rocks and Minerals, v. 23, p. 916–918.

Hawley, David and Potter, Donald B. (1960) Guidebook for field trips, 32nd Annual Meeting, N.Y. State Geol. Ass'n., Hamilton College, Clinton, New York.

Heinrich, E. William (1946) Studies in the mica group. The biotite-phlogopite series; Amer. Jour. Sci., vol. 244, p. 836–848.

(1958) Mineralogy and Geology of Radioactive Raw Materials, 654 p.; McGraw-Hill, New York.

(1976) The Mineralogy of Michigan; Geological Survey Division, Bull. 6, 225 p.

Heinrich, E. Wm., Levinson, A. A., Levandowski, D. W. and Hewitt, C. H. (1953) Studies in the natural history of micas; Univ. of Michigan Eng. Res. Inst. Project M 978.

Hess, H.H. (1962) A. F. Buddington, an appreciation: Petrologic Studies; Geol. Soc. Amer., Buddington Volume, p. VI–XI.

Heusser, George (1976) An update on collecting around Ellenville; Rocks and Minerals, vol. 51, p. 339–340.

(1977) The Shawangunk Mountain Lead-Zinc Deposit: Rocks and Minerals, Vol. 52, No. 10, Dec. 1977.

Hewitt, Phillip C., McClennan, William E. Jr., Nilsson, Harold (1965) Geological Phenomena in the Schenectady area; Geyser Park and the Vale of Springs; Guidebook to Field Trips in the Schenectady area: 37th Annual Meeting, N.Y. State Geol. Ass'n., p. D1–D13.

Hey, Max H. (1955) An Index of Mineral Species and Varieties Arranged Chemically with an Alphabetical Index of Accepted Mineral Names and Synonyms, Second Ed., 728 p.; British Museum, London.

(1963) Appendix, 135 p.; British Museum, London.

(1966) Catalog of Meteorites, 3rd Edition, 637 p.; British Museum, London.

Hey, Max H. and Embrey, Peter G. (1974) A Second Appendix to the Second Edition of An Index of Mineral Species and Varieties arranged chemically, British Museum, 168 p.

Hidden, William E. (1888) Xenotime from New York City; Amer. Jour. Sci., Ser. 3, 36, p. 380.

Hillebrand, W. F. (1896) Wollastonite, Oneida County, N.Y.; Amer. Jour. Sci., Ser. 4, p. 323.

Hills, Allan and Gast, P. W. (1964) Age of Pyroxene-hornblende granite gneiss of the eastern Adirondacks by the rubidum-strontium whole-rock method; Geol. Soc. Amer. Bull. v. 75, p. 759–766.

Hoadley, Charles W. (1928) Some mineral localities in Orange County, New York; Rocks and Minerals, v. 3, p. 33–34.

Hogarth, Donald D. (1977) Personal Communication.

Hogarth, Donald D. and Griffin, W. L. (1976) New data on Lazurite; Lithos, 9, p. 39–54.

Holden, Edward F. (1924) The cause of color in rose quartz; Amer. Miner, 9, p. 75–88, 101–107.

(1925) The cause of color in smoky quartz and amethyst; Amer. Mineral., 10, p. 203–252.

Hollick, Charles Arthur (1893) Mineralogical notes (Staten Island, N.Y.); Nat. Sci. Ass'n., Staten Island, 4, p. 6–7.

(1905) A recent discovery of amber on Staten Island; Jour. N.Y. Bot. Garden, vol. VI, no. 63.

(1905a) Additional notes on the occurrence of amber at Kreischerville; Proc. Nat. Sci. Ass'n of Staten Island, vol. IX, p. 35–36.

(1906) Origin of the amber found on Staten Island, N.Y.; Bot. Garden Jour., 7, p. 11–12.

(1908) Chemical analyses of Cretaceous amber from Kreischerville (Staten Island, N.Y.); Staten Island Ass'n., Proc. 2, p. 34.

(1910) Notes in connection with specimens recently obtained from serpentines of Staten Island; Abst., N.Y. Acad. Sci., Ann., 19, p. 315–317.

Holmes, Chauncey D. (1952) Drift dispersion in west central New York; Geol. Soc. Amer., v. 63, p. 993–1010.

(1960) Evolution of till-stone shapes, Central New York; Geol. Soc. Amer. Bull., v. 71, p. 1645–1660.

Hopkins, T. C. (1914) The Geology of the Syracuse quadrangle; N.Y. State Mus. Bull. 171.

Hornaday, W. T. (1896) The King of Museum Builders; The Commercial Travelers Home Magazine, Feb. 1896.

Horton, William (1843) List of minerals found in Orange County, N.Y.; Geol. Surv., N.Y. District, p. 577.

(1848) Mineral localities in New York; Amer. Jour. Sci., Ser. 2, 5. p. 132.

Hough, Franklin B. (1948) Mineral localities in New York; Amer. Jour. Sci., Ser. 2, 5, p. 132.

(1850) On the discovery of sulphuret of nickel in northern New York; Amer. Jour. Sci., Ser. 2, 9, p. 287.

(1850a) New Mineral Localities in New York; Amer. Jour. Sci., Ser. 2, 9, p. 288.

(1850b) On existing mineral localities of Lewis, Jefferson and St. Lawrence counties, New York; Amer. Jour. Sci., Ser. 2, 9, p. 424–430.

(1853) History of St. Lawrence and Franklin counties, New York, 719 p. Little & Co., Albany, N.Y.

(1854) A History of Jefferson County in the State of New York, 601 p. Sterling & Riddell; Watertown, N.Y.

Hovey, Edmund O. (1895) Notes on some specimens of minerals from Washington Heights, N.Y. City; Amer. Mus. Nat. Hist., Bull. 7, p. 341.

(1896) Notes on some specimens of minerals from Washington Heights, N.Y. City; The Mineral Collector, v. II, no. 11, p. 175–176.

Hubbard, O. P. (1837) Geological and mineralogical notices (Northern New York); Amer. Jour. Sci., Ser. 1, 32, p. 230–235.

Hunt, T. S. (1849) On the acid springs amd gypsum deposits of the Onondaga salt group; Amer. Jour. Sci., Ser. 2, 7, p. 175.

(1851) On the chemical constitution of the mineral warwickite; Amer. Jour. Sci., Ser. 2, 11, p. 352.

Hurlbut, Cornelius S. Jr. (1968) Minerals and Man, 304 p.; Random House, New York.

(1971) Dana's Manual of Mineralogy, 18th Ed., 579 p. Wiley, New York.

Hurlbut, Cornelius S. Jr. and Klein, Cornelis (1977) Manual of Mineralogy, 19th ed. Wiley, 532 p.

Hyde, Floy S. (1974) Adirondack Forests, Fields, and Mines, 223 p. North Country Books, Lakemont.

Ingham, Albert Irwin (1940) The zinc and lead deposits of Shawangunk Mountains, New York; Econ. Geol., v. 35, p. 751-760.

Isachsen, Ingvar W. (1965) Field trips in the Schenectady area, Albany to the Glen via Lake George; N.Y. State Geol. Ass'n., 37th Annual meeting, p. B1 to B17.

        (1969) Editor, Origin of Anorthosite and Related Rocks; N.Y. State Mus. Memoir 12, 466 p.

Isachsen, Ingvar W. and Moxham, R. L. (1969) Chemical variation in plagioclase megacripts from two vertical sections in the main Adirondack metamorthosite massif.; N.Y. State Museum and Science Service Memoir 18, p. 255-265.

Izard, John E. and Clemancy, Charles V. (1967) X-ray study of the sedimentary pyrite of western New York; Jour. Sed. Petr., p. 221-225.

Jackson, C. J. (1851) On eupyrchroite of Crown Point, N.Y.; Amer. Jour. Sci., Ser. 2, 12, p. 73.

Jackson, Charles T. (1866) On calcite from Martinsburg, New York; Boston Soc. Nat. Hist. Proc. 10, p. 97.

Jaffe, Howard W. and Jaffe, Elizabeth B. (1975) Preliminary report on bedrock geology of the 15' Mount Marcy quadrangle, New York; Empire State Geogram, v. 11, no. 1, p. 3.

Jahns, Richard H. (1955) The study of pegmatites; Econ. Geol., Fiftieth Anniversary volume, Part II, p. 1025-1130.

Januzzi, Ronald E. (1959) The minerals of western Connecticut and southeastern New York.

Jensen, David E. (1942) Minerals of the Lockport dolomite in the vicinity of Rochester, N.Y.; Rocks and Minerals, v. 17, no. 6, p. 199-203.

        (1954) The Septaria of Bare Hill; Rocks and Minerals, v. 29, nos. 5-6, p. 241-244.

        (1955) Gem and Ornamental Minerals of New York State; Lapidary Journal, v. 9, no. 1, p. 24-28.

        (1961) Memorial to Harold Lattimore Alling; Amer. Miner. v. 46, p. 471-474.

        (1976) Minerals and Gem Materials from New York State; Lapidary Journal, vol. 30, no. 1, p. 82-94.

        (1977) 114 years of a business started with a pebble; Lapidary Journal, vol. 30, no. 11, p. 2486-2494.

        P.O. Personal observation.

Jensen, David E. and Wishart, James S. (1956) Personal notes.

Jessup, A. E. (1822) Geological and mineralogical notice of a portion of the northeastern part of the state of New York; Philadelphia Acad. Sci., Jour., 2, p. 185.

Johnson, S. W. (1851) On Houghite of Prof. Shepard; Amer. Jour. Sci., Ser. 2, 12, p. 361.

Judd, Edward K. (1908) An arsenic mine in Putnam County, New York; Eng. Min. Jour., 85, p. 306.

Julien, A. A. (1882) On the serpentine of Staten and New York Islands; N.Y. Acad. Sci., trans., 1, p. 58.

Kaplan, Stuart A. (1965) A Guide to Information Sources in Mining; Minerals and Geosciences, 599 p. Wiley, New York.

Kay, Marshall and Grossman, William L. (1953) Geology of the Utica quadrangle, New York; N.Y. State Mus. Bull. 374.

Kays, M. Allan (1965) Petrographic and Modal relations, Sanford Hill Titaniferous magnetite deposit; Econ. Geol., v. 60, p. 1261–1297.

Kearns, Lance E. (1978) The Amity Area, Orange County, New York; The Mineralogical Record, Vol. 9, No. 2, Mar.–Apr. 1978, p. 85–90.

Kemp, James Furman (1890) Notes on the minerals occurring near Port Henry, N.Y.; Amer. Jour. Sci., Ser. 3, 40, p. 62.

(1894) Gabbros on the western shore of Lake Champlain; Geol. Soc. Amer., Bull. v. 5, p. 213–224.

(1895) The geology of the Moriah and Westport Townships, Essex County, N.Y.; N.Y. State Mus. Bull. 14.

(1895a) Preliminary report on the geology of Essex County; N.Y. State Mus., 49th Ann. Report, p. 579–614.

(1898) Geology of the magnetites near Port Henry, N.Y. and especially those of Mineville; Amer. Inst. Mining Eng., trans. 27, p. 146.

(1898a) Geology of the Lake Placid Quadrangle; N.Y. State Mus. Bull. 21.

(1906) The ore deposits of the United States and Canada, 481 p.; McGraw-Hill, New York.

(1912) The Mineral Springs of Saratoga; N.Y. State Mus. Bull. 159.

(1920) Geology of the Mount Marcy quadrangle, Essex County, New York; N.Y. State Mus. Bull. 229–230.

Kemp, James F. and Alling, Harold L. (1925) Geology of the Ausable quadrangle; N.Y. State Mus. Bull. 261.

Kemp, James F. and Hollick, Arthur (1894) The Granite of Mounts Adam and Eve. Warwick, Orange Co., N.Y. and its contact phenomena; Ann. N.Y. Acad. Sci., v. VII, p. 638–650.

Kemp, James F. and Ruedemann, Rudolf (1910) Geology of the Elizabethtown quadrangle; N.Y. State Mus. Bull. 138.

Kerr, Paul F. (1930) Kaolinite from a Brooklyn subway tunnel; Amer. Mineral., v. 15, p. 144–158.

(1932) Kaolinite from the terminal moraine of Staten Island; Amer. Mineral., v. 17, no. 1, p. 29–34.

(1935) U-Galena and uraninite in Bedford, New York, Cyrtolite; Amer. Mineral., v. 20, p. 443–450.

(1959) Optical Mineralogy; McGraw-Hill, New York.

Kerr, Paul F. and Hamilton, P. K. (1949) Glossary of Clay Mineral names; Preliminary Report No. 1, Amer. Petroleum Inst., Project 49, Clay Mineral Standards.

Kinney, H. D. (1910) A new anthophyllite occurrence on Manhattan Island: N.Y. Acad. Sci., trans. 19, p. 308.

Kirchoff, Oscar (1933) Personal communication—Fresh water molluscs containing pearls from Flint Creek, Ontario Co.

Knight, Nicholas (1903) Apatite crystals, Antwerp, New York; The American Geologist, 31, p. 62.

Koeberlin, F. R. (1909) The Brewster Iron-bearing district of New York; Econ. Geol. v. XI, p. 713–754.

Kostov, Ivan (1968) Mineralogy; translation by Peter Embry, 587 p. Oliver & Boyd, Edinburgh.

Kraus, Edward H. (1904) The occurrence of celestite near Syracuse, N.Y. and its relation to the vermicular limestones of the Salina epoch; Amer. Jour. Sci., 18, p. 30–39.

Kraus, Edward Henry and Slawson, Chester Baker (1947) Gems and gem materials; p. 332; McGraw Hill, 2nd ed.

Kreidler, William L. (1957) Occurrence of Silurian salt in New York State; N.Y. State Mus. and Science Service Bull. 361.

Kreiger, Medora Hooper (1937) Geology of the Thirteenth Lake quadrangle, N.Y.; N.Y. State Mus. Bull. 308.

Kunitz, W. (1929) Uvite (a var. of Tourmaline); Chem. Erde IV, no. 5, p. 214, no. 9, p. 217.

Kunz, George Frederick (1886) An almandite garnet crystal found in New York City (Thirty-fifth Street between Broadway and Seventh Avenue); N.Y. Acad. Sci., trans., 5, p. 265–266.

(1887) Minerals from Fort George, New York City; N.Y. Acad. Sci. trans., 7, p. 48–49.

(1888) Apatite from Yonkers, N.Y.; Amer. Jour. Sci., Ser. 3, p. 72.

(1889) Mineralogical notes on fluorite, etc.; Amer. Jour. Sci., Ser. 3, v. 38, p. 72–73.

(1892) Gems and Precious Stones of North America, 367 p. Scientific Publishing Co., New York.

Kunz, George F. and Stevenson, Charles H. (1908) The Book of the Pearl.

La Buz, Adrian L. (1968) Sphalerite-galena occurrences in central New York; Rocks and Minerals, v. 43, no. 5, p. 323–378.

(1969) The "Herkimer diamond" grounds; Rocks and Minerals, v. 44, no. 4, p. 243–250.

LaChapelle, Edward R. (1969) Field Guide to Snow Crystals, University of Washington Press, Seattle, 101 p.

Landis, E. K. (1900) The Tilly Foster mine (New York); Franklin Inst. Jour., 150, p. 223.

Lange, Ervin F. (1975) The Founders of American Meteorites; Meteoritics, v. 10, no. 3.

Lapham, Jerome F. (1955) Overlook feldspar quarry; Rocks and Minerals, p. 484.

Larsen, Esper S. (1921) The Microscopic determination of the Nonopaque minerals; U.S. Geol. Surv. Bull. 679.

(1928) The optical properties of the humite group; Amer. Mineral., v. 13, p. 354–359.

Larsen, Esper S. and Berman, Harry (1934) The microscopic determination of the non opaque minerals; U.S. Geol. Surv. Bull. 848.

Larsen, Esper S. and Schaller, Waldemar T. (1932) Serendibite from Warren County, New York and its paragenesis; Amer. Mineral., v. 17, p. 457–465.

Lea, Edgar R. and Dill, David B. (1968) Zinc deposits of the Balmat-Edwards district; Amer. Inst. Mining Eng., Graton-Sales volume, p. 20–48.

Leake, Bernard E. (1968) A catalog of analysed calciferous and sub-calciferous amphiboles together with their nomenclature and associated minerals; Geol. Soc. Am., Special paper 98.

Lee, C. A. (1824) Notice of the Ancram lead mine; Amer. Jour. Sci., Ser. 1, 8. p. 247–250.

Lee, O. Ivan (1928) The Mineralogy of hafnium; Chemical Reviews, 5:17–37.

Leeds, A. (1873) Augite from Amity, N.Y.; Amer. Jour. Sci., Ser. 3, 6, p. 24.

Leonard, Benjamin F. III (1951) Magnetite deposits of the St. Lawrence County District, New York; unpublished PhD dissertation, Princeton University, Princeton, N.J.

Leonard, Benjamin F. III, Hildebrand, Fred A. and Vlisidis, Angelina C., (1962) Members of the ludwigite-vonsenite series and their distinction from ilvaite; Petrologic Studies; Geol. Soc. Amer., Buddington volume, p. 523–568.

Leonard, Benjamin F. III and Vlisidis, A. C. (1960) Vonsenite from St. Lawrence County, New York; Amer. Mineral., v. 45, p. 439–442.

Lessing, Peter (1969) Jordanite at Balmat, New York; Econ. Geol., v. 64, p. 932.

Lessing, Peter and Grout, C. MacDonald (1971) Haüynite from Edwards, New York; Amer. Mineral., v. 56, p. 1096–1100.

Levin, S. B., (1950) Genesis of some Adirondack garnet deposits; Geol. Soc. Amer. Bull., v. 61, p. 519–566.

Levinson, A. A. and Heinrich, E. W. (1954) Studies in the mica group; Single crystal data on phlogopites; biotites and manganophyllites; Amer. Mineral., v. 39, p. 937–945.

Levinson, Wallace Gould (1901) Crystals of chrysoberyl from the Borough of Manhattan, New York City; Published by the author.

⸻ (1916) The New York Mineralogical Club; Amer. Mineral., Vol. 1, No. 1, p. 10–11.

Lindgren, Waldemar (1937) Mineral Deposits, 930 p.; McGraw-Hill, New York.

Loomis, F. B. (1903) The dwarf fauna of the pyrite layer at the horizon of the Tully limestone in western New York; N.Y. State Mus. Bull. 69.

Loveman, Michael H. (1911) Geology of the Philips pyrite mine near Peekskill, New York; Econ. Geol., 6, p. 231–246.

Lowe, Kirt Emil (1950) Storm King Granite at Bear Mountain, New York; Geol. Soc. Amer., v. 61, p. 137–190.

Luedke, Elaine M., Wrucke, Chester T., and Graham, John A. (1959) Mineral occurrences of New York State with selected references to each locality; U.S. Geol. Surv. Bull. 1072F.

Luquer, Lea McIlvane (1893) Mineralogical Notes (minerals from Kings Bridge, Amity and Sing Sing, N.Y.); School of Mines Quarterly 14, p. 327–329.

⸻ (1896) The minerals of the pegmatite veins at Bedford, N.Y.; Amer. Geologist, 18, p. 259–261.

⸻ (1904) Bedford cyrtolite; Amer. Geologist, 36, p. 17–19.

Luquer, Lea McIlvane and Ries, Heinrich (1896) The "Augen" gneiss area, pegmatite veins and diorite dikes at Bedford, New York; Amer. Geol., vol. 18, p. 239–261.

Luther, D. Dana (1894) Geology of the Livonia Salt shaft; N.Y. State Mus., 47th Ann. Rep't., p. 219–257.

Luther, Frank R. (1976) A chemical reaction for formation of the Gore Mountain garnet deposit, Warren County, New York; Geol. Soc. Amer., Northeast Section, Abstracts, 11th Annual Meeting, vol. 8, no. 2, Feb. 1976.

Mac Farland, J. (1878) Discovery of rock salt at Wyoming in western New York; Amer. Jour. Sci., Ser. 3, 16, p. 144.

Manchester, James G. (1910) Asterated rose quartz in (Bedford) New York State; Miner. World, 32, p. 1185–1186.

⸻ (1912) A new discovery of gemstones on Manhattan Island; Abst. N.Y. Acad. Sci., Ann., 21, p. 206.

⸻ (1914) The minerals of Broadway, New York City; published by the New York Mineralogical Club, No. 3.

⸻ (1931) The Minerals of New York City and its Environs; Bulletin of the New York Mineralogical Club, v. 3, no. 1, 165 p., 127 plates.

Manchester, James G. and Stanton, Gilman S. (1917) A discovery of gem garnet in New York City; Amer. Miner., vol. 11, no. 7, p. 85–86.

Manley, Frederick Harrison, Jr. (1959) Heavy mineral study of the Upper Devonian Catskill facies of south central New York; Unpublished M.S. thesis, University of Rochester, Rochester, New York.

Marble, John P. (1943) Possible age of allanite from Whiteface Mountain, Essex County, New York; Amer. Jour. Sci., v. 241, no. 1, p. 32–42.

Martens, James H. C. (1924) Scorodite from Putnam County, New York; Amer. Mineral., v. 9, p. 27–28.

        (1924) Igneous Rocks by Ithaca, New York and Vicinity; Geol. Soc. Amer. Bull. 35, p. 305–320.

        (1925) Sulfate minerals from the weathering of shale near Ithaca, New York; Amer. Mineral., v. 10, p. 175–176.

        (1927) Note on minerals from the Mahopac mine, Putnam County, New York; Amer. Mineral., v. 12, p. 56.

Martin, James C. (1916) The Precambrian rocks of the Canton quadrangle; N.Y. State Mus. Bull. 185.

Martin, R. Torrence (1954) Illite in the Enfield shale from southern New York; Amer. Mineral., v. 39, p. 149.

Mason, Brian (1962) Meteorites, 274 p., Wiley, New York.

Mason, Brian and Berry, Leonard G. (1968) Elements of Mineralogy, 550 p.; Freeman, San Francisco.

Mason, Brian and Wiik, H. B. (1960) The Tomhannock Creek, New York chondrite; Min. Mag., v. 32, p. 528–534.

Mather, J. H. and Brockett, L. P. (1848) A Geographical History of New York.

Mather, William Williams (1830) On xanthite and its crystalline form, with a notice of mineral localities (Orange County, N.Y.); Amer. Jour. Sci., Ser. 1, 18, p. 359–361.

        (1843) Geology of New York, Part I, Geology of the First Geological District, Albany.

Maynard, J. E. and Ploger, Louis W. (1946) A study of the Salt Springs road peridotite dike in Syracuse, New York; Amer. Mineral., v. 31, p. 471–485.

McElroy, Egbert (1939) Some old mineral localities; The Mineralogist, vol. VII, no. 6, p. 239.

McKelvey, Blake (1946) When Science was on trial in Rochester: 1850–1890; Rochester History, vol. VIII, no. 4, p. 1–24.

McKeown, F. A. and Klemic, Harry (1956) Rare earth-bearing apatite at Mineville, Essex County, New York; U.S. Geol. Surv. Bull., 1046B.

Meade, William (1830) New locality of zircon (Orange County, N.Y.); Amer. Jour. Sci., Ser. 1, 17, p. 196–197.

Merrill, Frederick James Hamilton (1895) Mineral resources of N.Y. State; N.Y. State Mus. Bull., 15, p. 365–395.

Merrill, G. P. (1889) On the ophiolite of Thurman, Warren County, New York with remarks on the Eozoon Canadense; Amer. Jour. Sci., Ser. 3, 37, p. 189.

        (1890) Notes on the serpentinous rocks of Essex County, N.Y.; from Aqueduct Shaft 26, N.Y. City and from near Easton, Pa.; U.S. Nat. Mus. Proc. 12, p. 595.

        (1906) Contributions to the history of geology; Report of the U.S. Nat. Mus. for 1904, p. 187–734.

        (1924) The first one hundred years of American geology; Yale University Press, New Haven, 773 p.

Miller, William J. (1910) Geology of the Port Leyden Quadrangle, Lewis County, New York; N.Y. State Mus. Bull. 135.

(1911) Geology of the Broadalbin Quadrangle, Fulton, Saratoga Counties, New York; N.Y. State Mus. Bull. 153.

(1912) The garnet deposits of Warren County, New York; Econ. Geol., VII, p. 493–501.

(1913) The Garnet deposits of Warren County; N.Y. State Mus. Bull. 164.

(1914) Geology of the North Creek quadrangle, Warren County, New York; N.Y. State Mus. Bull. 170.

(1916) Geology of the Lake Pleasant quadrangle, Hamilton County, New York; N.Y. State Mus. Bull. 182.

(1916a) Geology of the Blue Mountain Lake; N.Y. State Mus. Bull. 192.

(1917) The Adirondack Mountains; N.Y. State Mus. Bull. 193.

(1918) Geology of the Lake Placid Quadrangle; N.Y. State Mus. Bull. 211–212.

(1918a) Geology of the Schroon Lake Quadrangle; N.Y. State Mus. Bull. 213–214.

(1918b) Adirondack anorthosite; Geol. Amer. Bull. v. 29, p. 399–462.

(1921) Some crystal localities in St. Lawrence County, New York; Amer. Mineral., v. 6, p. 77–79.

(1921a) Geology of the Luzerne quadrangle; N.Y. State Mus. Bull. 245–246.

(1926) Geology of the Lyon Mountain quadrangle; N.Y. State Mus. Bull. 271.

Mills, F. S. (1908) The Economic Geology of Northern New York; Eng. and Mining Jour., v. 85, p. 396–398.

Milner, Henry G. (1962) Sedimentary Petrography, 4th Ed., Vol. I, Methods, 643 p.

Vol. II Principles and Applications, 715 p. MacMillian, N.Y.

Ming, Li-Chung (1971) Green Phlogopite in Talcville, New York; Unpublished M.S. thesis at University of Rochester, Rochester, New York.

Mitchill, Samuel L. (1797) A sketch of the mineralogical history of the State of New York. Description of the Islands; Medical Repository, v. 1, IV.

(1810) Descriptive Catalogue accompanying a suite of mineral specimens presented to the Editor by his colleague, S. L. Mitchill, M.D., Professor of Natural History and Botany, in the University of the State of New York. (These pieces were collected during a tour made, in the summer of 1809, to Niagara (Bruce, 1810) The American Mineralogical Journal, Vol. 1, p. 1–5).

Monahan, Joseph W. (1928) Minerals in eastern exposures of the Lockport in eastern New York State; Amer. Mineral., v. 13, no. 2, p. 70–71.

Moore, E. S. (1952) Memorial to Heinrich Ries; Proceedings Volume of the Geol. Soc. Amer. for 1951, p. 141–144.

Moses, Alfred J. (1893) Mineralogical notes; pyrite from Kings Bridge, New York; Amer. Jour. Sci., Ser. 3, 45, p. 488.

Moyd, Louis (1976) Personal Communication.

Muench, O. B. (1931) Analysis of cyrtolite for lead and uranium; Amer. Jour. Sci., 5th Ser. v. 21, p. 350–357.

Nason, F. L. (1888) Some New York minerals and their localities; N.Y. State Mus. Bull. 4.

(1893) Notes on some of the iron-bearing rock of the Adirondack Mountains; Amer. Geologist, 17, p. 75.

Navias, Robert A. and Ostrom, John H. (1951) The occurrence of Chrysoberyl at Greenfield, N.Y.; Amer. Jour. Sci., v. 249, p. 308–311.

Nelson, Arthur E. (1968) Geology of the Ohio quadrangle, southwestern part of the Adirondack Mountains, New York; U.S. Geol. Surv. Bull., 1251 F.

Nevius, J. Nelson (1899) Talc industry of St. Lawrence County, N.Y.; N.Y. State Mus., 51st Ann. Report, p. 1–121.

(1901) Emery mines of Westchester County (New York); N.Y. State Mus. Ann. Report 53, p. 151–154.

Newland, David Hale (1901) The serpentines of Manhattan Island and their accompanying minerals; Sch. Mines Quarterly 22, p. 307–317, 399–410.

(1905) The mining and quarry industry of New York State 1904; N.Y. State Mus. Bull. 93.

(1906) The mining and quarry industry of New York State; N.Y. State Mus. Bull. 102.

(1908) Geology of the Adirondack Magnetic Iron Ores; N.Y. State Mus. Bull. 119.

(1909) Gypsum Deposits of New York; N.Y. State Mus. Bull. 143.

(1910) Mining and quarry industry of New York State during 1907; N.Y. State Mus. Bull. 120.

(1916) The Quarry Materials of New York; granite, gneiss, trap and marble; N.Y. State Mus. Bull. 181.

(1919) The Mineral resources of the State of New York; N.Y. State Mus. Bull. 223, 224.

(1929) The gypsum resources and gypsum industry of New York; N.Y. State Mus. Bull. 283.

(1933) The prospects for gold discoveries in New York State; N.Y. State Mus. Circular 12.

(1935) Minerals of Whiteface Mountain; Rocks and Minerals, v. 10, no. 6, p. 81–82.

(1936) Mineralogy and origin of the taconic limonites; Econ. Geol., vol. 31, p. 133–135.

(1937) Herkimer County quartz crystals; Rocks and Minerals, vol. 12, p. 36–37.

(1942) The geology of the Catskill and Kaaterskill quadrangles; Part I, Cambrian and Ordovician geology of the Catskill quadrangle; N.Y. State Mus. Bull. 331. (Economic Geology, p. 239–241.)

Newland, David H. and Hartnagel, C.A. (1908) Iron ores of the Clinton formation in New York State; N.Y. State Mus. Bull. 123.

(1932) The mining and quarry industries of New York for 1927 to 1929; N.Y. State Mus. Bull. 295.

(1936) Mining and Quarry Industries of New York State for 1930–1933; N.Y. State Mus. Bull. 305.

(1939) The mining and quarry industries of New York State for 1934 to 1936; N.Y. State Mus. Bull. 319.

Newland, David H. and Kemp, James F. (1908) Geology of the Adirondack magnetite iron ores—with a report on the Mineville-Port Henry group; N.Y. State Mus. Bull. 119.

Newland, David H. and Leighton, Henry (1910a) Gypsum deposits of New York; N.Y. State Mus. Bull. 143.

Newland, David H. and Vaughn, D. (1942) Guide to the Geology of the Lake George region; N.Y. State Mus. Handbook 19.

Nier, A. O. (1939) The isotopic composition of lead and the measurement of geologic time III; Phy. Rev., v. 60, p. 112–116.

Nininger, Harvey H. (1933) Our stone pelted planet; Amer. Meteorite Mus., Ariz.

Nininger, Harvey H. and Nininger, Addie D. (1959) The Nininger Collection of Meteorites; Amer. Meteorite Mus., Sedona, Ariz.

Niven, William (1895) On a new locality for xenotime, monazite, etc. on Manhattan Island; Amer. Jour. Sci., Ser. 3, 50, p. 75.

    (1930) My mineral discoveries since 1879; Rocks and Minerals, v. 5, no. 3, p. 73–76.

Nuwer, Henry J. (1971) The Tilly Foster Mine; Rocks and Minerals, v. 46, no. 3, p. 147–154.

Ogilvie, Olga H. (1904) The geology of the Paradox Lake quadrangle, New York; N.Y. State Mus. Bull. 96.

Okulewicz, Steven C. (1977) Petrology of The Staten Island Alpine Ultramafic, Staten Island, New York; Geol. Soc. Amer., Abstracts Northeast Section 12th Annual Meeting, p. 307.

Onyeagocha, Anthony C. and Seifert, Karl E. (1971) Optical properties of Adirondack plagioclases; Amer. Miner., v. 56, p. 1199–1207.

Page, L. R. (1950) Uranium in pegmatites; Econ. Geol., 45, 12–34.

Palache, Charles, Berman, Harry, and Frondel, Clifford; The System of Mineralogy—Seventh Edition: Wiley, New York.

    (1944) Volume I, Elements, Sulfides, Sulfo-salts, Osides, 834 p.

    (1951) Volume II, Halides, Nitrates, Borates, Carbonates, Sulfates, Phosphates, Arsenates, Tungstates, Molybdates, etc., 1124 p.

Palmer, Donald F. (1970) Geology and ore deposits near Benson Mines, New York; Econ. Geol., v. 65, p. 31–39.

Parker, Arthur E. (1920) Archaeological History of New York, Parts I & II; N.Y. State Mus. Bull. 235–236.

    (1924) The great Algonquin flint mines at Coxsackie; Researches and trans. N.Y. State Arch. Ass'n, Lewis Henry Morgan Chapter.

Payne, Thomas G. (1938) The Genesee Country; Guide Bulletin No. 5, Rochester Museum of Arts and Sciences.

Pearl, Richard (1971) Cleaning and Preserving Minerals, 810 p. Maxwell.

Pegau, A. A. and Bates, J. D. (1941) Some little known minerals of the Bear Mountain section of the Hudson Highlands, New York; Amer. Mineral., v. 26, no. 11, p. 673–674.

Penfield, Samuel Lewis (1888) A very pure magnesian mica, phlogopite, from Edwards, St. Lawrence County, N.Y.; Amer. Jour. Sci., Ser. 3, 36, p. 329.

Penfield, Samuel Lewis and Foote, H. W. (1896) Hortonolite from Orange County, New York; Amer. Jour. Sci., Ser. 4, 1, p. 131.

Penfield, Samuel Lewis and Ford, Wm E. (1900) Calcite crystals from Union Springs, New York; Amer. Jour. Sci., Ser. 4, 10, p. 237.

Penfield, Samuel Lewis and Howe, W. T. H. (1894) On the chemical composition of chondrodite, humite and clinohumite; Amer. Jour. Sci., Ser. 3, 47, p. 188.

Penfield, Samuel Lewis and Stanley, F. C. (1907) On the chemical composition of amphibole (describes edenite, hornblende and hudsonite from Orange County, New York); Amer. Jour. Sci., Ser. 4, 23, p. 38–51.

Phair, George (1969) The founding of the Mineralogical Society of America; Amer. Mineral., v. 54, p. 1244–1255.

Philips, Alexander H. (1924) Thompsonite from Peekskill, New York; Amer. Mineral., v. 9, no. 12, p. 240–241.

Platt, Robert Melvin (1949) Lead and zinc occurrence in the Lockport dolomite of New York State; unpublished M.S. thesis at the University of Rochester, Rochester, New York.

Pough, Frederick H. (1936) Bertrandite and epistilbite from Bedford, New York; Amer. Mineral., v. 21, p. 264–265.

——— (1940) Willemite morphology and paragenesis at Balmat, New York; Amer. Mineral., v. 25, p. 488–496.

——— (1941) Occurrence of willemite; Amer. Mineral., v. 26, p. 92–102.

——— (1949) Memorial of Herbert Percy Whitlock; Amer. Mineral., vol. 34, p. 261–266.

——— (1953) A field guide to rocks and minerals, 333 p.; Houghton-Mifflin, Cambridge.

Prucha, John J. (1953) The white crystal dolomite near Gouverneur, New York: N.Y. State Sci. Service Report, Inv. 9, 13 p., 2 maps.

——— (1956) Geology of the Brewster magnetite district of southeastern New York; N.Y. State Mus. and Sci. Service circular 43.

——— (1957) Pyrite deposits of St. Lawrence and Jefferson Counties, New York; N.Y. State Mus. and Sci. Service Bull. 357.

Rabbitt, John C. (1948) A study of the anthrophyllite series; Amer. Mineral., v. 33, p. 263–323.

Ramdohr, Paul (1969) The Ore Minerals and their Intergrowths, 1174 p., English Translation of the 3rd Ed.; Pergamon Press, Oxford.

Ransome, Jay Ellis (1974) Gems and minerals of America, 705 p.; Harper and Row, New York.

Raymond, R. W. (1876) Spathic iron ores of the Hudson River; Amer. Inst. Min. Eng., trans. 4, p. 339–343.

——— (1894) Pyrrotite deposits at Anthony's Nose, N.Y.; Amer. Inst. Min. Eng., trans. 24, p. 886–888.

Reasenberg, Julian (1968) New artinite find on Staten Island, New York; Rocks and Minerals, v. 43, no. 9, p. 643–647.

Reimann, Irving (1938) The Geological Collection: Seventy-five years, A history of the Buffalo Society of Natural Sciences, 1861–1936, v. XVIII, p. 106–110; Buffalo Society of Natural Sciences, Buffalo, N.Y.

Richardson, Charles H. (1917) Building Stones and Clays, 437 p.; Published by the author, Syracuse, N.Y.

Rickard, Lawrence V. (1975) Correlation of the Silurian and Devonian rocks in New York State; N.Y. State Mus. and Science Service, map and chart, series no. 24.

Rickard, Lawrence V. and Zenger, Donald H. (1964) Stratigraphy and paleontology of the Richfield Springs and Cooperstown quadrangles, New York; N.Y. State Mus. Bull. 396.

Ries, Heinrich (1894) List and Bibliography of the minerals occurring in Warwick Township; Ann. N.Y. Acad. Sci., v. VIII, p. 651–653.

——— (1895) The Monoclinic pyroxenes of New York State; Ann., N.Y. Acad. Sci., (Lyceum Nat. Hist. N.Y.) v. IX, p. 124–180. (Publ. 1896–1897).

——— (1895a) Geology of Orange County; N.Y. State Mus., 49th Ann. Rep't., v. 2, p. 393–476.

——— (1898) Allanite crystals from Mineville, Essex County, N.Y.; N.Y. Acad. Sci., 16, p. 327.

——— (1898a) Note on beryl crystal from N.Y. City; N.Y. Acad. Sci., Trans. 16, p. 329.

——— (1900) Clays of New York, Their properties and use; N.Y. State Mus.

Bull. 35, v. 7, p. 493, 944.

    (1930) Economic Geology, 860 p.; Wiley, New York.

Ritchie, William A. (1957) Traces of Early Man in the northeast; N.Y. State Mus. and Science Service Bull. 358.

    (1965) The Archaeology of New York State, 355 p.; Natural History Press, Garden City, N.Y.

Roberts, Willard L., Rapp, George and Weber, Julius (1974) Encyclopedia of Minerals, 693 p.; Van Nostrand Reinhold, New York.

Robinson, George (1971) Geological studies in the northwest Adirondacks, New York; 43rd Annual Meeting, The New York State Geological Association; Trip F, Mineral Collecting in St. Lawrence Co., p. F1–F9.

    (1973) DeKalb diopside; Lapidary Journal, p. 1040–1042, 1058–1059.

    (1975) Tremolite-Actinolite series, Euhedra et Cetera; The St. Lawrence Co. Rock and Mineral Club.

Robinson, George and Alverson, Schuyler (1971) Minerals of the St. Lawrence Valley.

Robinson, Samuel (1825) A Catalog of American Minerals with their localities.

Rodgers, John (1952) Absolute ages of radioactive minerals from the Appalachian region; Amer. Jour. Sci., v. 250, p. 411–427.

Roe, Arthur (1975) The C. U. Shepard Mineral Collection and the two Drs. Shepard: Mineralogical Record, v. 6, no. 5, Sept.-Oct. 1976, p. 253–257.

Rogers, Austin Flint (1929) Polysynthetic twinning in dolomite; Amer. Mineral., V. 14, p. 245–250.

Rogers, Gaillard Sherburne (1911) Geology of the Cortlandt series and its emery deposits; N.Y. Acad. Sci., A.N.N., 21, p. 11–86.

Root, E. W. (1868) On Wilsonite from St. Lawrence County, N.Y.; Amer. Jour. Sci., Ser. 2, 45, p. 47–48.

Root, O. (1852) On a mass of meteoric iron from near Seneca River; Amer. Jour. Sci., Ser. 2, 14, p. 439–440.

Rowley, Elmer B. (1942a) Huge tourmaline crystals discovered; The Mineralogist, v. X, no. 2, p. 42–48, 63–64.

    (1942b) A New York Find: The Mineralogist, v. X, no. 3, p. 96.

    (1948) Vesuvianite crystals from Essex County, New York; Rocks and Minerals, v. 23, nos. 11–12, p. 906–907.

    (1951) Crystal collecting at Saratoga Springs, N.Y.; Rocks and Minerals, v. 26, nos. 9–10, p. 528–532.

    (1955) Brown tourmaline, A new American locality; Rocks and Minerals, v. 30, nos. 9–10, p. 461–463.

    (1957) Epidote and allanite at Schroon Lake, New York; Rocks and Minerals, v. 32, nos. 9–10, p. 451–461.

    (1960) Monazite and cyrtolite at Day, New York pegmatite; Rocks and Minerals, v. 35, nos. 7–8, p. 328–330.

    (1962) Rare earth pegmatite discovered in Adirondack Mountain area, Essex County, New York; Rocks and Minerals, v. 37, nos. 7–8, p. 341–347; Part II, v. 37, nos. 9–10, p. 453–460.

    (1963) Rare earth pegmatite discovered in Adirondack Mountain area, Essex County, New York, Parts I and II; Geology and Mineralogy of the Adirondack Mountain region.

    (1967) Apatite crystals in pyrrhotite from Essex County, New York; Rocks and Minerals, v. 42, no. 2, p. 85–88.

    (1976) Personal communication.

Ruedemann, Rudolf (1930) Geology of the Capital District (Albany, Cohoes, Troy, and Schenectady quadrangles); N.Y. State Mus. Bull. 285.

(1931) Age and origin of the siderite and limonite of the Burden Iron Mines near Hudson, New York; N.Y. State Museum Bull. 286, p. 135–152.

Ruedemann, Rudolf and Goldring, Winifred (1944) Memorial to David H. Newland; Proceedings Volume of the Geol. Soc. Amer., Ann. Rept. for 1943, p. 209–216.

Sack, Richard O. (1977) Oxidation of Magnetite and Garnet-forming Reactions, Split-Rock magnetite mine, Westport, N.Y.: Geol. Soc. Amer. Abstracts Northeast Section 12th Annual Meeting, p. 315.

Sahlin, A. (1893) The talc industry of the Gouverneur District, St. Lawrence County, New York; Amer. Inst. Mining Eng., trans., 21, p. 583–588.

Sapozhnikov, A. P. and Ivanov, V. G. (1976) Occurrence of a triclinic (Pseudo-orthorhombic) modification of lazurite: Soveshchanie Molodykh Uchenykh Mineral., Geokhim, Metod. Issled. Mineralov (Tezisy Dokladov), Primorsk, Otdel, Vses, Mineralog. Obshch., Dal'nevostochn. Geol. Inst., Vladivostok, pp. 81–82 (Abstract; In Russian).

Schaller, Waldemar T. (1905) Dumortierite; U.S. Geol. Surv. Bull. 262, p. 94–95.

(1916) Peristerite from Valhalla, New York; U.S. Geol. Surv. Miner. Res. (1915), p. 850.

Schaller, Waldemar T. and Hildebrand, F. A. (1955) A second occurrence of the mineral sinhalite; Amer. Mineral., v. 40, p. 453–457.

Schlegel, Dorothy M. (1969) Gem Stones of the United States; U.S. Geol. Surv. Bull. 1042g.

Schneer, Cecil J. (1969) Ebeneezer Emmons and the Foundation of American Geology; Isis, Vol. 60, 4, No. 204, p. 439–450.

Schuberth, Christopher J. (1968) The Geology of New York City and environs, 304 p.; Natural History Press, New York.

Scott, George S. (1918) Iridescent quartz from New York City; Amer. Mineral., v. 3, p. 183.

Segeler, Curt G. (1959) Notes on a second occurrence of groutite; Amer. Mineral., v. 44, p. 877–878.

(1961) First occurrence of manganoan cummingtonite, tirodite; Amer. Mineral., v. 46, p. 637–641.

Seybert, H. (1822) Note on green pyroxene from Willsboro on Lake Champlain; Amer. Jour. Sci., Ser. 1, 5, p. 115–116.

Seyfert, Carl K. and Leveson, David J. (1968) Structure and Petrology of Pelham Bay Park; Guidebook to Field Excursions, 40th Annual Meeting, N.Y. State Geol. Ass'n., p. 175–195.

Shand, S. James (1942) Phase geology in the Cortlandt complex, New York; Geol. Soc. Amer. Bull., v. 53, p. 409–428.

Shaub, Benjamin M. (1929) A unique feldspar deposit near the DeKalb Junction, New York; Econ. Geol., v. 24, p. 68–89.

(1940) Age of the uraninite from the McLear pegmatite near Richville Station, St. Lawrence County, New York; Amer. Mineral., v. 25, p. 480–487.

(1949) Paragenesis of the garnet and associated minerals of the Barton Mines, near North Creek, New York; Amer. Mineral., v. 34, p. 573–582.

(1951) The cause of radial fracturing around some rock minerals; Rocks and Minerals, v. 26, nos. 7–8, p. 345–347.

(1953) Moonstone from Olmsteadville, New York; Rocks and Minerals, v. 28, nos. 9–10, p. 451–455.

(1975) Treasures from the Earth; The Rocks and Minerals, 223 p.; Crown, New York.

Shepard, Charles Upham (1832) A sketch of the mineralogy and geology of the counties—Orange (New York) and Sussex (New Jersey); Amer. Jour. Sci., Ser. 1, 21, p. 321–334.

(1835) On the strontianite of Schoharie, N.Y.; Amer. Jour. Sci., Ser. 1, 27, p. 363–368.

(1938) Notice of warwickite, a new mineral species; Amer. Jour. Sci., Ser. 1, 36, p. 85–87.

(1851) Mineralogical Notices; Amer. Jour. Sci., Ser. 2, 12, p. 200.

(1852) Treatise on Mineralogy, Third Edition.

(1852) Two new minerals from Monroe, Orange Co., N.Y.; Amer. Jour. Sci., Ser. 2, 13, p. 392.

(1853) Notice of the meteoric iron found near Seneca River, Cayuga County, N.Y.; Amer. Jour. Sci., Ser. 2, 15, p. 363–366.

Silliman, Benjamin (1819) Quartz from West Canada Creek; Amer. Jour. Sci., Ser. 1, p. 241.

(1821) Fluorspar on the Genesee River; Amer. Jour. Sci., Ser. 1, 3, p. 235.

(1829) Fibrous gypsum of Onondaga County; Amer. Jour. Sci., Ser. 1, 16, p. 377.

(1844) Analysis of meteoric iron from Burlington, Otsego County, New York; Amer. Jour. Sci., Ser. 1, 46, p. 401–403.

(1845) Notice of a mass of meteoric iron found at Cambria, near Lockport in the State of New York; Amer. Jour. Sci., 1st Ser., v. 48, p. 388–392.

Silver, Leon T. (1965) U-Pb Isotopic data in Zircons of the Grenville series of the Adirondack Mountains, New York (abs.): Amer. Geophys. Union Trans. 46: 1:164.

(1969) A Geochronological investigation of the Anorthosite complex, Adirondack Mountains, New York; N.Y. State Mus. and Science Service Memoir 18, p. 233–251.

Sims, P. K. and Hotz, P. E. (1951) Zinc-Lead deposits at Shawangunk Mine, Sullivan County, New York; U.S. Geol. Surv. Bull. 978D.

Sinkankas, John (1951) Some cutting material localities around New York City; Rocks and Minerals, vol. 26, nos. 11–12, p. 587–591.

(1959) Gemstones of North America, 675 p.; Van Nostrand, Princeton, N.J.

(1966) Mineralogy. A First Course for Amateurs, 582 p., 327 fig., Van Nostrand, Princeton, N.J.

(1968) Van Nostrand's Standard Catalog of Gems, 286 p.; Van Nostrand, New Jersey.

(1976) Gemstones of North America, vol. II, 494 p., 16 color plates, 110 fig., maps, drawings. Van Nostrand.

Skinner, Brian J. (1956) Physical properties of end members of the garnet group; Amer. Mineral., v. 41, p. 428–436.

Slocum, Horace W. (1948) Rambles of a Collector; Rocks and Minerals, vol. 23, no. 6, p. 497–503.

Smith, Burnett (1931) Note on the Clintonville dikes, Onondaga County, New York; N.Y. State Mus. Bull. 286, p. 119–126.

Smith, C. H. (1952) Recent Herkimer "diamond" hunting: Rocks and Minerals, v. 27, p. 272–275.

Smith, Edward S. C. and Kruesi, O. (1947) Polycrase in New York State; Amer. Mineral., v. 32, p. 585–587.

Smith, H. P. (Editor) (1885) History of Essex County 1885, 754 p. Mason, Syracuse, N.Y.

(1885) History of Warren County, 702 p. Mason, Syracuse, N.Y.

Smith, John Lawrence (1856) Warwickite, a borotantalite (from Orange County, New York); Amer. Jour. Sci., Proc. 7, p. 147–148.

(1874) Warwickite (from Orange County, New York); Amer. Jour. Sci., Ser. 3, 8, p. 432–434.

Smith, John Lawrence and Brush, George Jarvis (1853) Hydrous anthophyllite from New York Island; Amer. Jour. Sci., 16, p. 49.

Smith, Joseph V. (1974) Feldspar Minerals, vol. 1, Crystal Structure and Properties, 622 p.

(1974) Feldspar Minerals, vol. 2, Chemical and Textural Properties, 690 p.

(197) Feldspar Minerals, vol. 3, Occurrences. (In press).

Smith, Orsino C. (1953) Identification and qualitative chemical analysis of minerals, 2nd Ed., 385 p.; D. VanNostrand, New York.

Smith, Stephen (1829) Notice of the Salt Springs and manufacture of salt at Salina, Syracuse, N.Y.; Amer. Jour. Sci., Ser. 1, p. 6–12.

Smock, J. C. (1889) Iron mines and iron ore districts in the state of New York; Bull. of N.Y. State Mus. no. 7.

Smyth, C. H., Jr. (1893) Alnoite containing an uncommon variety of melilite; Amer. Jour. Sci., Ser. 3, p. 104–107.

(1893) A third occurrence of peridotite in central New York; Amer. Jour. Sci., Ser. 3, 43, p. 322–327.

(1894) Crystalline limestones and associated rocks of the northwestern Adirondack region; Geol. Soc. Amer. Bull., v. 6, p. 263–284.

(1895) Report on the talc industry of St. Lawrence County; N.Y. State Mus., 49th Ann. Report, p. 665–671.

(1896) Genetic relations of certain minerals of northern New York; N.Y. Acad. Sci., trans. 15, p. 266.

(1897) Talc of St. Lawrence County, N.Y.; Amer. Jour. Sci., Ser. 4, p. 76.

(1897a) Pseudomorphs of northern New York; Amer. Jour. Sci., Ser. 4, p. 309–312.

(1902) Petrography of recently discovered dikes in Syracuse, N.Y.: with note on the occurrence of melilite in the Green Street dike: Amer. Jour. Sci., 4th Ser. 14, p. 465–493.

(1911) A new locality for pyrrhotite crystals and their pseudomorphs; Amer. Jour. Sci., Ser. 4, 32, p. 156–160.

(1917) Genesis of the zinc ores of the Edwards district, St. Lawrence County, New York; N.Y. State Mus. Bull. 201.

Smyth, C. H. Jr. and Buddington, Arthur F. (1926) Geology of the Lake Bonaparte quadrangle; N.Y. State Mus. Bull. 269.

Sparrow, Ruth A. (Compiler) (1972) Milestones of Science; Epochal books in the history of science; Buffalo Society of Natural Sciences, Collection Catalog, no. 1.

Stamper, John W. (1970) Mineral facts and problems, Titanium; U.S. Bur. Mines Bull., 650, p. 773–794.

Stanton, Gilman Shattuck (1891) The occurrence of beryls and garnets on New York Island; N.Y. Acad. Sci., trans. 10, p. 50–51.

Steacy, H. R. (1976) Personal Communication.

Steel, J. H. (1822) A new locality of chrysoberyl; Amer. Jour. Sci., Ser. 1, 4, p. 37–38.

Steinocher, V. and Novacek, R. (1939) On Beta-uranotile; Amer. Mineral., v. 24, no. 5, p. 324–338.

Stephenson, Robert C. (1945) Titaniferous magnetite deposits of the Lake Sanford area, New York; N.Y. State Mus. Bull. 340.

Stockman, Harlan (1975) Personal Communication.

Stoltz, Guy C. (1908) The forest of Dean iron mine, New York; Eng. Mining Jour. 85, p. 1091–1093.

Strunz, Hugo (1970) Mineralische Tabellen, 5th Edition, 621 p.

Swift, J. Otis (1929) Kensico quarry (Valhalla, New York); West. Mag. 1, p. 104.

Sylvester, Nathaniel Bartlett (1878) History of Saratoga County 1609 to 1878, 514 p.

Szenics, Terry (1968) World-famous lost American gem diopside locality rediscovered: Lapidary Journal, Vol. 21, p. 1232–1239.

Tan, Li-Ping (1966) Major pegmatite deposits of New York State; N.Y. State Mus. Bull. 408.

Tesmer, Irving H. (1975) Geology of Cattaraugus County; Buffalo Soc. Natural Sciences, Bull. 27.

Thibault, N. W. (1935) Celestite from Chittenango Falls, New York; Amer. Mineral., v. 20, p. 147–152.

Thompson, Bruce (1957) Personal communication.

Thurston, Anthony (1942) Some New York Caves; Rocks and Minerals, v. 17, no. 12, p. 410–411.

Torrey, J. (1848) Discovery of Vauquelinite a rare ore of chromium, in the United States; Ann. N.Y. Acad. Sci., (Lyceum Nat. Hist. N.Y.) v. IV, p. 76–79.

Trainer, David W. (1932) The Tully limestone of central New York; N.Y. State Mus. Bull. 291.

Toulmin, Piestley, 3rd (1963) Proustite-pyrargyrite solid solutions: Amer. Miner., v. 48, p. 725–735.

Trainer, John N. (1938) Tilly Foster up-to-date; Rocks and Minerals, v. 13, no. 10, p. 291–303.

    (1939) Rocks and Minerals, v. 14, no. 2, p. 50–52.

    (1940) Another year at Tilly Foster; Rocks and Minerals, v. 15, no. 4, p. 126–128.

    (1941) The fifth year at Tilly Foster; Rocks and Minerals, v. 16, no. 4, p. 122–126.

    (1942) Sixth year at Tilly Foster; Rocks and Minerals, v. 17, no. 1, p. 8–9.

    (1943) More about Tilly Foster; Rocks and Minerals, v. 18, no. 6, p. 168–169.

Troost, Gerard (1824) Description of a new crystalline form of chrysoberyl; Acad. Nat. Sci., Philadelphia, Jour., 4, p. 122.

Turner, Francis J. and Verhoogen, John (1960) Igneous and Metamorphic Petrology, 694 p.; McGraw Hill, New York.

Tuttle, Donald L. (1973) Inclusions in "Herkimer Diamonds", Herkimer County, New York quartz crystals; Lapidary Journal, v. 27, no. 6, p. 966–976.

(1977) Shades of Adirondack Iron: The Conservationist, March–April 1977, p. 33–35: Latham, N.Y.

Valley, John W. and Essene, Eric J. (1977) Regional metamorphic wollastonite in the Adirondacks; Geol. Soc. Amer. Abstracts Northeast Section 12th Annual Meeting, p. 326–327.

Valiant, William S. (1899) A collector's paradise; several articles; The Mineral Collector.

(1900) The Lewis C. Beck Mineral Collection; The Mineral Collector, vol. VII, no. 2, p. 20–24, vol. VII, no. 3, p. 37–40.

Vanders, Iris and Kerr, Paul F. (1967) Mineral Recognition, 316 p., John Wiley & Sons, New York.

Van Diver, Bradford B. (1969) Meta-anorthosite of the Jay-Whiteface nappe, Ausable Forks-Lake Placid quadrangles, northeastern Adirondacks, New York; 41st Annual Meeting, New York State Geological Association, Trip H.

(1976) Rocks and Routes of the North Country, New York: 205 p., paper. W. F. Humphrey Press Inc., Geneva, New York.

Van Schmus, W. R. and Wood, J. A. (1967) A chemical-petrologic classification for the chondritic meteorites; Geochim. Cosmochim. Acta 31, p. 747–765.

Vanuxem, Lardner (1842) Geology of New York, Part III, Comprising the Survey of the Third District, 305 p.

Waite, Evelyn (1940) New localities in Westchester County, N.Y.; Rocks and Minerals, v. 15, no. 10, p. 327–329.

Ward, Henry A. (1904) Catalogue of the Ward-Coonley Collection of Meteorites, 113 p., 10 plates, Marsh, Aitkins & Curtis, Chicago.

Ward, Roswell (1933) (1948) Henry A. Ward, Museum builder to America; The Rochester Historical Society, Publication XXIV.

Watson, Thomas L. (1917) Weathering of allanite; Geol. Soc. Amer. Bull., v. 28, p. 470–471, 474.

Webster, John White (1824) Catalog of Minerals in The State of New York: 32 p. Albany, N.Y.

Webster, M. H. (1824) Catalogue of the minerals which have been discovered in the state of New York, arranged under the heads of the respective counties and towns in which they are found, 32 p., Albany.

Webster, Robert (1972) Gems, second edition, revised impression, 838 p. Archon Books, Hamden, Conn.

Weidhaas, Ernest (1959) The Large Bedford tourmaline group; Rocks and Minerals, v. 34, nos. 9–10, p. 390–392.

Weidman, S. (1903) Note on the amphibole Hudsonite previously called a pyroxene; Amer. Jour. Sci., Fourth Ser., v. XV, p. 227–232.

Wells, D. A. (1859) No title is found for this paper; Proc. Boston Soc. Nat. Hist., vol. 7, p. 176.

Wendt, Arthur F. (1885) The iron mines of Putnam County, New York; Amer. Inst. Mining Eng., trans. 13, p. 478–488.

Wheeler, Everett Pepperell, 2nd (1950) Massive leucoxene in Adirondack titanium deposit (N.Y.); Econ. Geol., v. 45, no. 6, p. 574–577.

White, George W. (Editor) (1968) Contributions to the History of Geology, vol. 1, "The American Mineralogical Journal" by Archibald Bruce, M.D., 270 p., a reprint by Hafner, New York.

White, J. S. (1971) Appendix to Glossary of Mineral Species by Fleischer (1971).

Whitfield, J. E. (1887) Danburite from Russell, St. Lawrence County, New York; Amer. Jour. Sci., Ser. 3, 34, p. 285.

Whitlock, Herbert P. (1902) Guide to the mineralogic collection at the New York State Museum; N.Y. State Mus. Bull. 58.

(1903) New York Mineral Localities; N.Y. State Mus. Bull. 70.

(1905) Contributions from the mineralogic laboratory; N.Y. State Mus. Bull. 98.

(1907) Minerals from Lyon Mountain, Clinton County; N.Y. State Mus. Bull. 107, p. 55–74, 11 plates.

(1910) Calcites of New York; N.Y. State Mus. Memoir 13, 190 p., 27 plates.

(1910a) Contributions to Mineralogy; N.Y. State Mus. Bull. 140, pp. 197–203.

(1912) Recent mineral occurrences in New York City and vicinity; N.Y. State Mus. Bull. 158, p. 183–187.

(1913) The Mount Morris meteorite; N.Y. State Mus. 9th Report of the Director of the Science Division, p. 78–79.

(1919) Pyrite crystals from Broadway and 207th Street, New York City; Amer. Miner., 4, p. 31–32.

Whitnall, Harold O. (1930) Howe Caverns; Rocks and Minerals, v. 5, no. 4, p. 109–115.

Williams, E. H. (1876) On crystals of tourmaline with enveloped orthoclase from Crown Point, N.Y.; Amer. Jour. Sci., Ser. 3, 11, p. 273.

Williams, George Huntington (1884) Barite crystals from DeKalb, New York; Johns Hopkins Univ. circ. 3, p. 61.

(1886) The peridotites of the Cortlandt series on the Hudson River near Peekskill, N.Y.; Amer. Jour. Sci., 3rd Ser. v. 31, p. 26–31.

(1887) On some remarkable crystals of pyroxene from Orange Co., N.Y.; Amer. Jour. Sci., Ser. 3, 34, p. 275–276.

Winchell, Alexander N. (1933) Elements of Optical Mineralogy, 3rd Ed., 551 p.; Wiley, New York.

Wray, Charles F. (1948) Varieties and sources of flint found in New York State; Pennsylvania Archaeologist, v. XVIII, nos. 1–2, p. 25–45.

Yedlin, Leo Neal (1940) Some notes on St. Lawrence Co., New York; Rocks and Minerals, v. 15, no. 6, p. 183–186.

(1976) Personal communication.

Zenger, Donald H. (1965) Stratigraphy of the Lockport formation (Middle Silurian) in New York State; N.Y. State Mus. Bull. 404, p. 1–210.

Zimmer, Paul W. (1947) Anhydrite and gypsum in the Lyon Mountain magnetite deposit of the northeastern Adirondacks; Amer. Mineral., v. 32, p. 647–653.

Zodac, Peter (1933) The Anthony's Nose pyrrhotite mine; Rocks and Minerals, v. 8, no. 2, p. 61–76.

(1939a) A remarkable melanterite; Rocks and Minerals, v. 14, no. 2, p. 53.

(1939b) A weird experience; Rocks and Minerals, v. 14, no. 8, pp. 244–245.

(1940) Atlas quarry near Pine Island, New York; Rocks and Minerals, v. 15, no. 5, p. 162–164.

(1941) Shaft 7 near Fishkill, N.Y.; Rocks and Minerals, vol. 16, p. 3–11.

(1951) Pectolite near Nyack, N.Y.; Rocks and Minerals, v. 26, nos. 5–6, p. 285.

(1951a) Turgite in Dutchess County, N.Y.; Rocks and Minerals, v. 26, nos. 7–8, p. 409.

Mineral Names That Are Now Obsolete or Seldom Used

This list only includes names that were used in the past for minerals from New York state localities and are now obsolete or seldom used.

(Ref. Dana–1892; Hey–1963).

Achmite = acmite
Actinote = actinolite
Adinole = albite
Aegirite = aegirine
Amiant = syn. of asbestos
Amianthus = syn. of asbestos
Aplome = andradite
Arragonite = aragonite

Baikalite = diopside
Barytine = barite
Bitter spar = dolomite
Black lead = graphite
Black manganese = psilomelane
Blue malachite = azurite
Blende = sphalerite
Boltonite = forsterite
Botryolite = datolite
Bucholzite = sillimanite

Calamite = tremolite
Calcedony = chalcedony
Cerine = allanite
Ceruse = cerussite
Chabazie = chabazite
Chalcodite = stilpnomelane
Chalkopyrite = chalcopyrite
Chalkosin = chalcocite
Chalybite = siderite
Chrysophane = seybertite = clintonite
Coccolite = diopside
Colophonite = andradite
Copperas = melanterite
Copper pyrites = chalcopyrite
Crichtonite = ilmenite
Cymophane = chrysoberyl

Datholite = datolite
Dimagnetite = pseudomorph of magnetite after ilvaite
Disthene = kyanite
Dysyntribite = an impure mica

Egeran = vesuvianite
Enceladite = warwickite
Eupyrchroite = carbonation fluorapatite

Fibrolite = sillimanite

Galenite = galena
Gigantolite = a mixture of muscovite and biotite
Grenat = garnet
Gurhofite = dolomite

Harmatome = harmotome
Holmesite = clintonite
Holmite = clintonite
Hornstone = chert
Houghite = pseudomorph of hydrotalcite after spinel
Hudsonite = hastingsite
Hydrodolomite = a mixture of hydromagnesite and calcite
Hydrophite = an iron serpentine
Hystatite = a mixture of ilmenite with hematite or mahnetite

Indicolite = tourmaline group

Lederite = titanite
Leucaugite = augite

210

Loxoclase = orthoclase

Marmolite = chrysolite
Menaccanite = ilmenite
Mesotype = mesolite
Metaxite = chrysotile
Mispickel = arsenopyrite
Monrolite = sillimanite

Necronite = orthoclase
Nemalite = brucite

Ophiolite = ophicalcite = serpentine + calcite or dolomite

Perofskite = perovskite
Prochlorite = chlorite
Pseudolite = talc pseudomorph after spinel
Pyrallolite = an altered pyroxene

Rastolyte = altered biotite
Rensselaerite = talc pseudomorph after pyroxene

Sahlite = salite
Schiller spar = altered enstatite
Sphaerosiderite = siderite
Spinelle = spinel
Sulphur = sulfur

Uranconite = an imperfectly described uranium sulfate

Washingtonite = a mixture of ilmenite with hematite or magnetite

Xanthitane = anatase
Xanthite = idocrase

Zanthithone = xanthithane

Alphabetical List of Minerals of New York State

Achroite—See Tourmaline
Acmite—See Pyroxene
Actinolite—See Amphibole
Adularia—See Orthoclase
Aegirine—See Pyroxene
Aeschynite—See Samarskite
Agate—See Quartz
Albite—See Plagioclase
ALLANITE
Almandine—See Garnet
ALUNOGEN
Amazonite—See Microcline
Amethyst—See Quartz
AMPHIBOLE
  Actinolite
  Anthophyllite
  Byssolite
  Crocidolite
  Cummingtonite
  Edenite
  Glaucophane
  Hastingsite
  Hexagonite
  Hornblende
  Mountain leather
  Pargasite
  Riebeckite
  Tirodite
  Tremolite
  Tschermakite
  Uralite
ANALCIME
ANATASE
ANDALUSITE
Andesine—See Plagioclase
Andradite—See Garnet
ANGLESITE
ANHYDRITE
ANKERITE
ANORTHOCLASE
Anthophyllite—See Amphibole
Antigorite—See Serpentine

APATITE
APOPHYLLITE
Aquamarine—See Beryl
ARAGONITE
ARSENOPYRITE
ARTINITE
Augite—See Pyroxene
AUTUNITE
AXINITE
AZURITE

BABINGTONITE
BARITE
Barytocelestite—See Celestite
BASTNAESITE
BERTRANDITE
BERYL
BETA-URANOPHANE
BIOTITE
BISMUTHINITE
BORNITE
BOURNONITE
BRAUNITE
Bronzite—See Pyroxene
BROOKITE
BRUCITE
Byssolite—See Amphibole
Bytownite—See Plagioclase

CACOXENITE
CALCITE
  Calc Tufa
  Stalactite
  Stalagmite
  Travertine
Calc Tufa—See Calcite
Carbonate-Fluorapatite—See Apatite
CARNALLITE
CELESTITE
CERITE
CERUSSITE
CHABAZITE

Chalcedony—See Quartz
CHALCOCITE
Chalcodite—See Stilpnomelane
CHALCOPYRITE
Chamosite—See Chlorite
Chert—See Quartz
CHLORITE
    Chamosite
    Clinochlore
    Leuchtenbergite
    Ripidolite
CHLORITOID
Clinochlore—See Chlorite
CHONDRODITE
Chromian Tremolite—See Tremolite
CHROMITE
CHRYSOBERYL
CHRYSOCOLLA
Chrysotile—See Serpentine
Citrine—See Quartz
Cleavelandite—See Albite
Clinochlore—See Chlorite
CLINOHUMITE
CLINOZOISITE
CLINTONITE
COBALTITE
Collophane—See Apatite
Colophonite—See Garnet
COALINGITE
COLUMBITE
COPIAPITE
CORDIERITE
CORUNDUM
Coulsonite—See Magnetite
COVELLITE
Crocidolite—See Amphibole
Cummingtonite—See Amphibole
Cyanite—See Kyanite
Cyrtolite—See Zircon

DANBURITE
DATOLITE
Diamond
Diopside—See Pyroxene
Diatomaceous Earth—See Opal
Dipyr—See Scapolite
DOLOMITE
Dravite—See Tourmaline
DUMORTIERITE

Edenite—See Amphibole
Elbaite—See Tourmaline

Emery—See Corundum
Enstatite—See Pyroxene
EPIDOTE
EPISTILBITE
EPSOMITE
ERYTHRITE
Eupyrochroite—See Apatite

FAYALITE
Feldspar
    Orthoclase
    Microcline
    Anorthoclase
    Plagioclase
    Albite
    Oligoclase
    Andesine
    Labradorite
    Bytownite
    Anorthite—absent in New York
      State
FERGUSONITE
Flint—See Quartz
Fluorapatite—See Apatite
FLUORITE
FORSTERITE
FOURMARIERITE
Francolite—See Apatite
Fuller's Earth—See MONTMORIL-
    LONITE

GALENA
GARNET
    Almandine
    Andradite
    Grossular
    Spessartine
GEOCRONITE
GIBBSITE
Gieseckite—See Nepheline
Glaucophane—See Amphibole
Goethite—See Limonite
GOLD
Golden beryl—See Beryl
GRAPHITE
Grossular—See Garnet
GROUTITE
Guitermanite—See Jordanite
GUMMITE
GYPSUM

HALITE

HARMOTOME
Hastingsite—See Amphibole
HAÜYNE (Haüynite)
Hedenbergite—See Pyroxene
HEMATITE
HEULANDITE
Hexagonite—See Amphibole
HISINGERITE
HOEGBOMITE
Hornblende—See Amphibole
HORTONOLITE
HUMITE
Hyalite—See Opal
HYDROMAGNESITE
HYDROTALCITE
HYDROZINCITE
Hypersthene—See Pyroxene

ICE
Iddingsite—See Olivine
Idocrase—See Vesuvianite
ILLITE
ILMENITE
Ilmeno-magnetite—See Magnetite
ILVAITE
Iolite—See Cordierite
IRON (Nickel-iron)

JAROSITE
Jasper—See Quartz
Jefferisite—See Vermiculite
Jenkinsite—See Serpentine
JORDANITE

KAOLINITE
KASOLITE
KYANITE

LABRADORITE—See Plagioclase
LANTHANITE
Lapis Lazuli—See Haüynite
LAUMONITE
LAZURITE—See under Haüynite
Leuchtenbergite—See Chlorite
Leucoxene—See Ilmenite
LIMONITE
LINNAEITE
Lizardite—See Serpentine
LOELLINGITE

MAGHEMITE
MAGNESITE

MAGNETITE
MALACHITE
Malacolite—See Pyroxene
MANASSEITE
MARCASITE
Marialite—See Scapolite
Marmolite—See Serpentine
Martite—See Hematite
Meionite—See Scapolite
MELANTERITE
MELILITE
Meta-autunite—See Autunite
Metabentonite—See Montmorillonite
Mica
  Biotite
  Clintonite
  Illite
  Muscovite
  Phlogopite
  Sericite
MICROCLINE
MICROLITE
MILLERITE
Mizzonite—See Scapolite
MOLYBDENITE
MONAZITE
MONTICELLITE
MONTMORILLONITE
MUSCOVITE

NATROLITE
NEPHELINE
Norbergite—See under Chondrodite

OLIGOCLASE—See Plagioclase
OLIVINE
OPAL
ORPIMENT
ORTHOCLASE

Pargasite—See Amphibole
PECTOLITE
Periclase—See Serpentine
PEROVSKITE
Pharmocolite
PHLOGOPITE
PHOSPHURANALYTE
PICKERINGITE
Picotite—See Spinel
Plagioclase
  Albite
  Oligoclase

Andesine
Labradorite
Bytownite
Anorthite (Absent in New York
State)
Pleonaste—See Spinel
POLYCRASE
POLYHALITE
Polylithionite—See Phlogopite
PREHNITE
PUMPELLYITE
PYRITE
PYROLUSITE
PYROMORPHITE
Pyrope—See Garnet
PYROXENE
  Aegirine
  Augite
  Diopside
  Enstatite
  Hedenbergite
  Hypersthene
PYRRHOTITE

QUARTZ
  Agate
  Amethyst
  Chalcedony
  Chert
  Citrine
  Flint
  Jasper
  Rose Quartz
  Smoky Quartz

REALGAR
Retinolite—See Serpentine
RHODONITE
Riebeckite—See Amphibole
Ripidolite—See Chlorite
Rose Quartz—See Quartz
RUTILE

SAMARSKITE
SAPPHIRINE
SCAPOLITE
  Marialite
  Dipyr
  Mizzonite
  Meionite
Schorl—See Tourmaline
Schroeckingerite—See under Beta-
  Uranophane

SCORODITE
Selenite—See Gypsum
SERENDIBITE
Sericite—See Muscovite
SERPENTINE
Seybertite—See Clintonite
SIDERITE
SILLIMANITE
SILVER
SINHALITE
SKLODOWSKITE
SMITHSONITE
Smoky Quartz—See Quartz
Spessartine—See Garnet
SPHALERITE
Sphene—See Titanite
SPINEL
SPODUMENE
Stalactite—See Calcite
Stalagmite—See Calcite
STAUROLITE
STEVENSITE
STILBITE
STILPNOMELANE
STRONTIANITE
SULFUR
SYLVITE

TALC
TENNANTITE
TETRAHEDRITE
THOMSONITE
THORITE
Thucholite—See Uraninite
Tirodite—See Amphibole
Titaniferous magnetite—See Magne-
  tite
TITANITE
TORBERNITE
TOURMALINE
  Achroite
  Dravite
  Elbaite
  Schorl
  Uvite
Travertine—See Calcite
Tremolite—See Amphibole
TROILITE
Tschermakite—See Amphibole
Turgite—See Hematite

Uralite—See Amphibole
URANINITE

URANOPHANE
Uranothorite—See Thorite
Uvite—See Tourmaline

VANADINITE
VAUQUELINITE
VERMICULITE
VESUVIANITE
VONSENITE

WAD
WARWICKITE
Wernerite—See Scapolite
WILLEMITE
Williamsite—See Serpentine
WOLLASTONITE
WULFENITE
WURTZITE

XENOTIME

Yttrian fluorite—See Fluorite

Zeolites
  Analcime
  Chabazite
  Epistilbite
  Harmotome
  Heulandite
  Laumontite
  Mesolite
  Natrolite
  Stilbite
  Thomsonite
ZIRCON
ZOISITE

Subject Index

He has written well over one hundred articles on geological topics for various publications. Some years ago, Mr. Jensen wrote a book on the hobby of rock and mineral collecting. He also revised the book, "Getting Acquainted With Minerals," by George L. English. Both of these books are now out of print.

Mr. Jensen is a Fellow of the Geological Society of America; a Fellow and Life Member of the Mineralogical Society of America; Fellow of the Rochester Museum and Science Center; Fellow of the Rochester Academy of Science; Research Associate of the Buffalo Museum of Science in Buffalo, New York; a Director of Friends of Mineralogy; and a past president of the Eastern Federation of Mineralogical and Lapidary Societies, Inc.

Many of the photographs in this book were taken by the author's wife, Katherine H. Jensen. She is a member of the Photographic Society of America, and is a noted photographer of minerals, fossils, and wildflowers. She is a Fellow of the Rochester Museum and Science Center, Fellow of the Rochester Academy of Science, and a past president of the Eastern Federation of Mineralogical and Lapidary Societies, Inc.